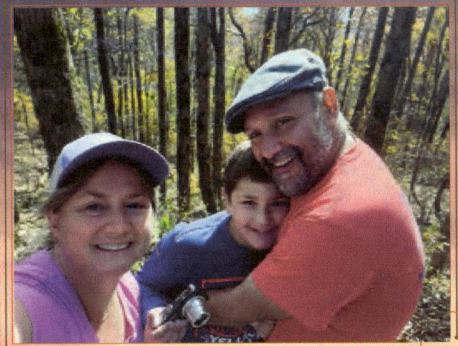

Owen with his parents, Israel and Renee

The cover photo of this book captures the joy I receive from my weekly visits to the Lake Apopka Wildlife Drive (LAWD) near my home in Central Florida! On one beautiful day, a female Boat-tailed Grackle joined me for part of the drive! No wonder I "Go Out with Joy!" (Isaiah 55:12).

I love sharing my enthusiasm for photography with my grandson, Owen, who shares my adoration for LAWD and the Lord! Perhaps, the next edition will be co-authored!

I'm dedicating this book to my mentor, Dr. O, and to my grandson, Owen Osvaldo Rodriguez.

Go Out With Joy!

Wildlife Photos & Encouraging Scriptures

Christine Clark Hammett
Dr. Phyllis M. Olmstead, Editor

I have clicked along the Lake Apopka Wildlife Drive in Central Florida for years! Out of which came the coffee table photo book, **Flora and Fauna of Lake Apopka Wildlife Drive** ©2021 by Dr. Phyllis M Olmstead, me, and Michelle McKee.

Since then, I have attended Tim Shield's **Photography Academy**, which I highly recommend. I utilized his mentor, Serge Ramelli's, Adobe Lightroom Classic filters on some of my photos.

101 Encouraging Bible Verses to Uplift and Inspire You was compiled by The Bible Study Tools staff and shared with their permission. Visit them online to discover even more edification.

My blog is Abolitionist Arise. A portion of the proceeds will be donated to Pro-Life Action Ministries (PLAM).

Heartfelt thanks to my editor and publisher, Dr. O, who coached me throughout this photographic and publishing journey with the patience of Job!

If you can enjoy the drive personally, I'm sure you will love it! It is open Friday, Saturday, Sunday, and national holidays. It takes two to three hours to complete. Please be patient with photographers and other nature lovers. I hope that your spirit will be uplifted! Blessings!

Go Out With Joy! Wildlife Photos & Encouraging Scriptures
By Christine Clark Hammett (Author, Photographer)
Dr. Phyllis M. Olmstead (Editor)
ISBN 978-193-419494-2
Fully copyrighted by Olmstead Publishing © 11/25/2025
(olmsteadpublishing.org)
Do not reproduce any part of this book in electronic or print form.

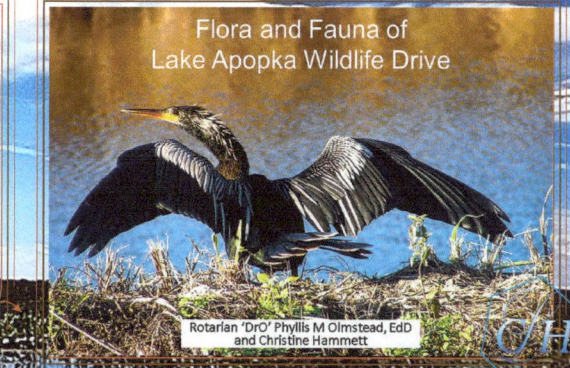

Flora and Fauna of Lake Apopka Wildlife Drive

Rotarian 'DrO' Phyllis M Olmstead, EdD and Christine Hammett

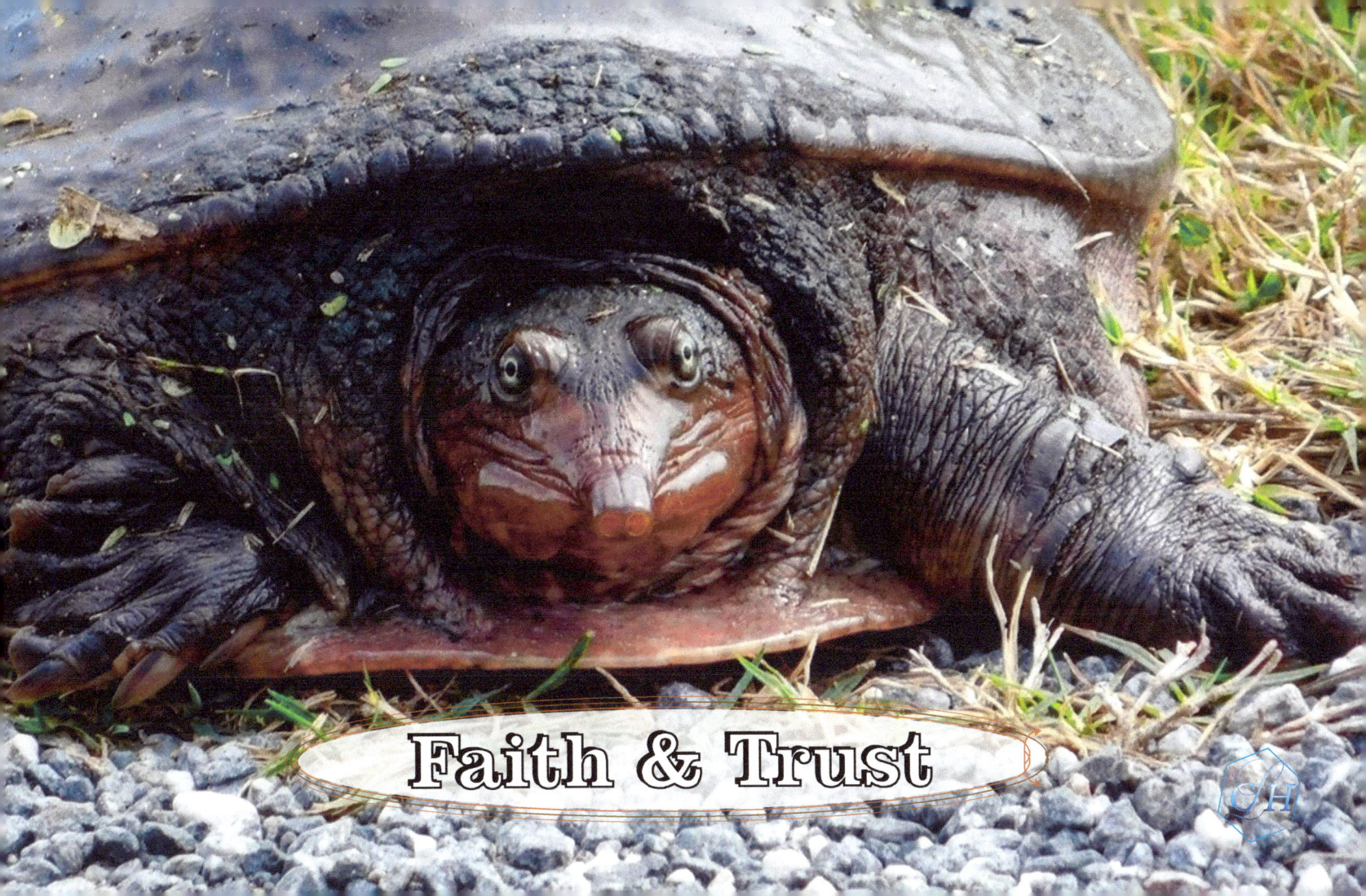

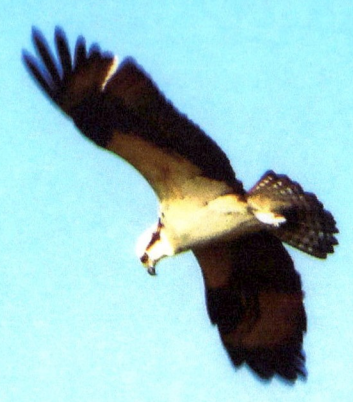

Ephesians 6:10
Proverbs 17:22
Luke 1:37
Proverbs 3:5-6
Hebrews 11:1
Matthew 6:31-32
1 Chronicles 16:27
Matthew 21:21-22
Hebrews 11:6
James 1:2-4
Ephesians 1:13
Proverbs 17:17
Jeremiah 29:11
Galatians 5:22
Ephesians 4:1-3
Matthew 6:33-34
Ephesians 3:17-19
Hebrews 10:23
2 Chronicles 7:14
Matthew 11:28

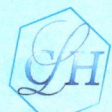

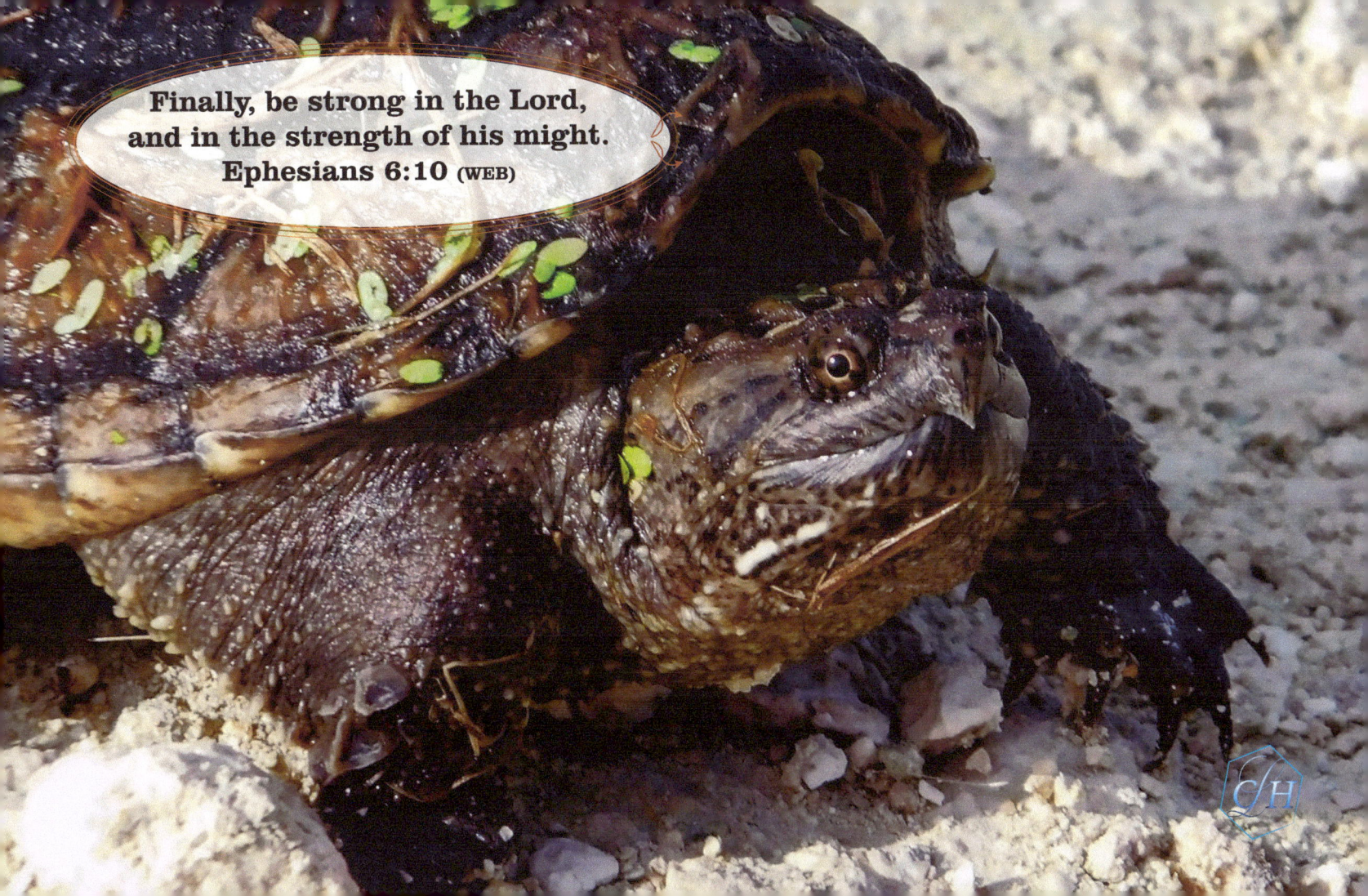

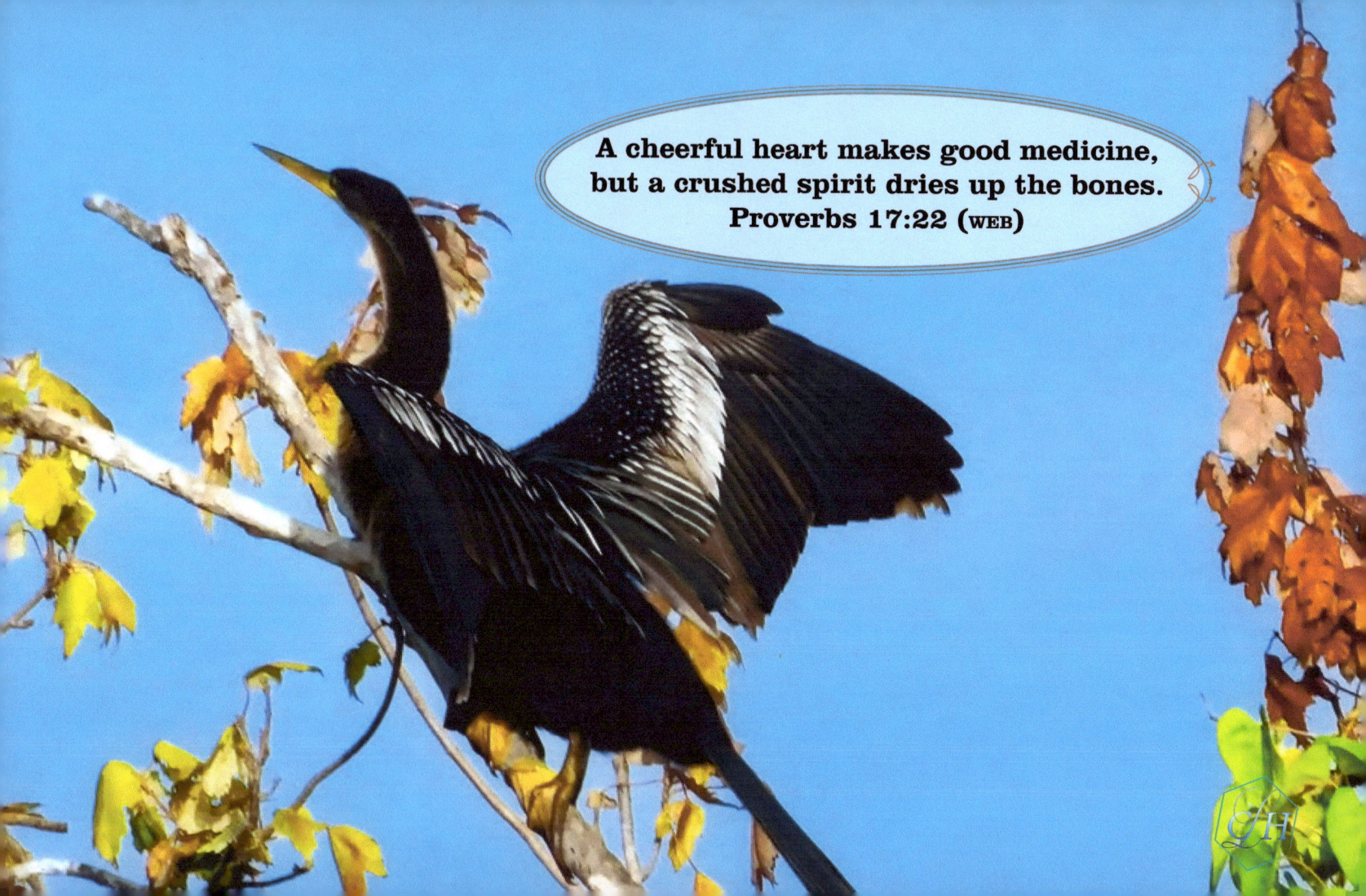

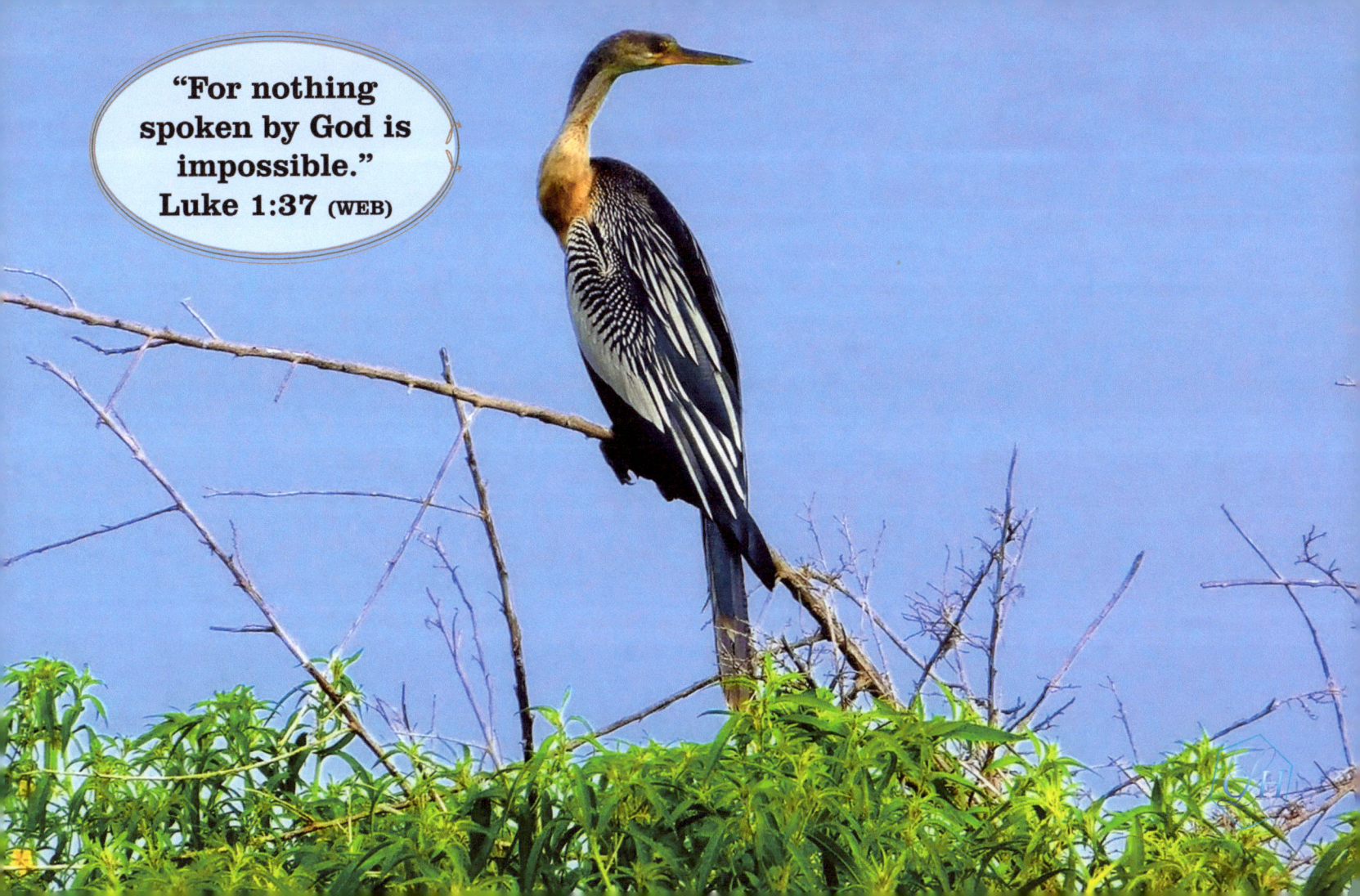

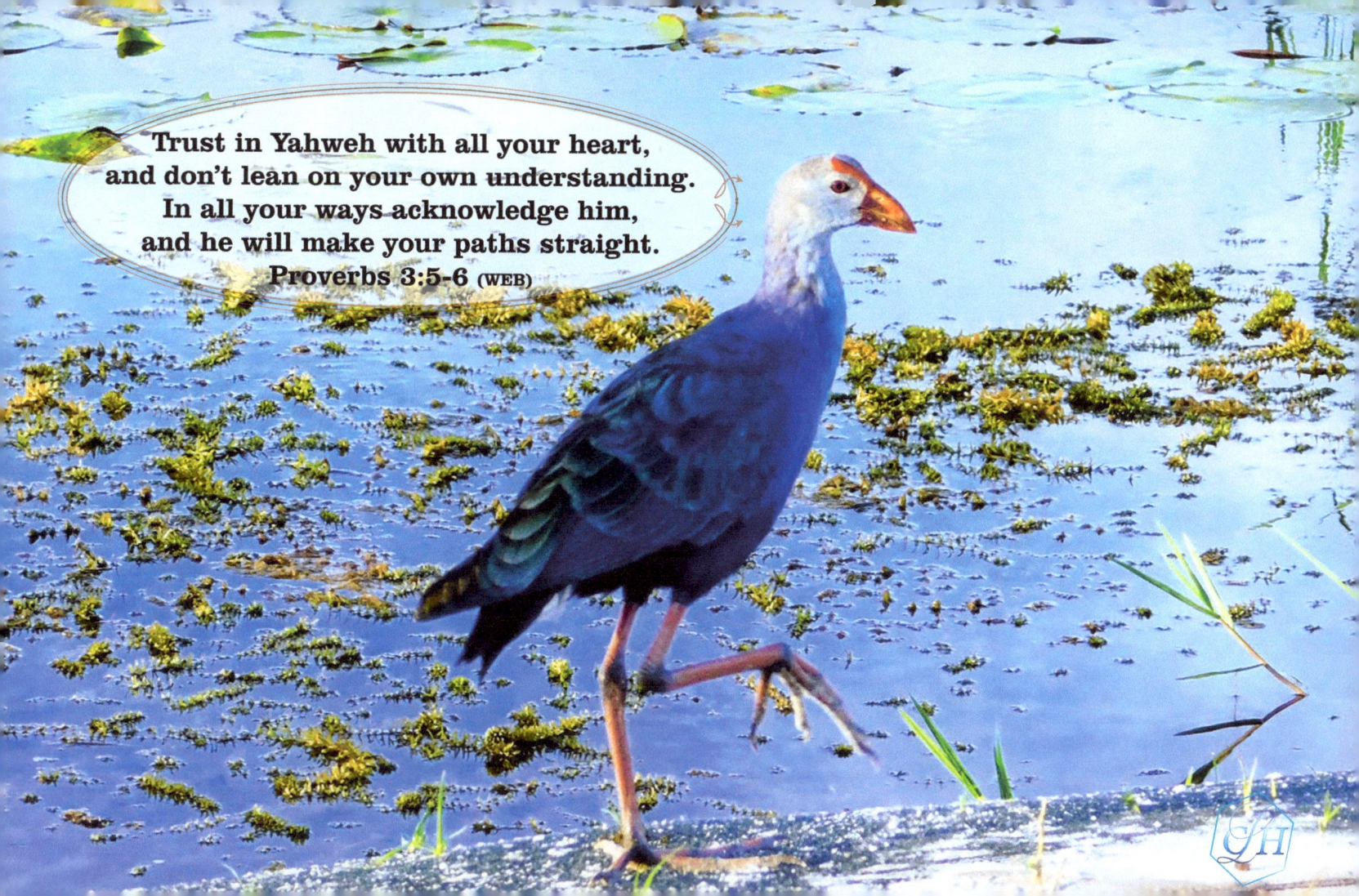

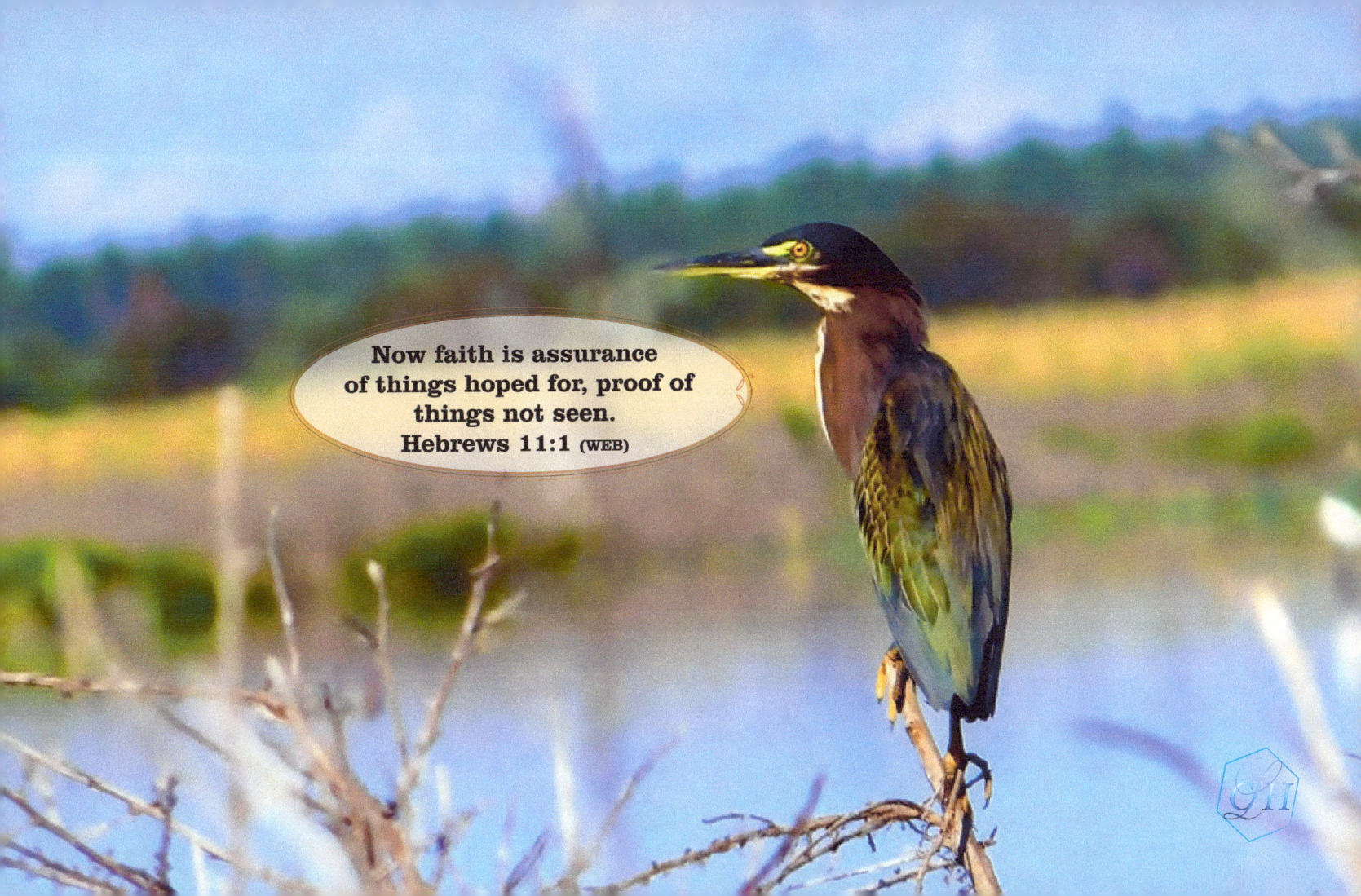

"Therefore don't be anxious, saying, 'What will we eat?', 'What will we drink?' or, 'With what will we be clothed?' For the Gentiles seek after all these things; for your heavenly Father knows that you need all these things.
Matthew 6:31-32 (WEB)

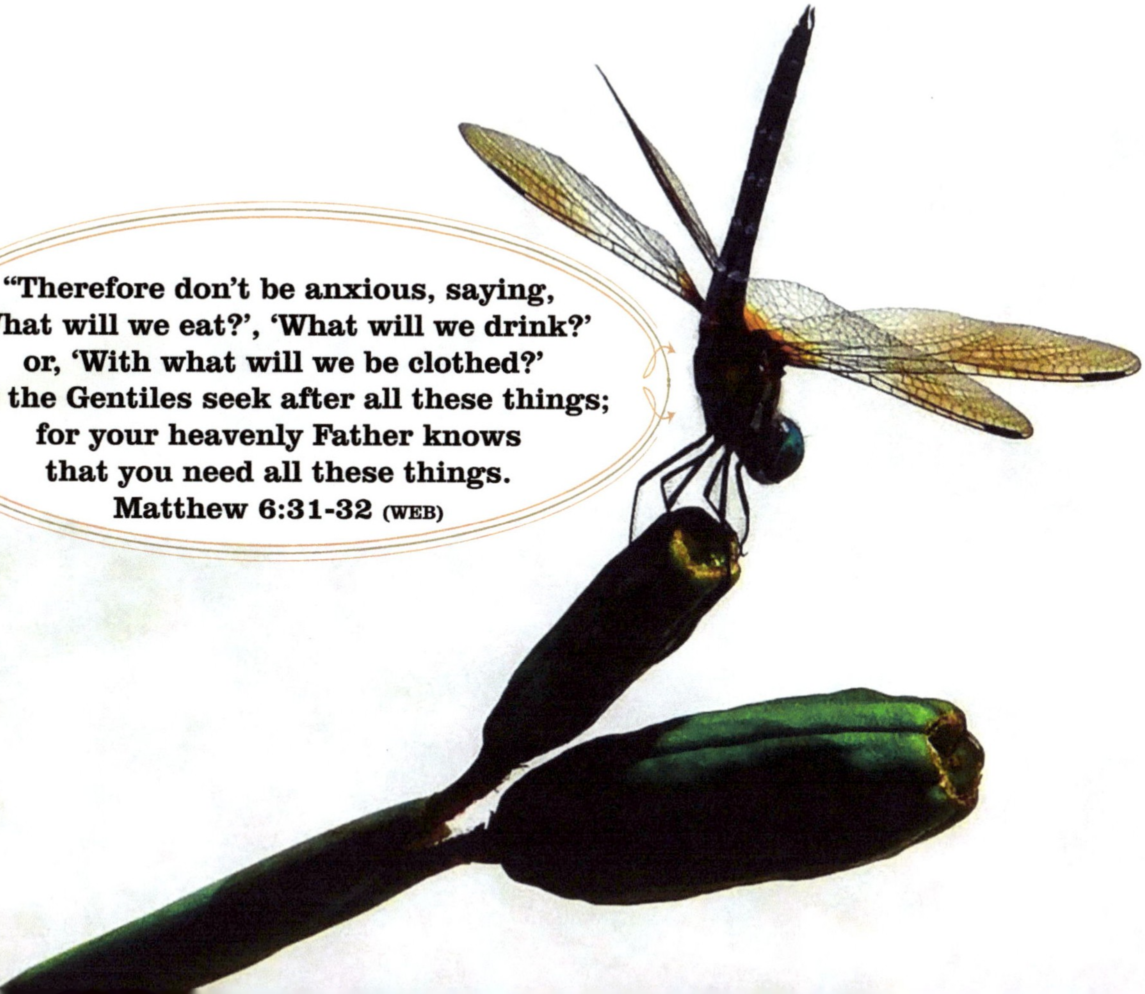

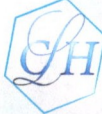

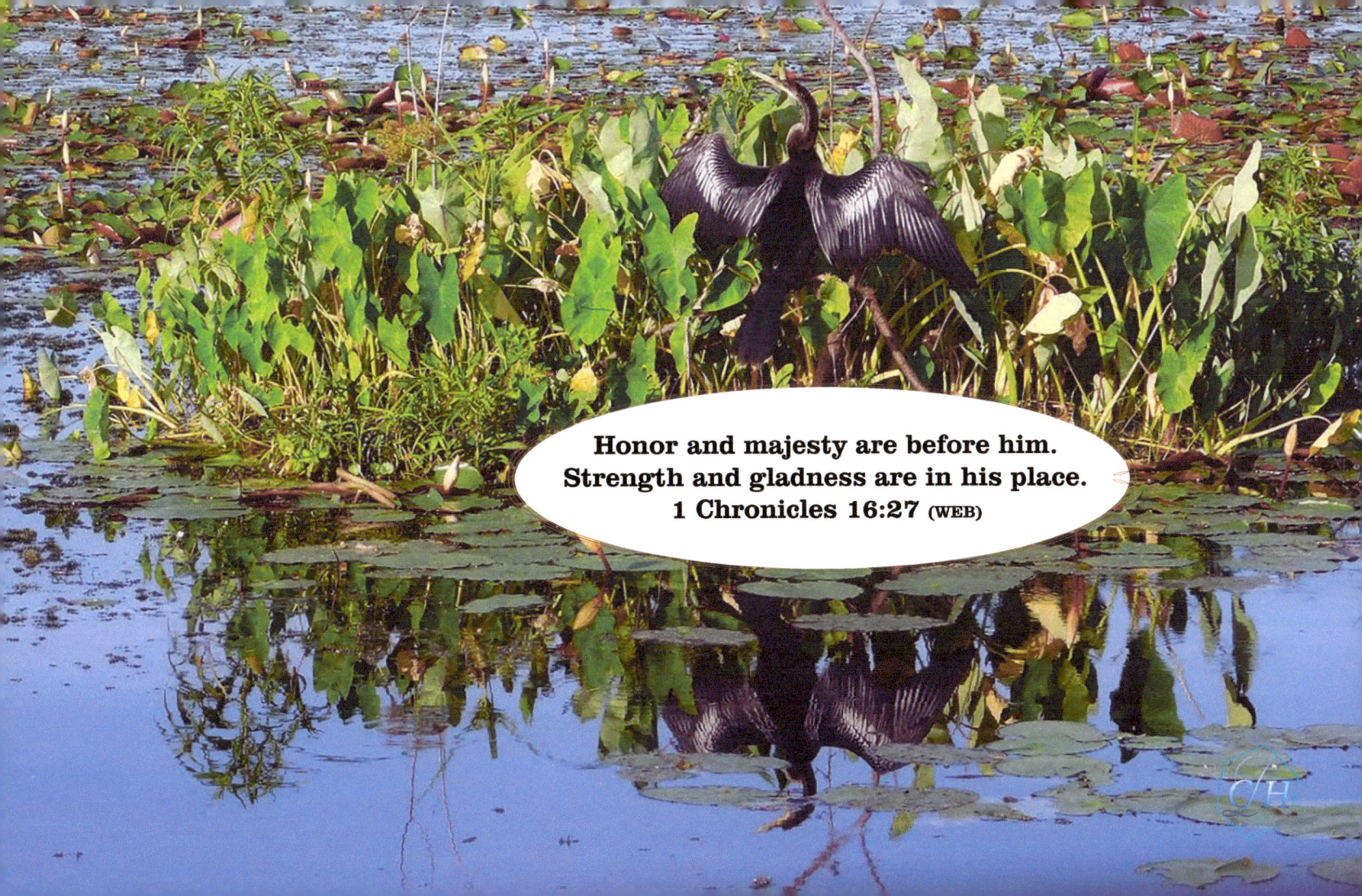

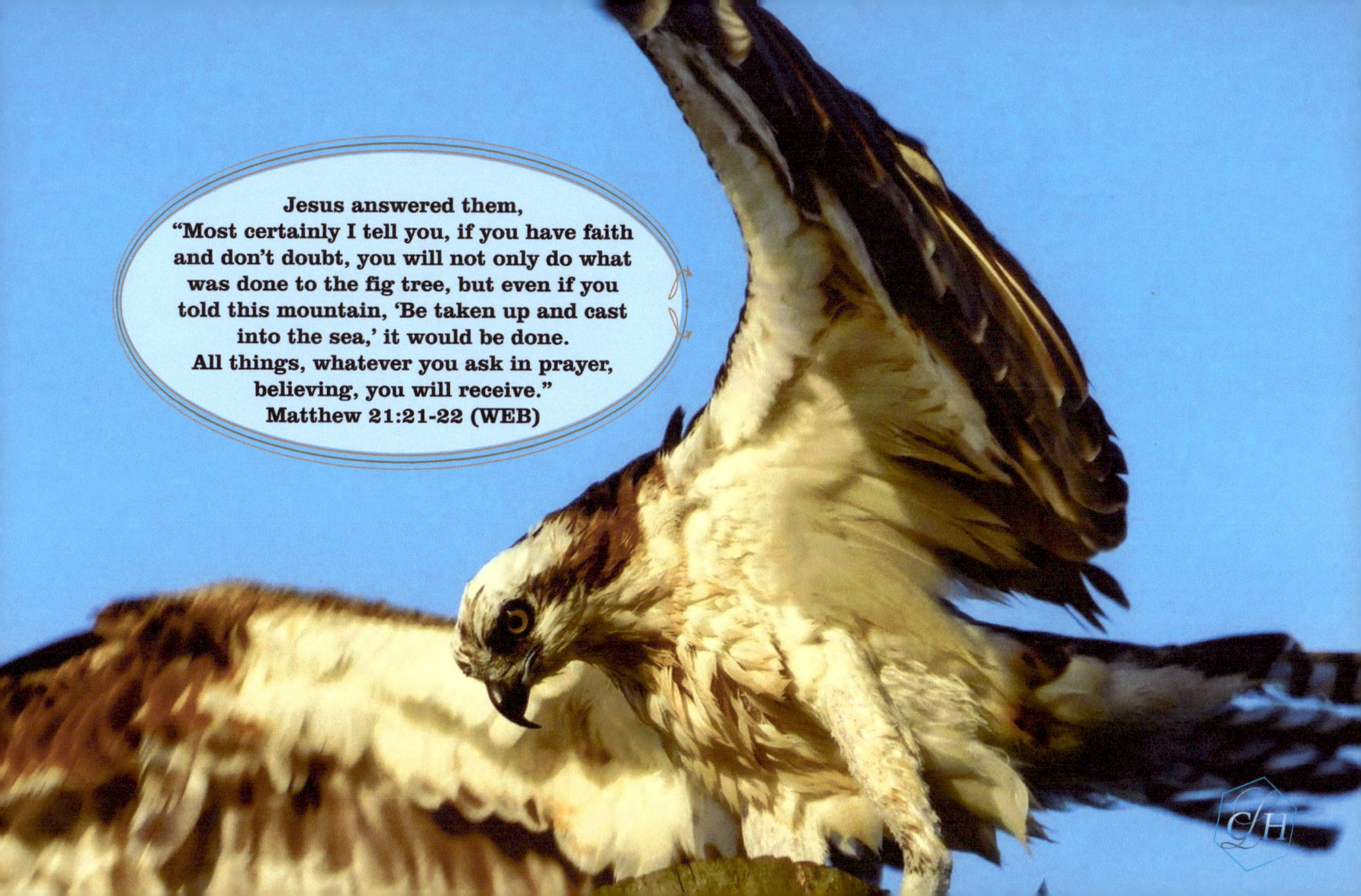

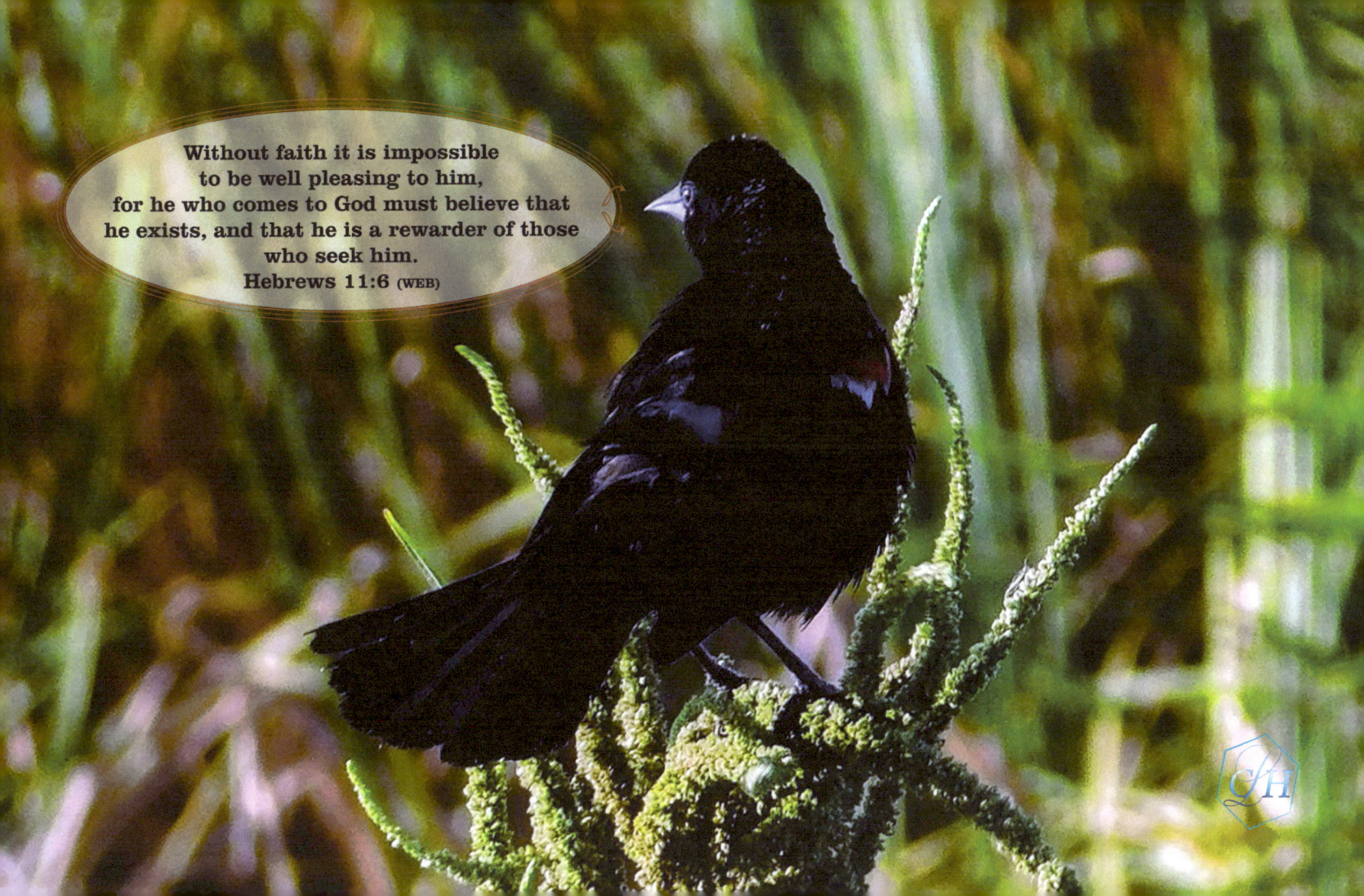

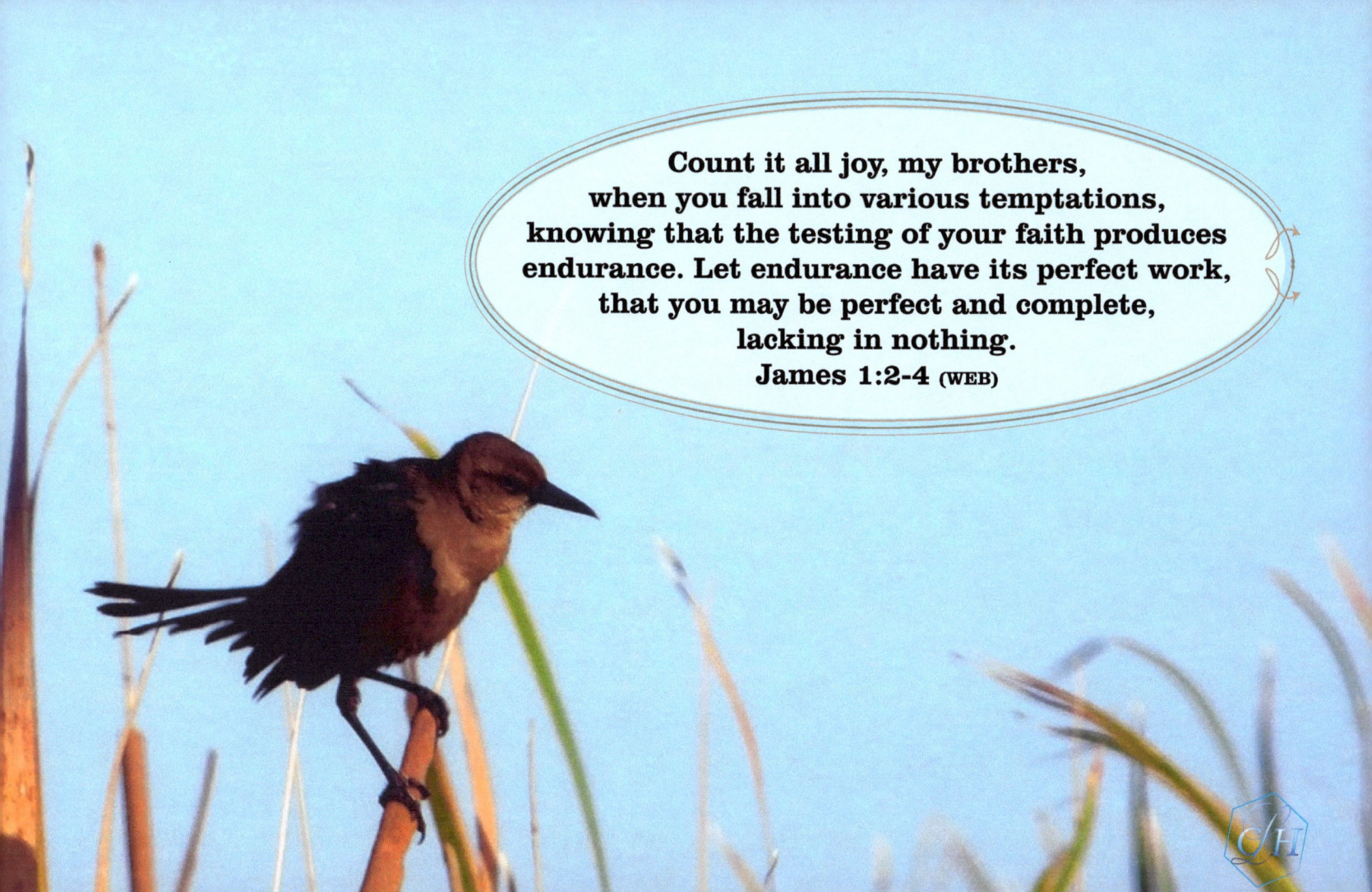

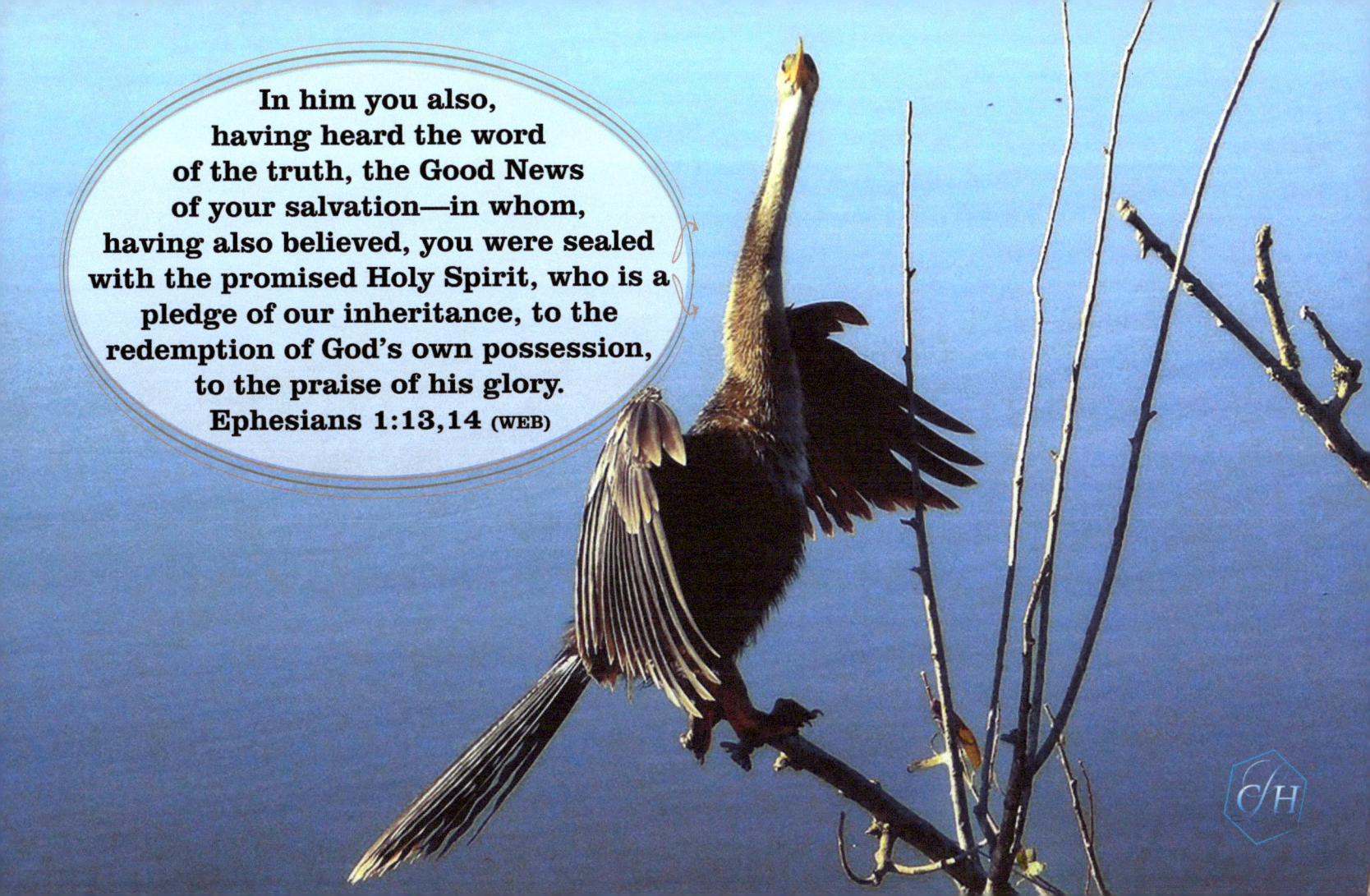

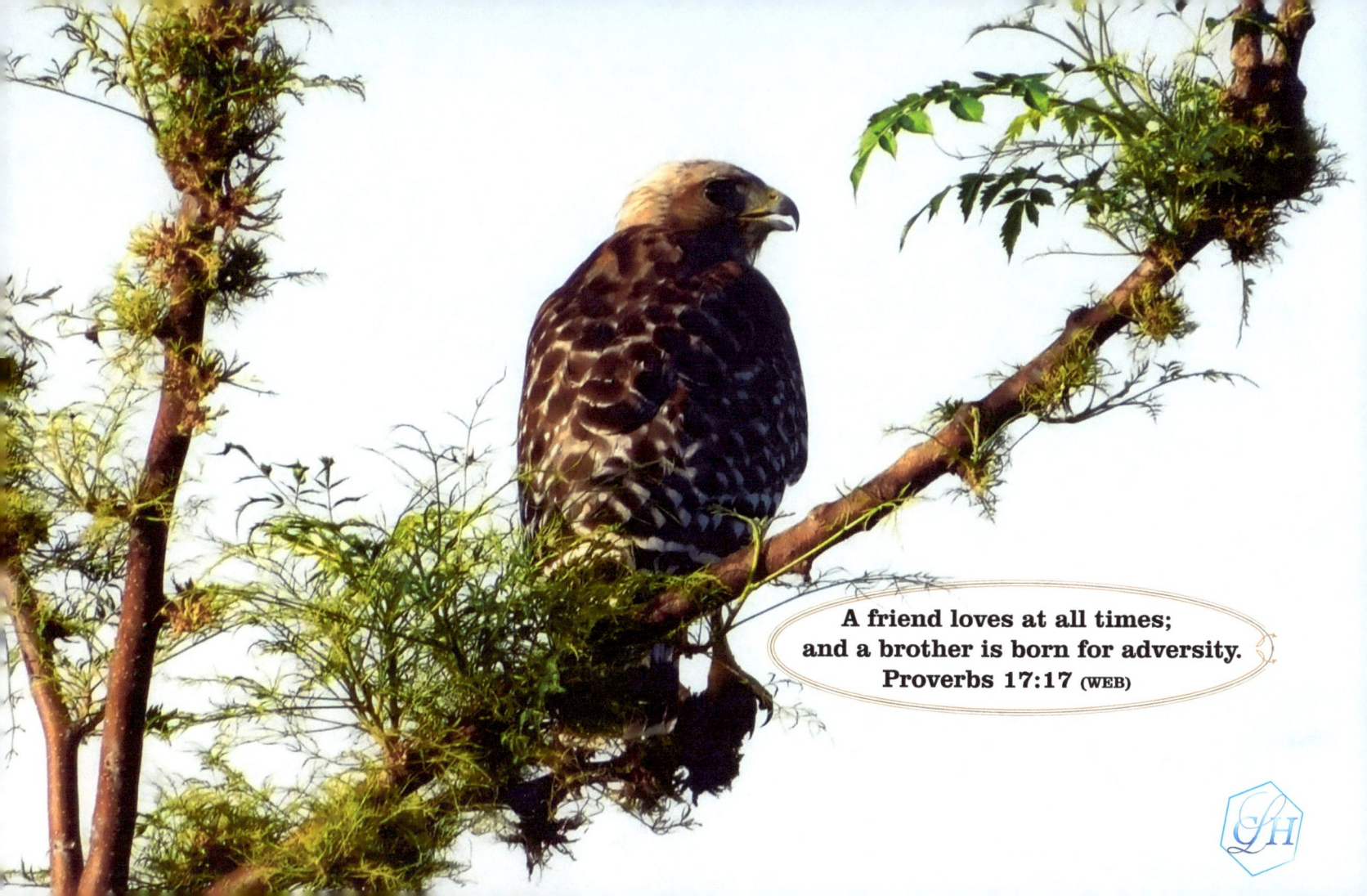

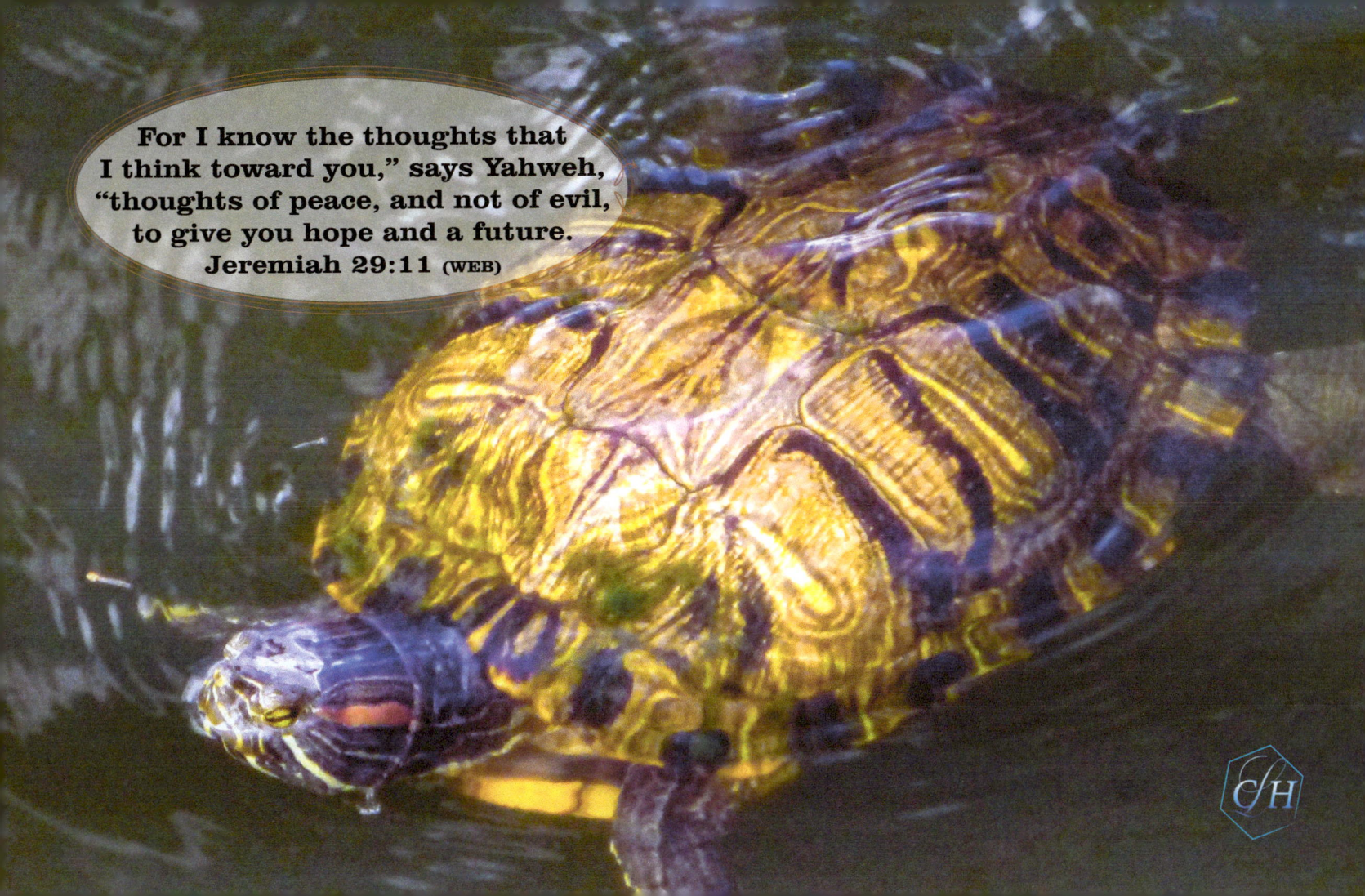

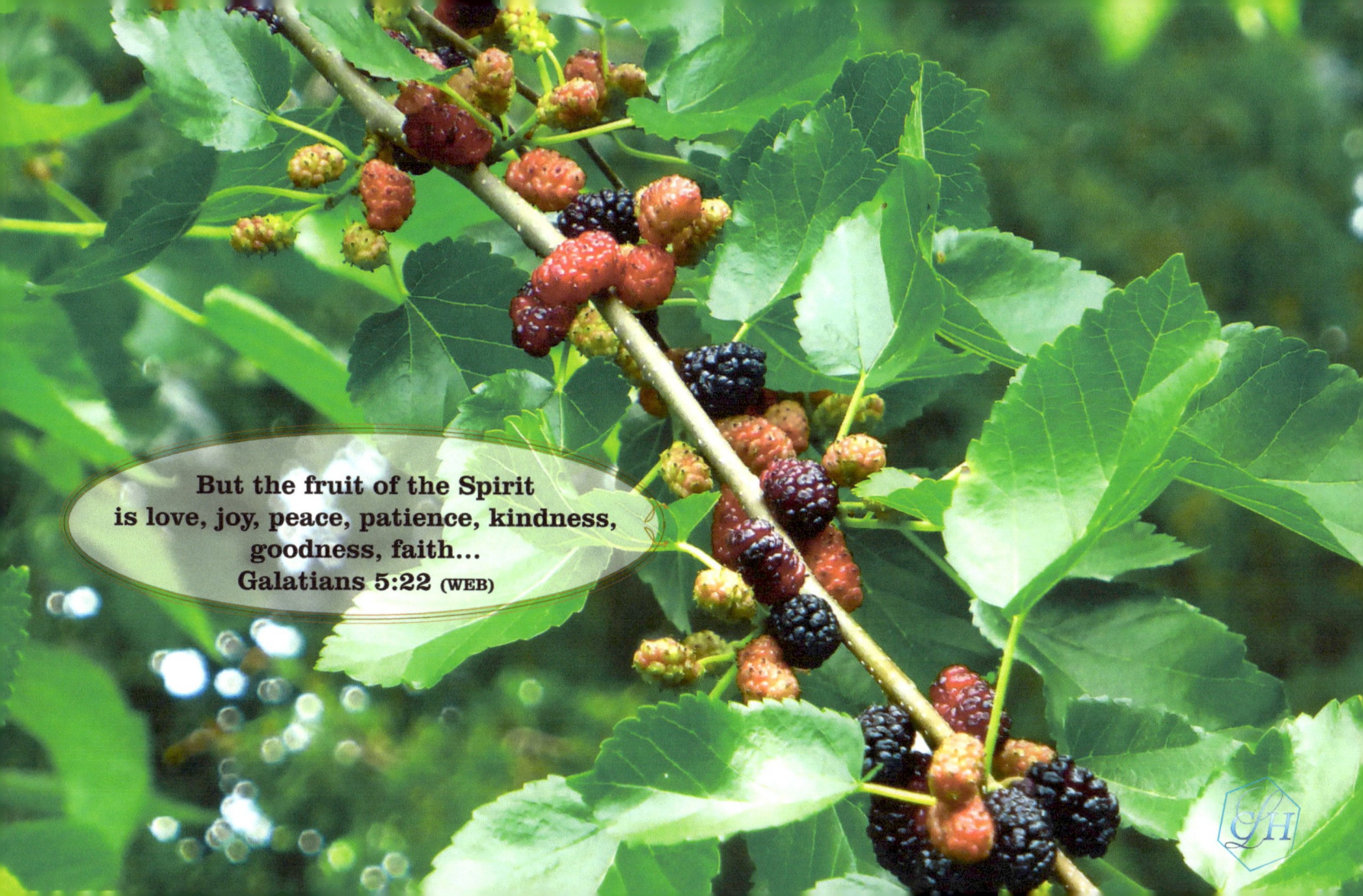

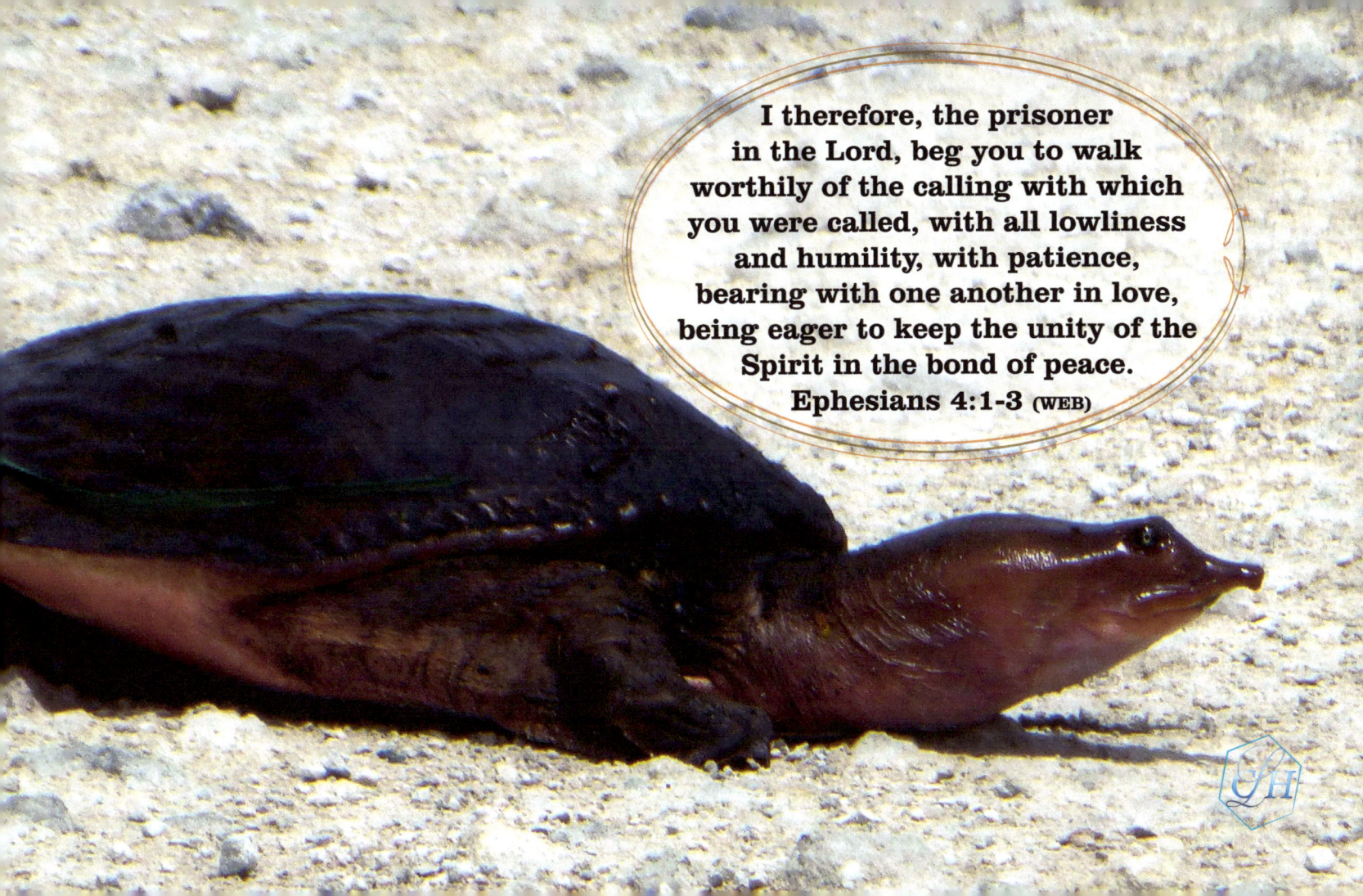

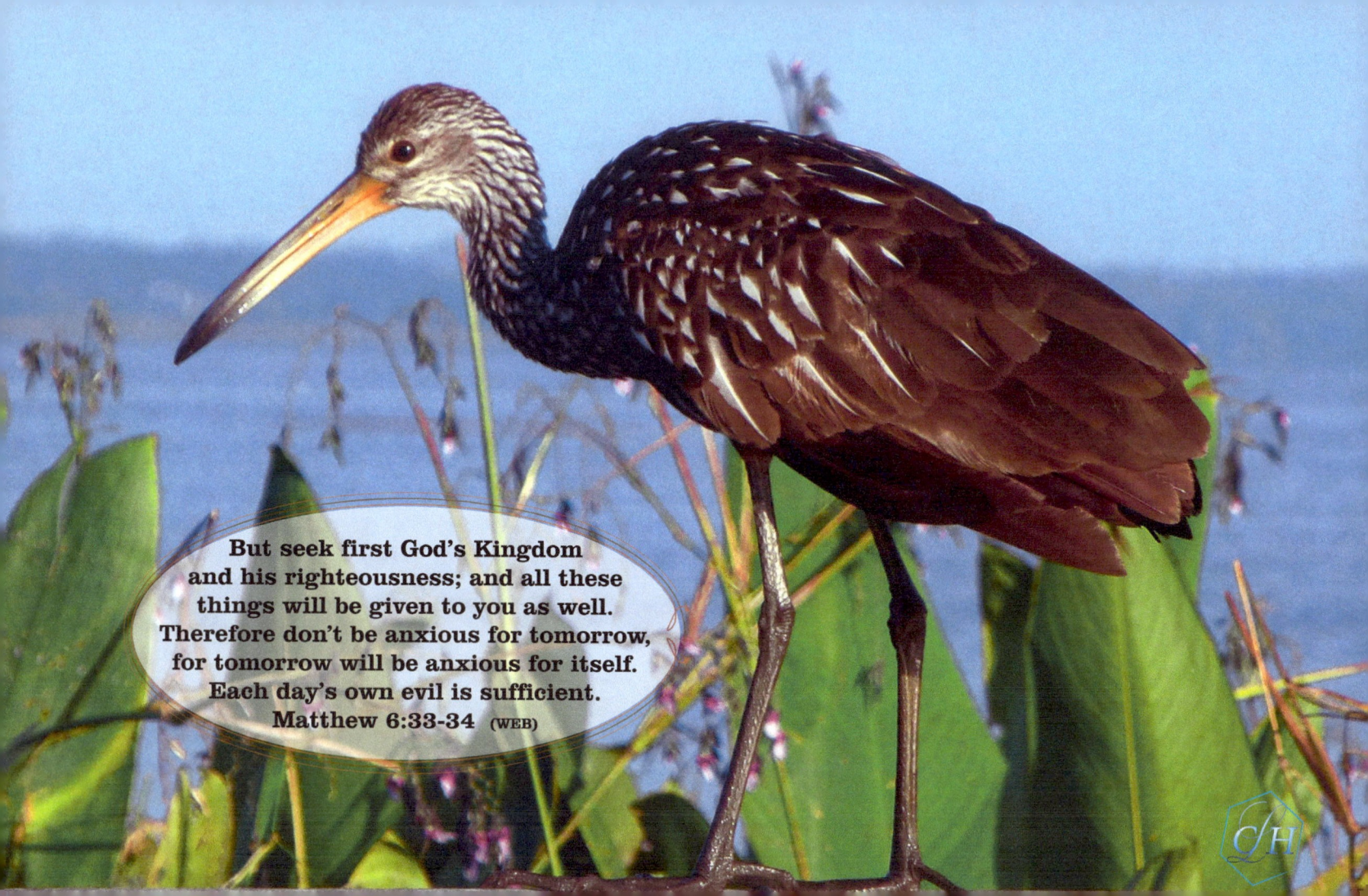

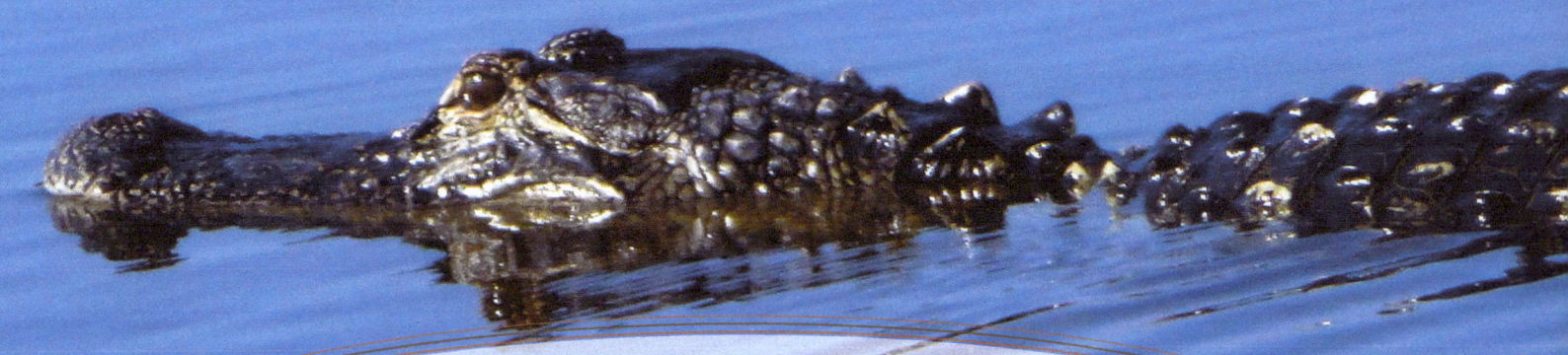

...that Christ may dwell in your hearts through faith,
to the end that you, being rooted and grounded in love,
may be strengthened to comprehend with all the saints
what is the width and length and height and depth, and to know
Christ's love which surpasses knowledge,
that you may be filled with all the fullness of God.
Ephesians 3:17-19 (WEB)

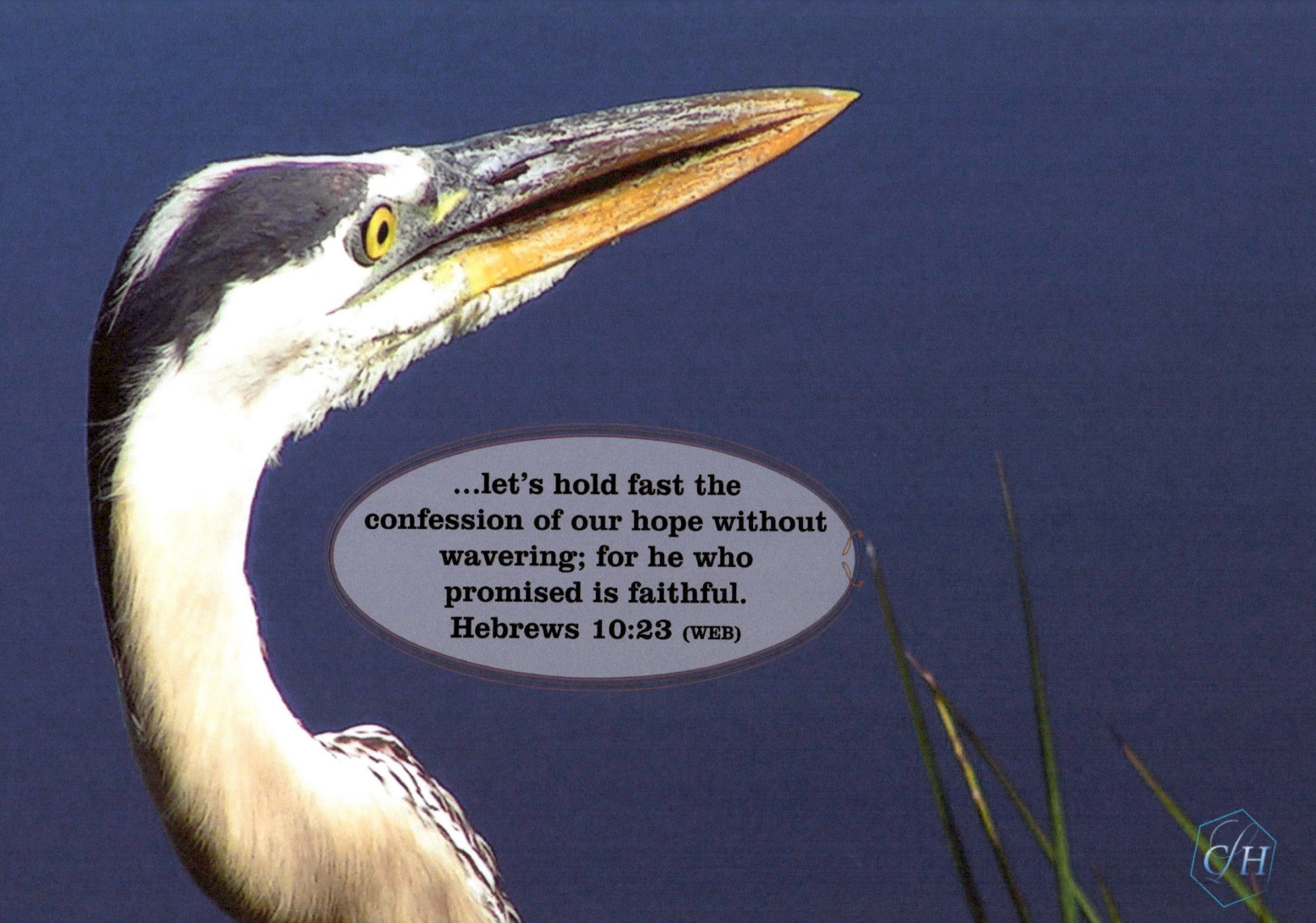

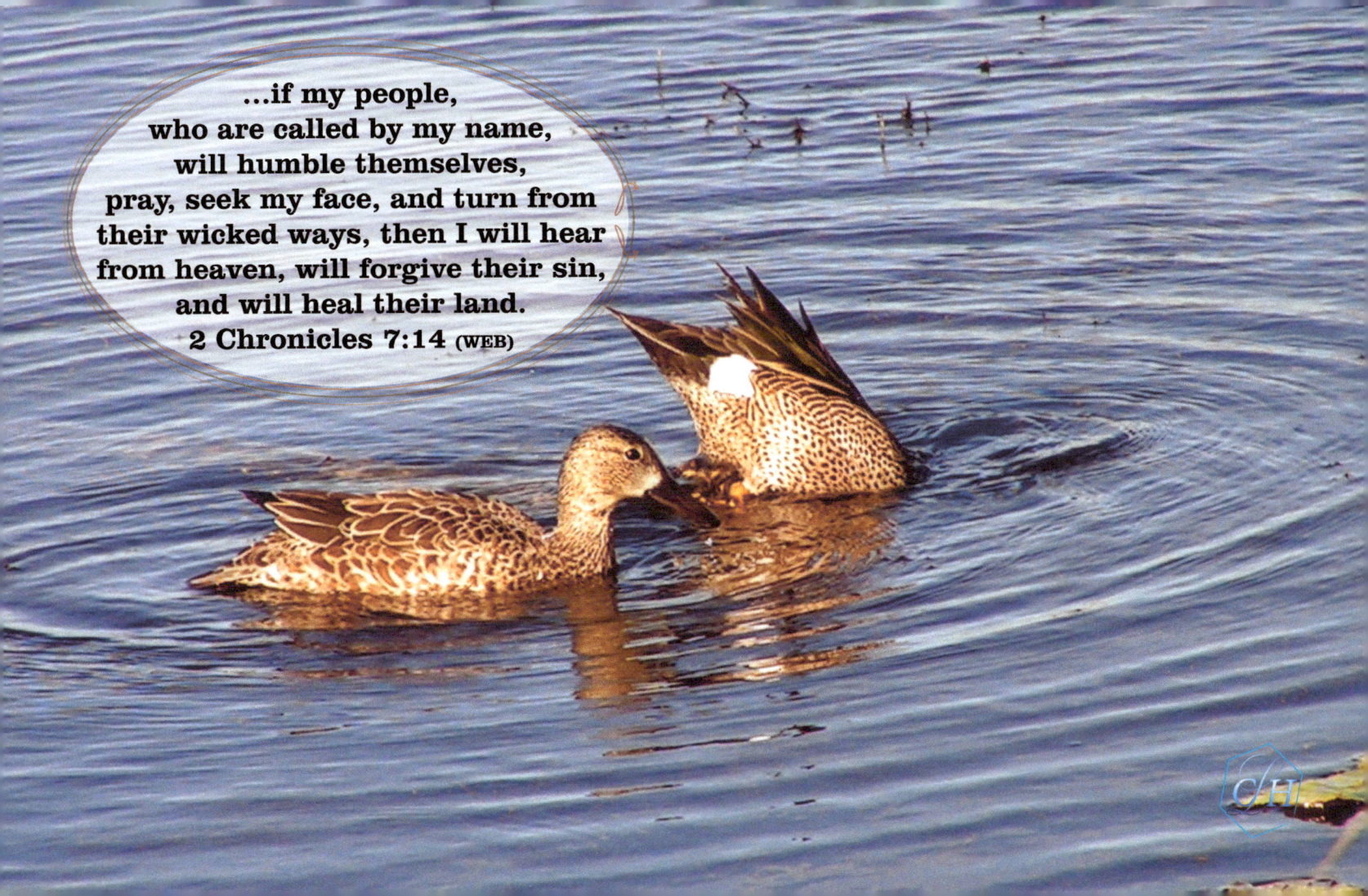

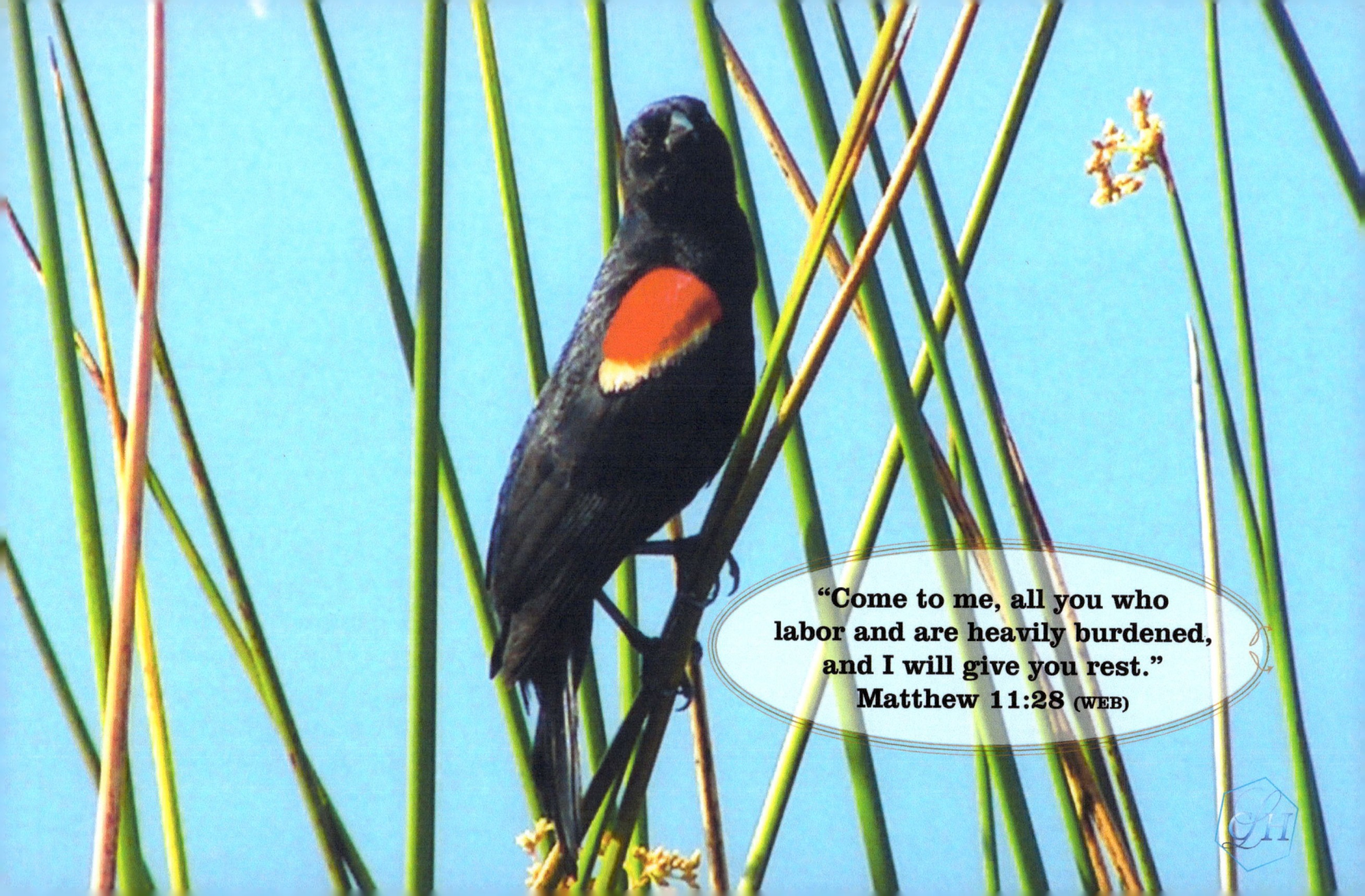

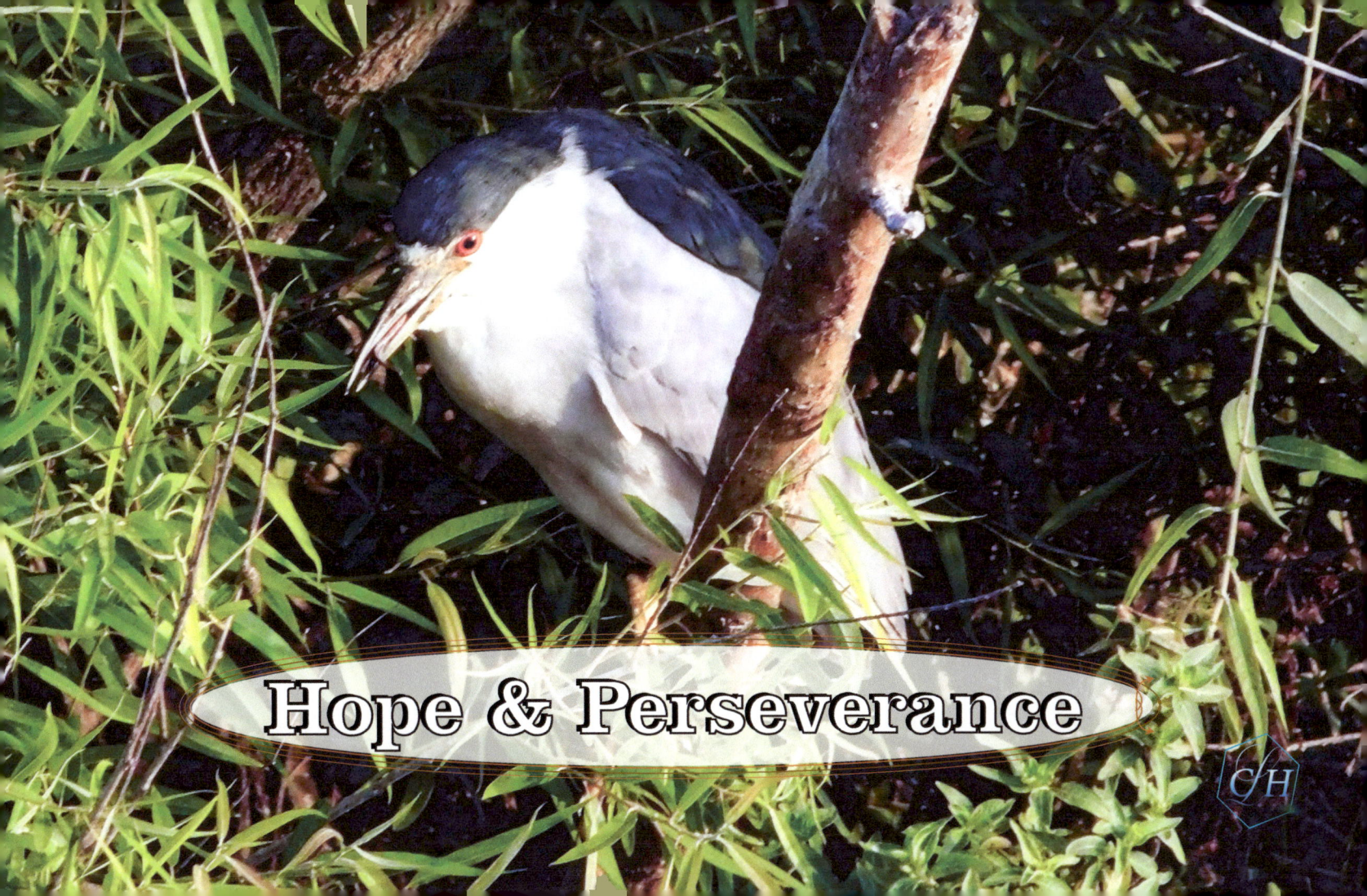

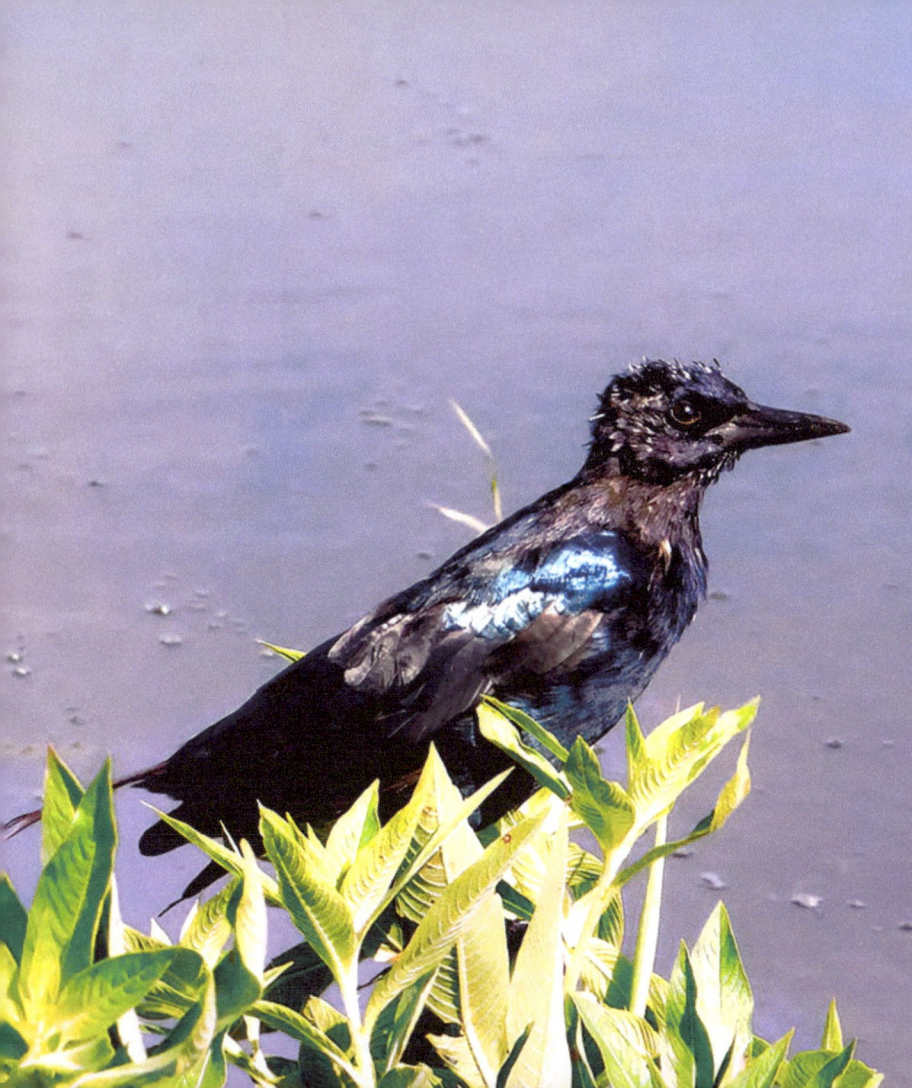

Philippians 4:13
2 Timothy 1:7
Psalms 27:1
1 Peter 1:8-9
Romans 12:12
Psalms 34:4-5
1 Thessalonians 5:16-18
1 Peter 5:10
1 Thessalonians 1:3
Romans 5:5
Romans 8:28
Romans 15:13
1 Peter 5:6-7
Revelations 21:4
1 Peter 4:8
Romans 13:8
Romans 5:8
Romans 12:9
Lamentations 3:22-23
Romans 8:38-39

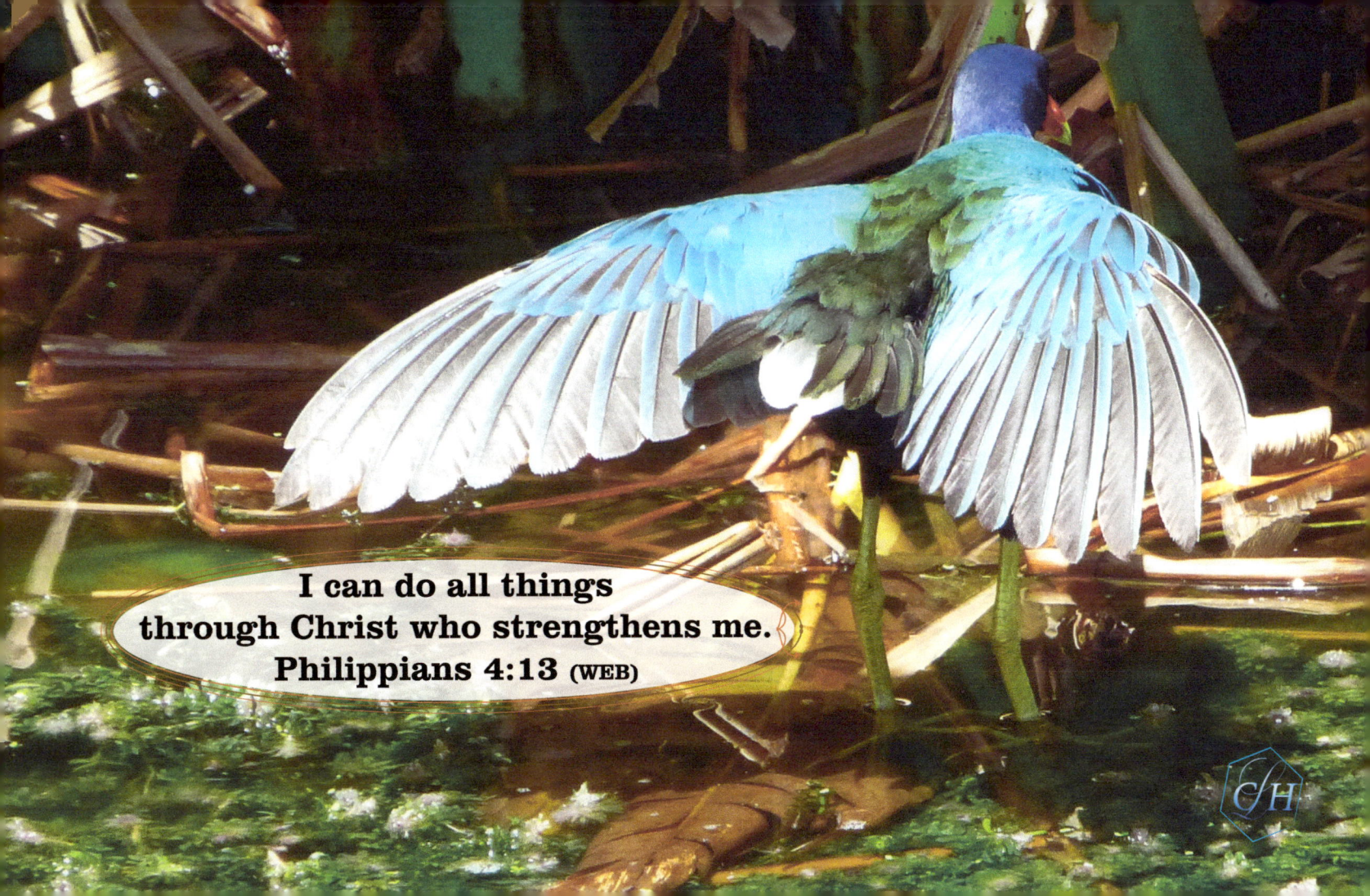

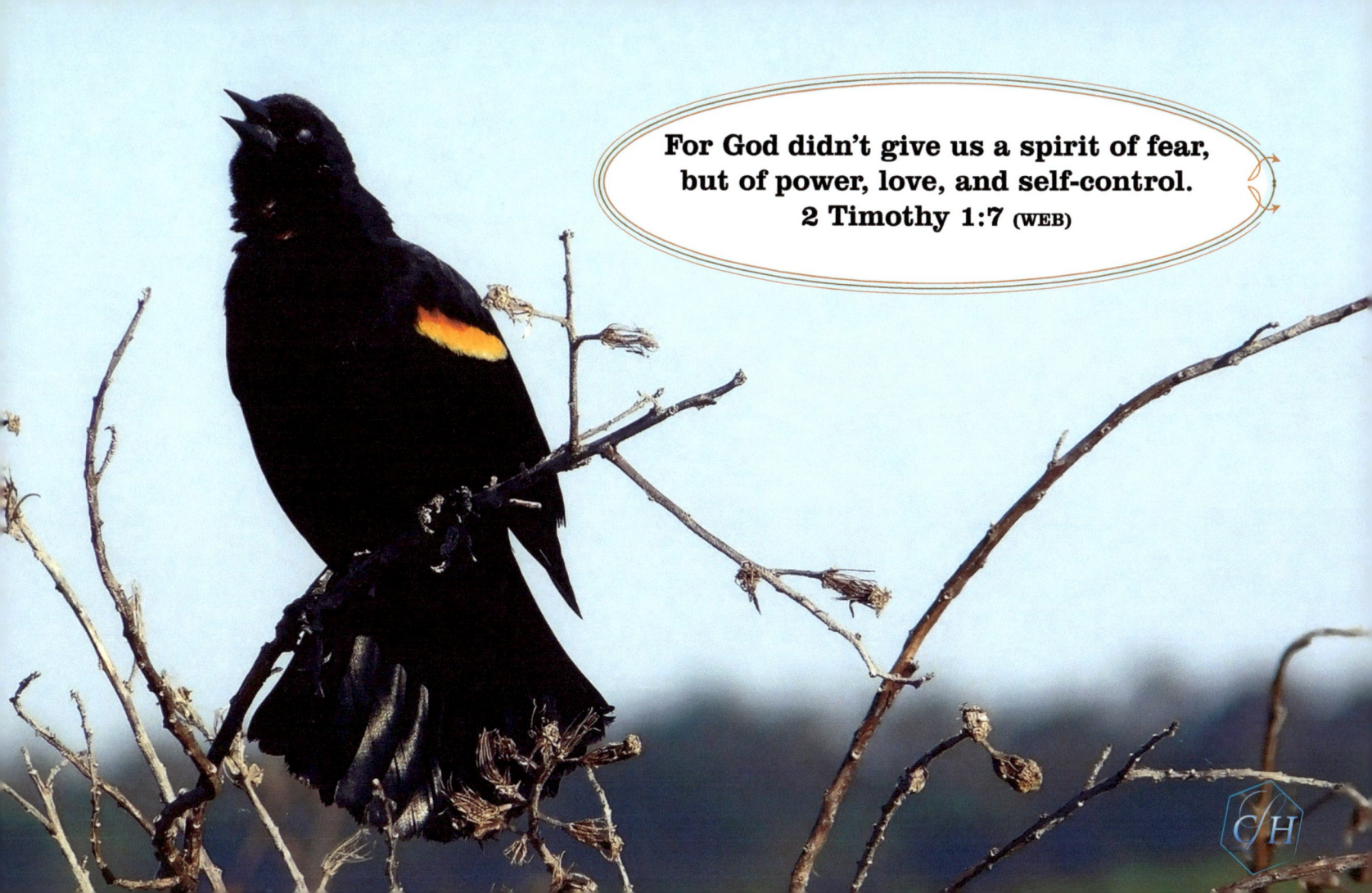

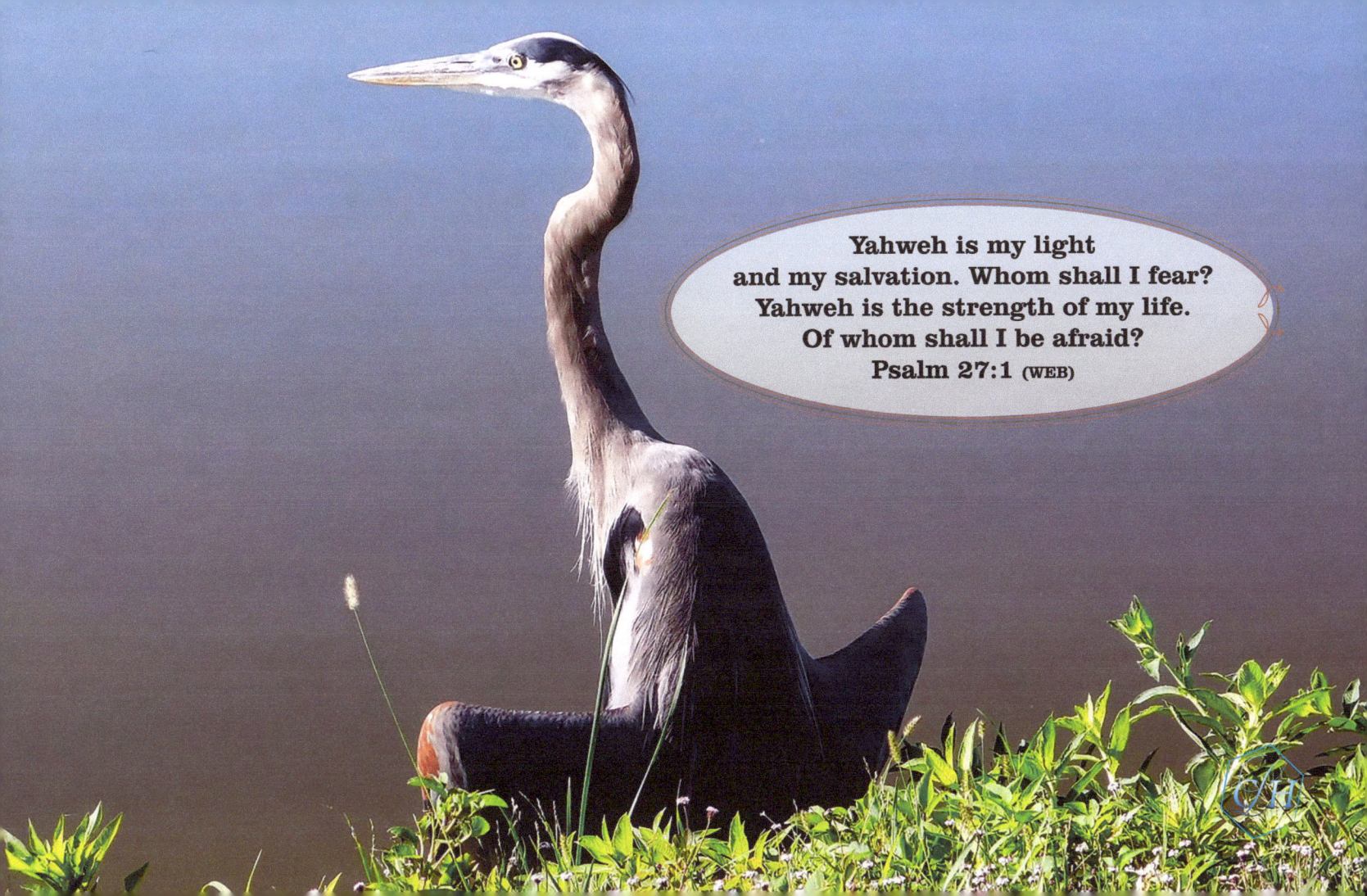

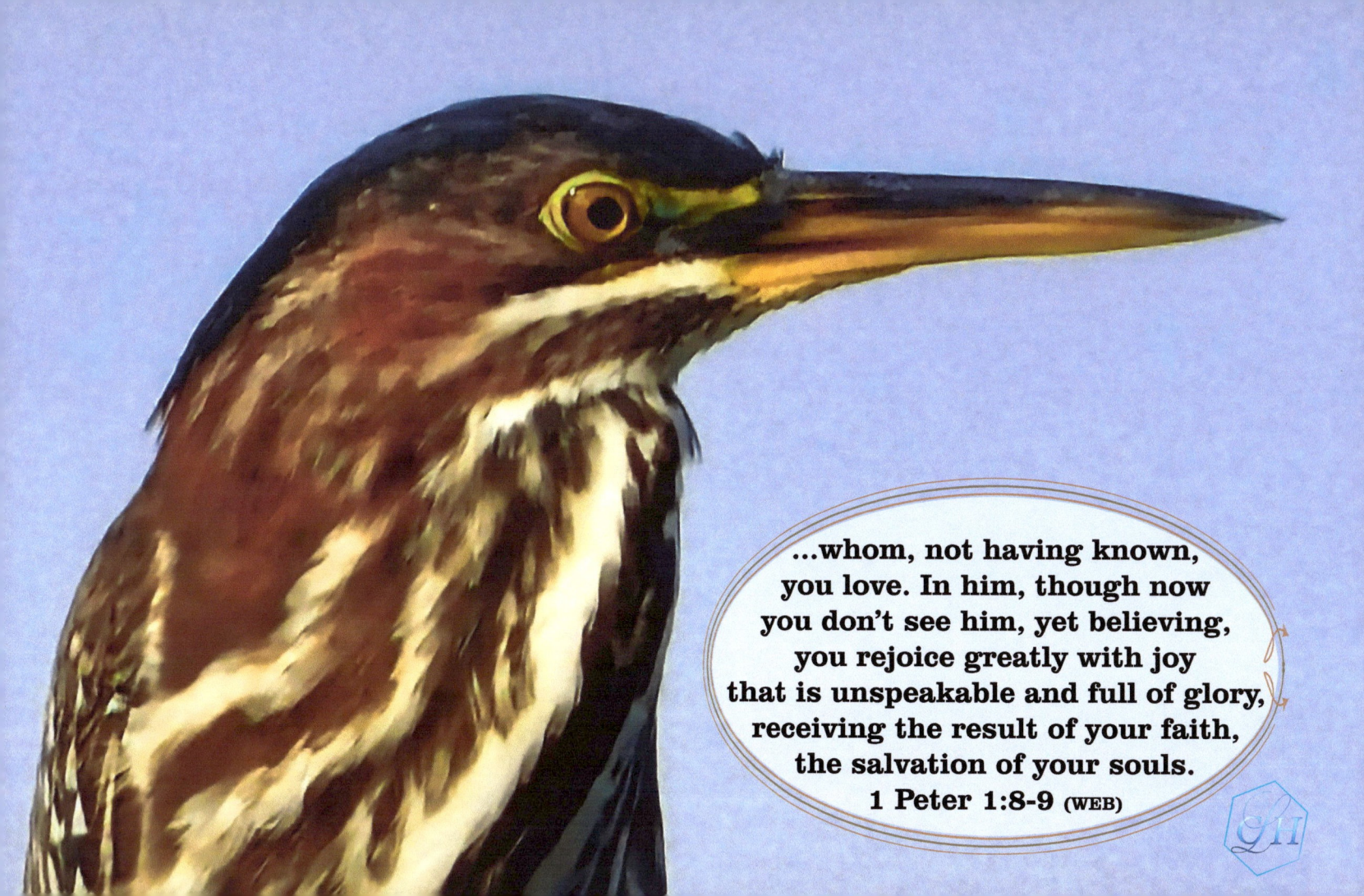

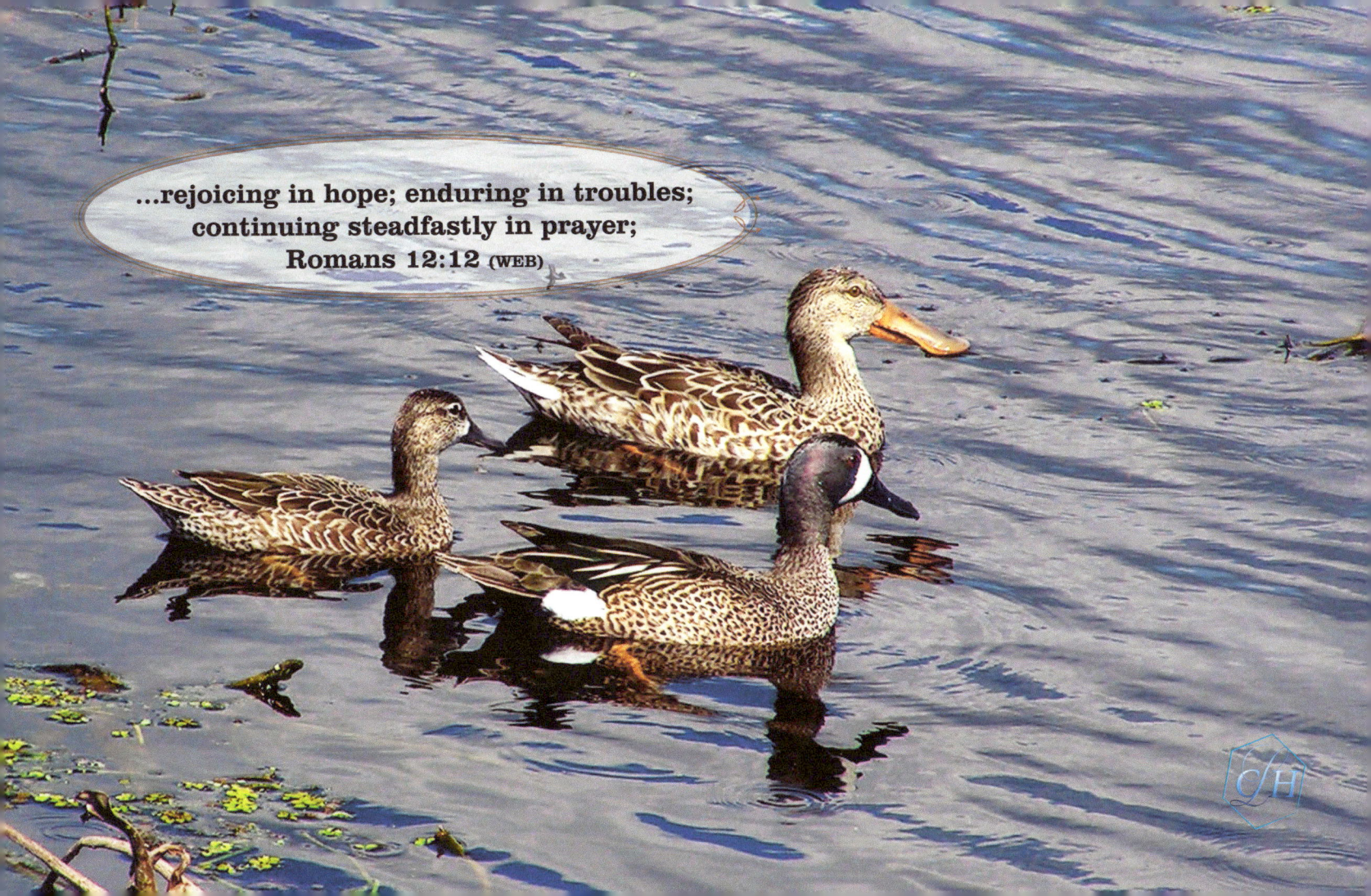

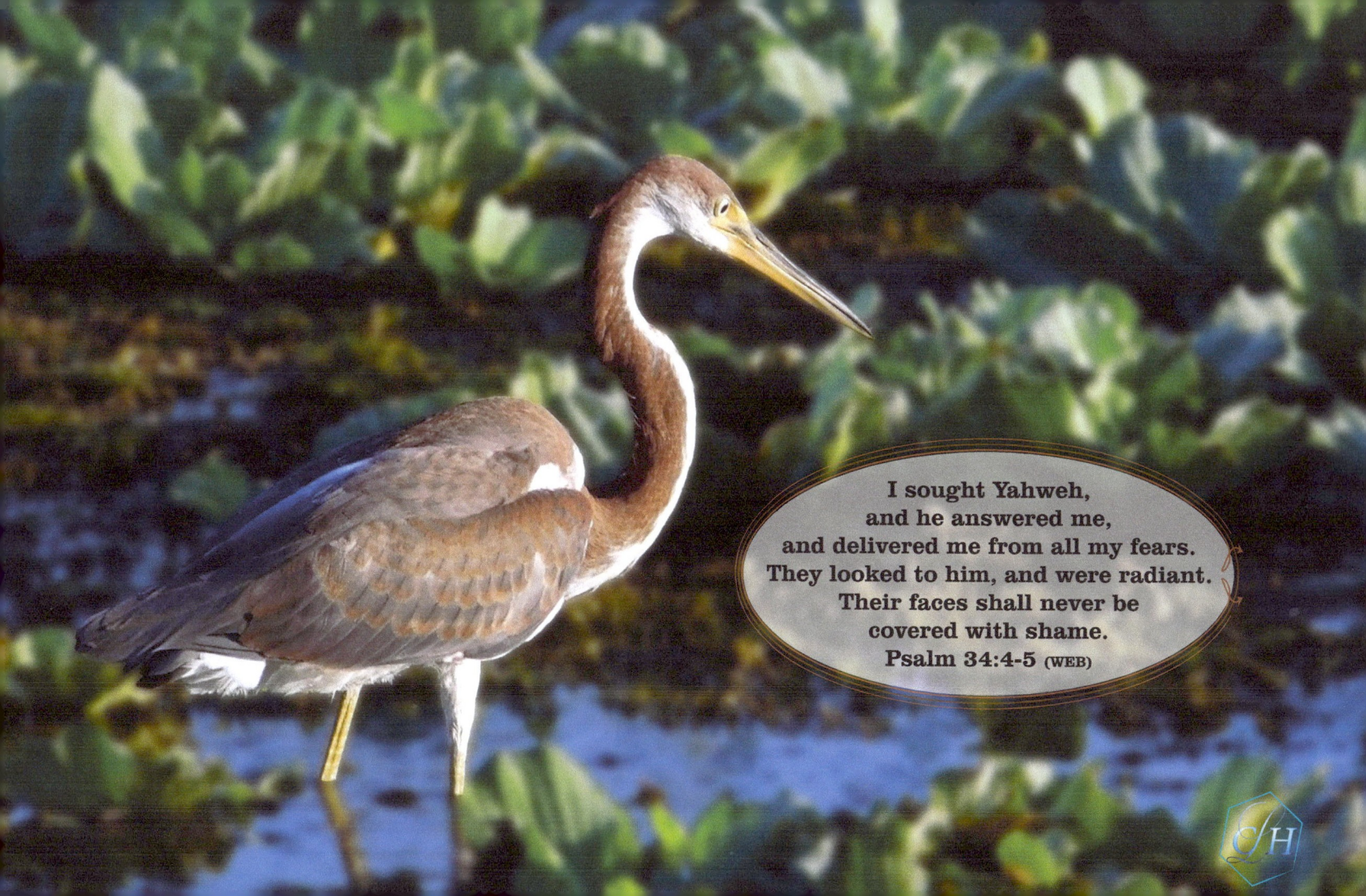

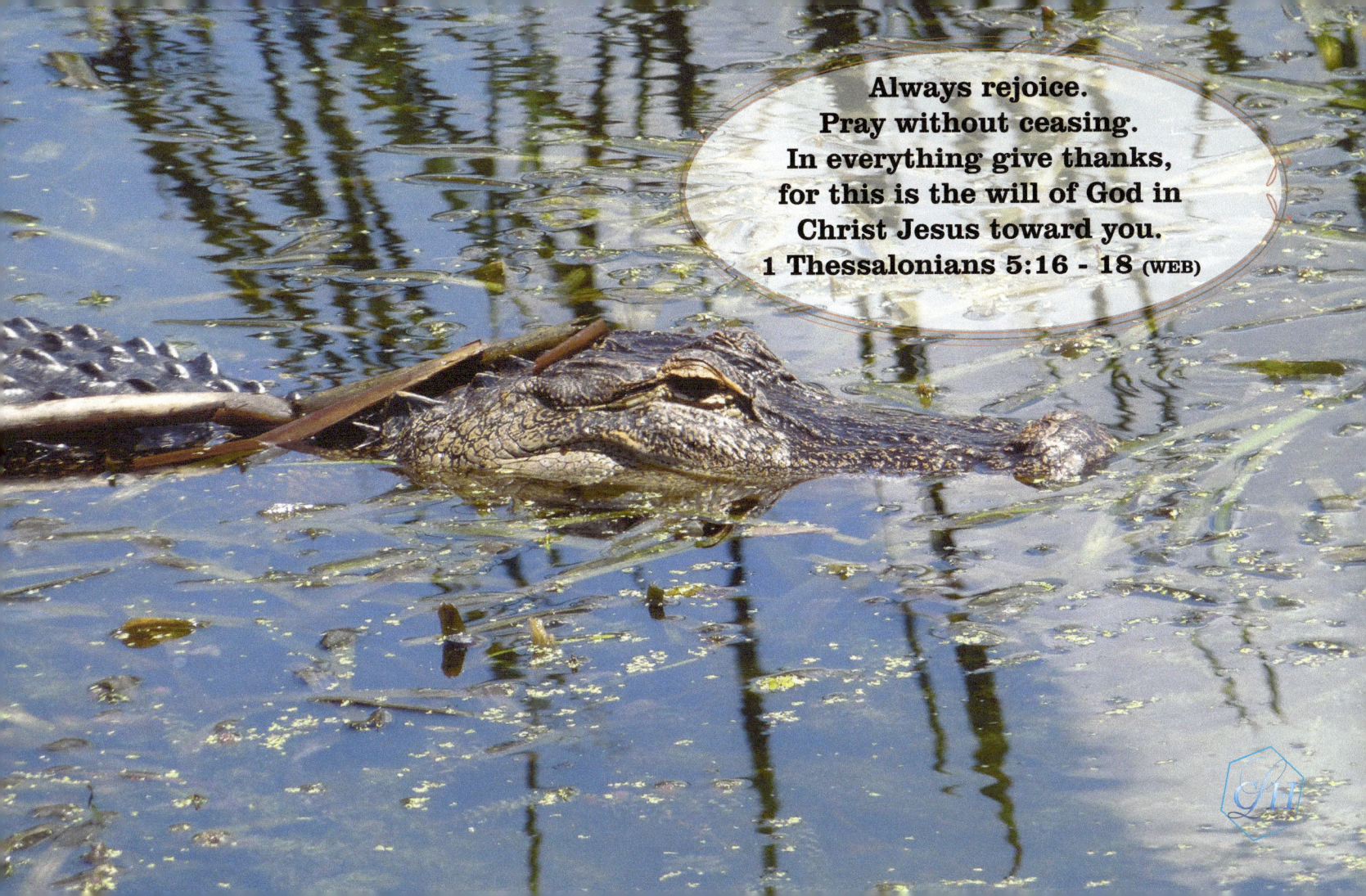

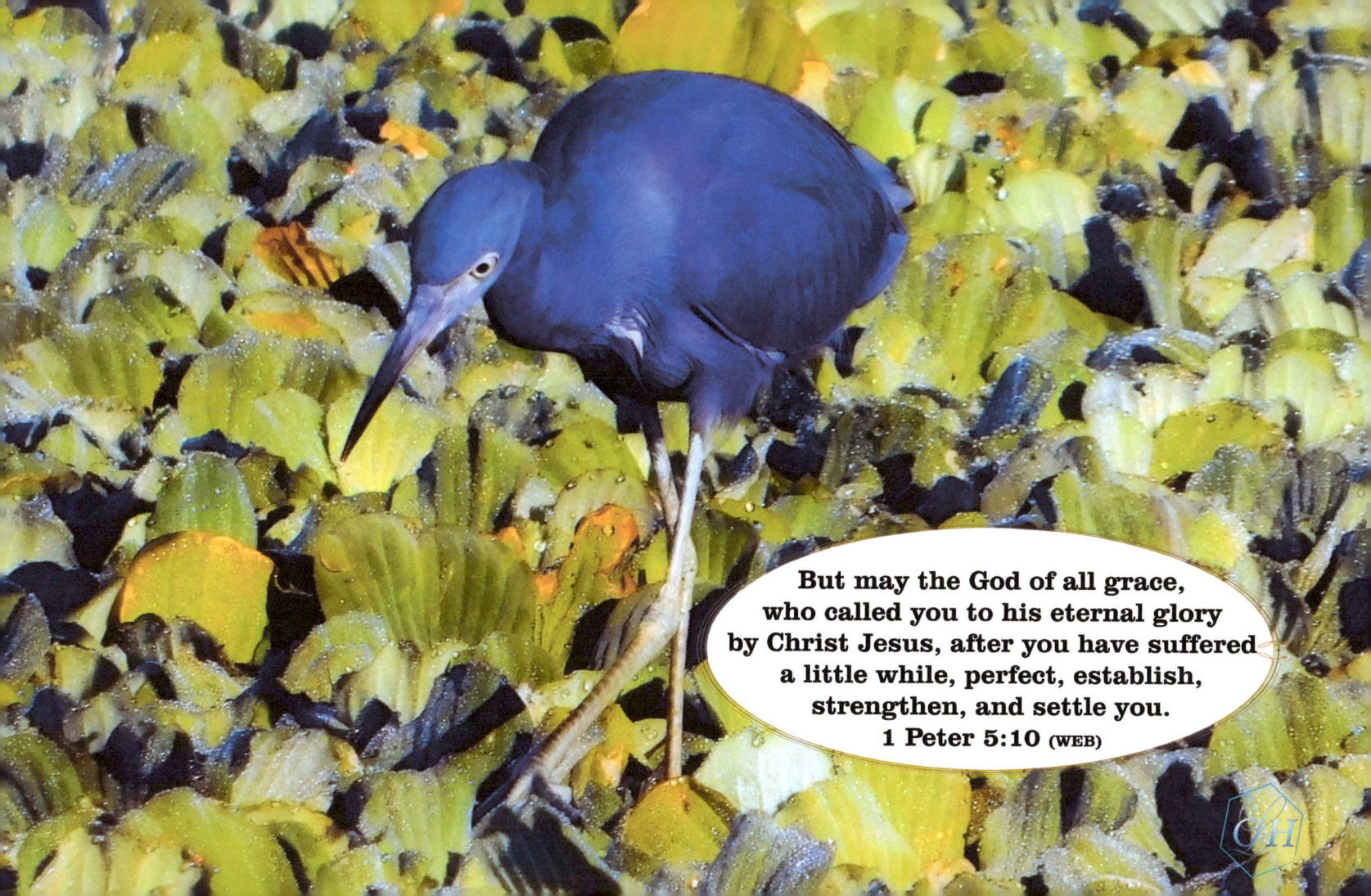

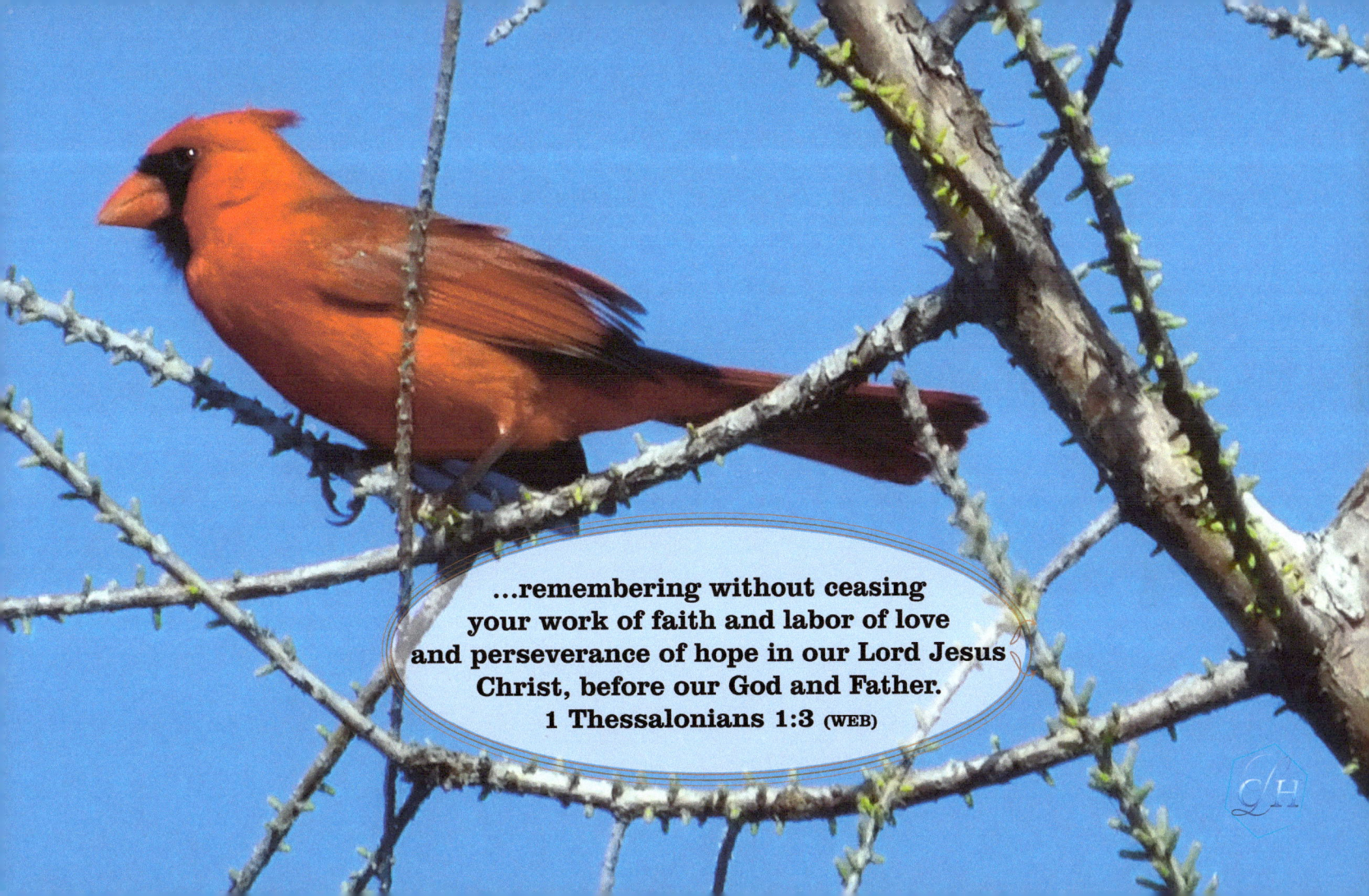

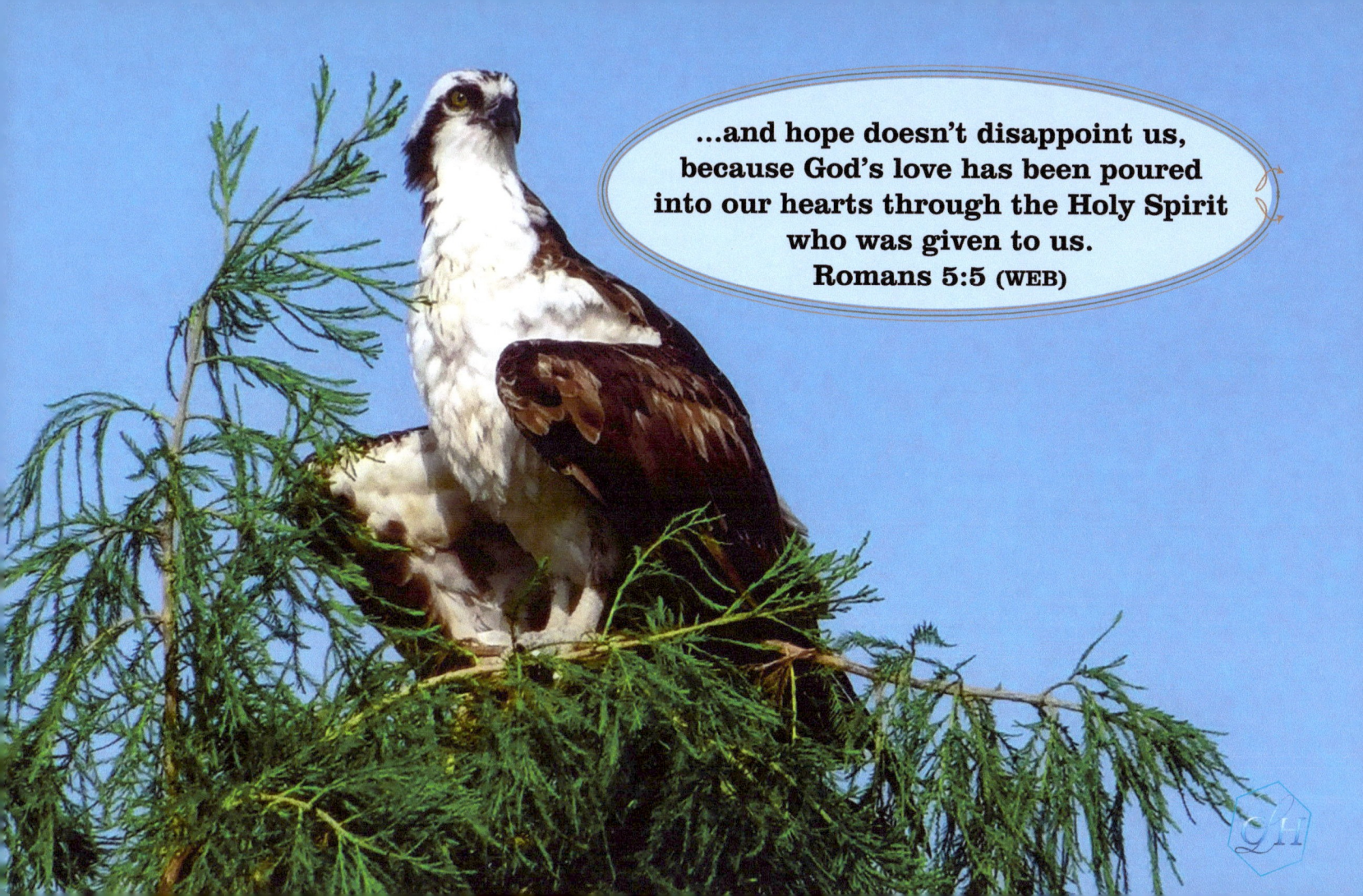

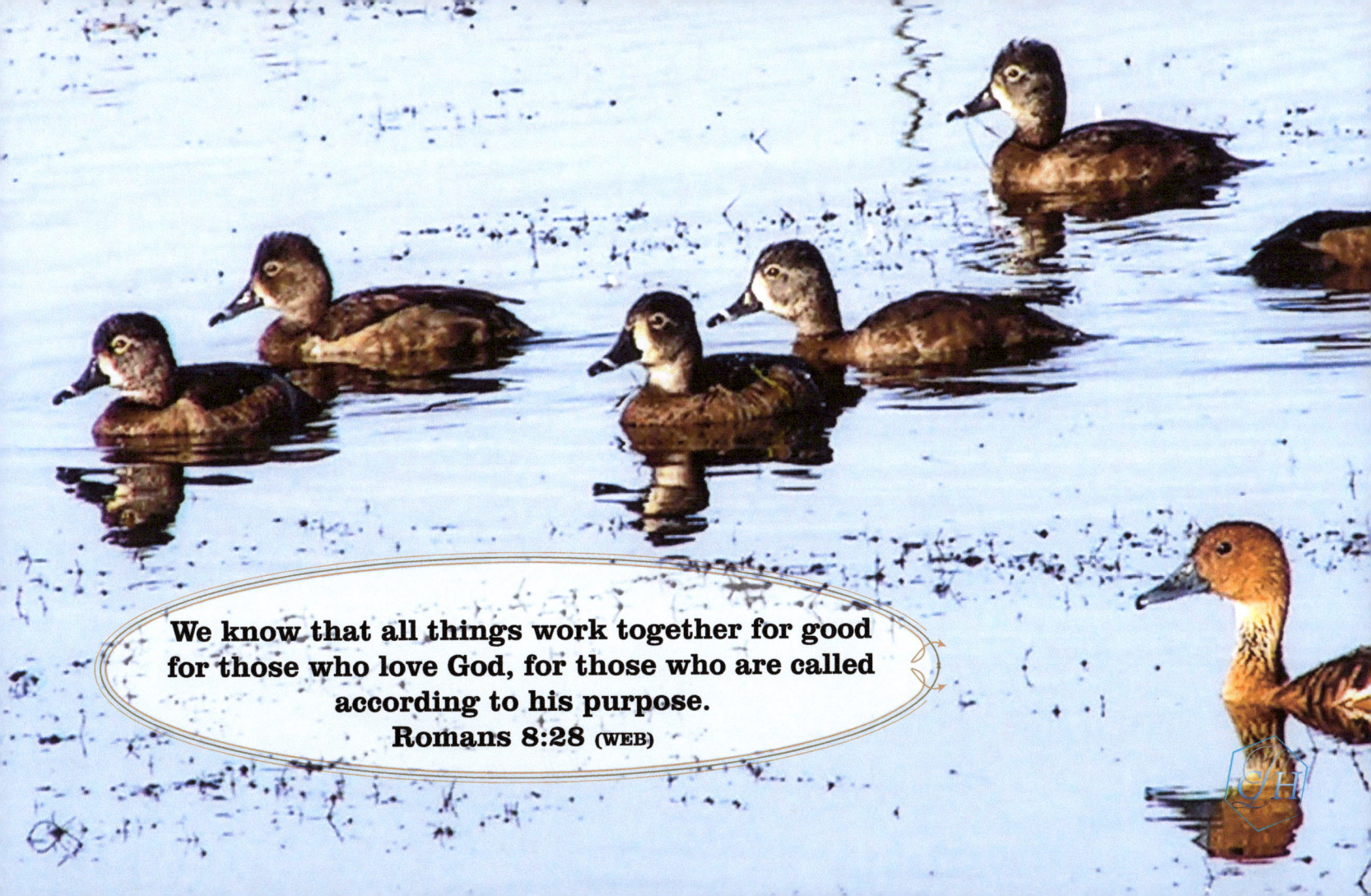

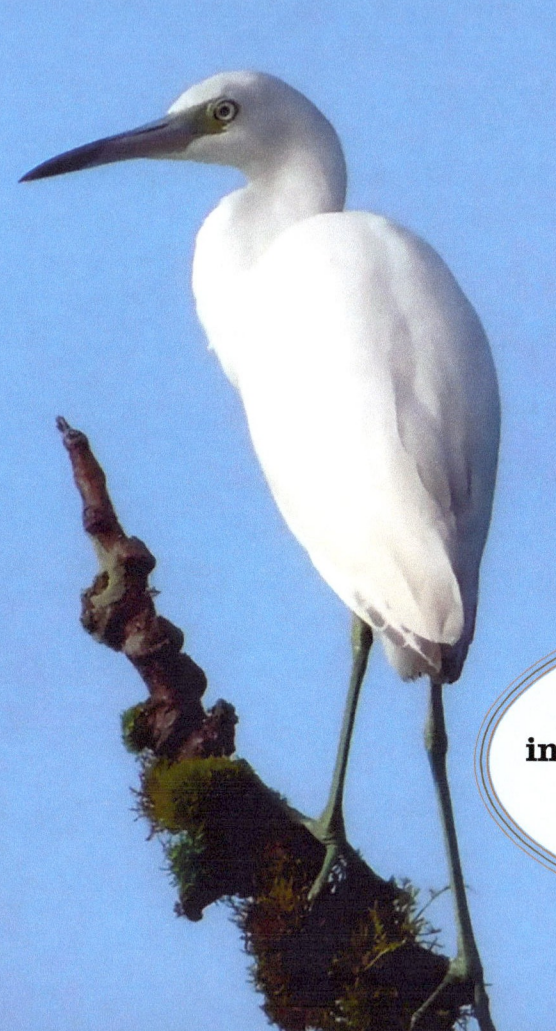

Now may the God of hope fill you with all joy and peace in believing, that you may abound in hope, in the power of the Holy Spirit.
Romans 15:13 (WEB)

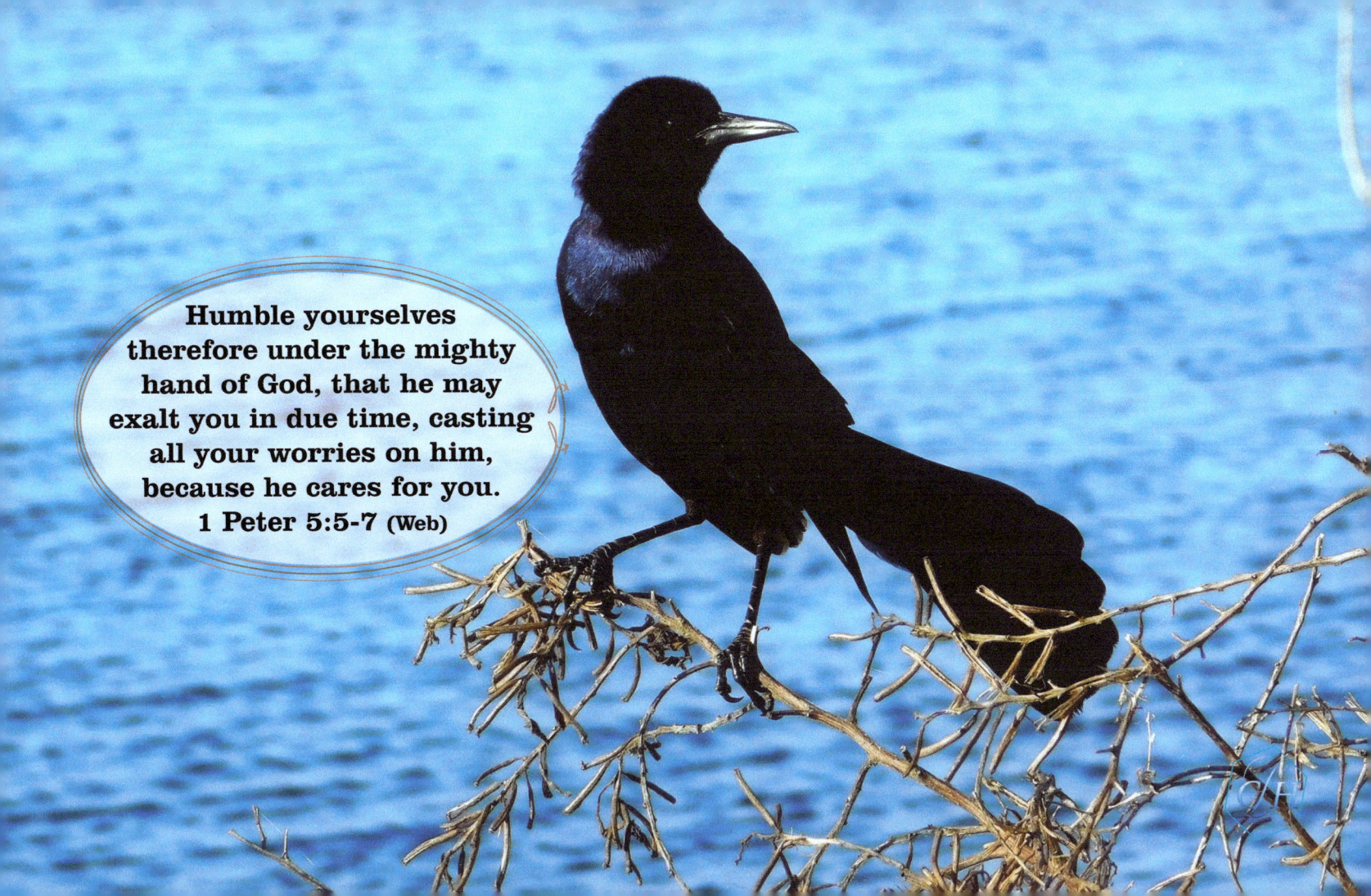

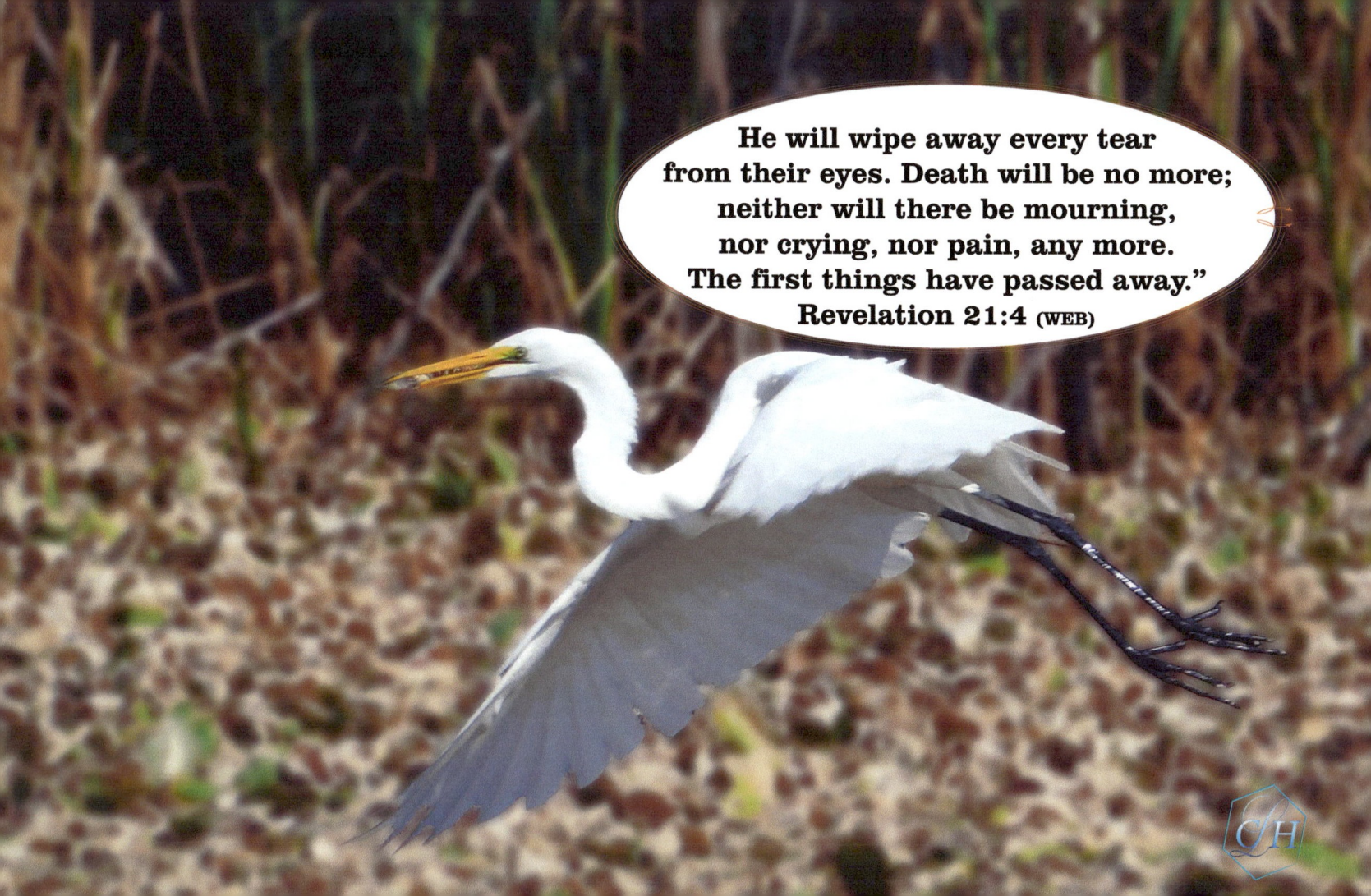

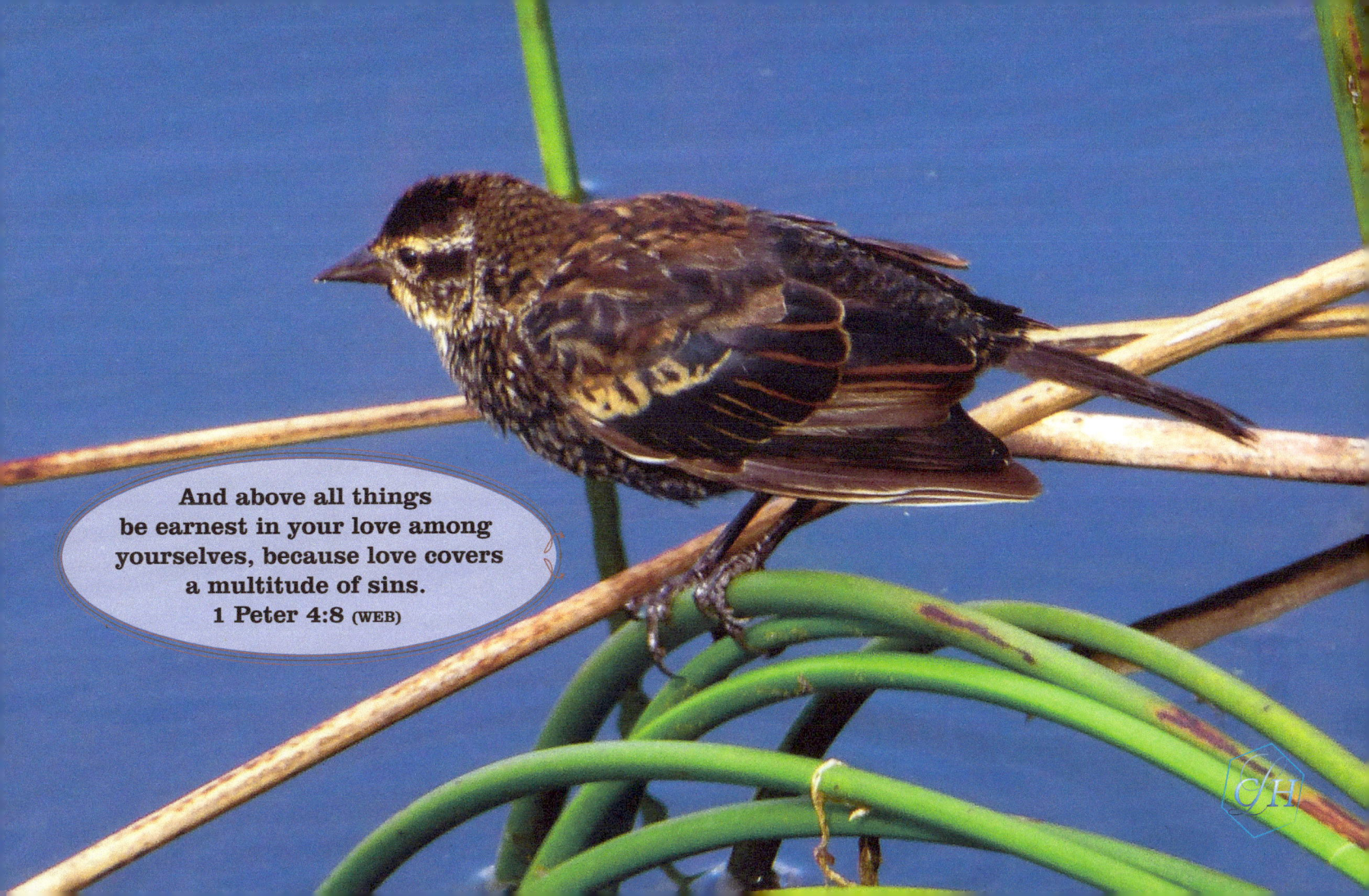

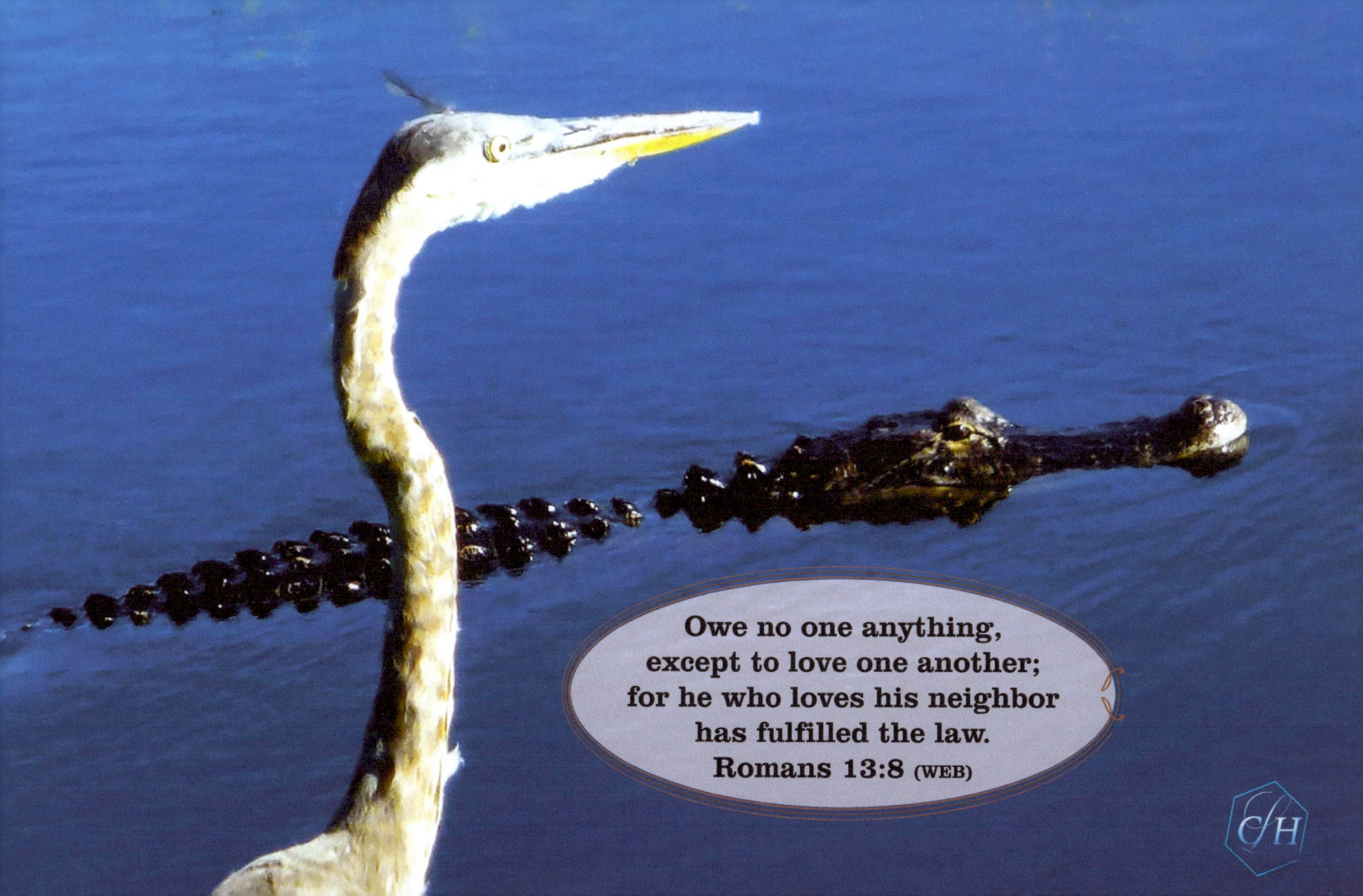

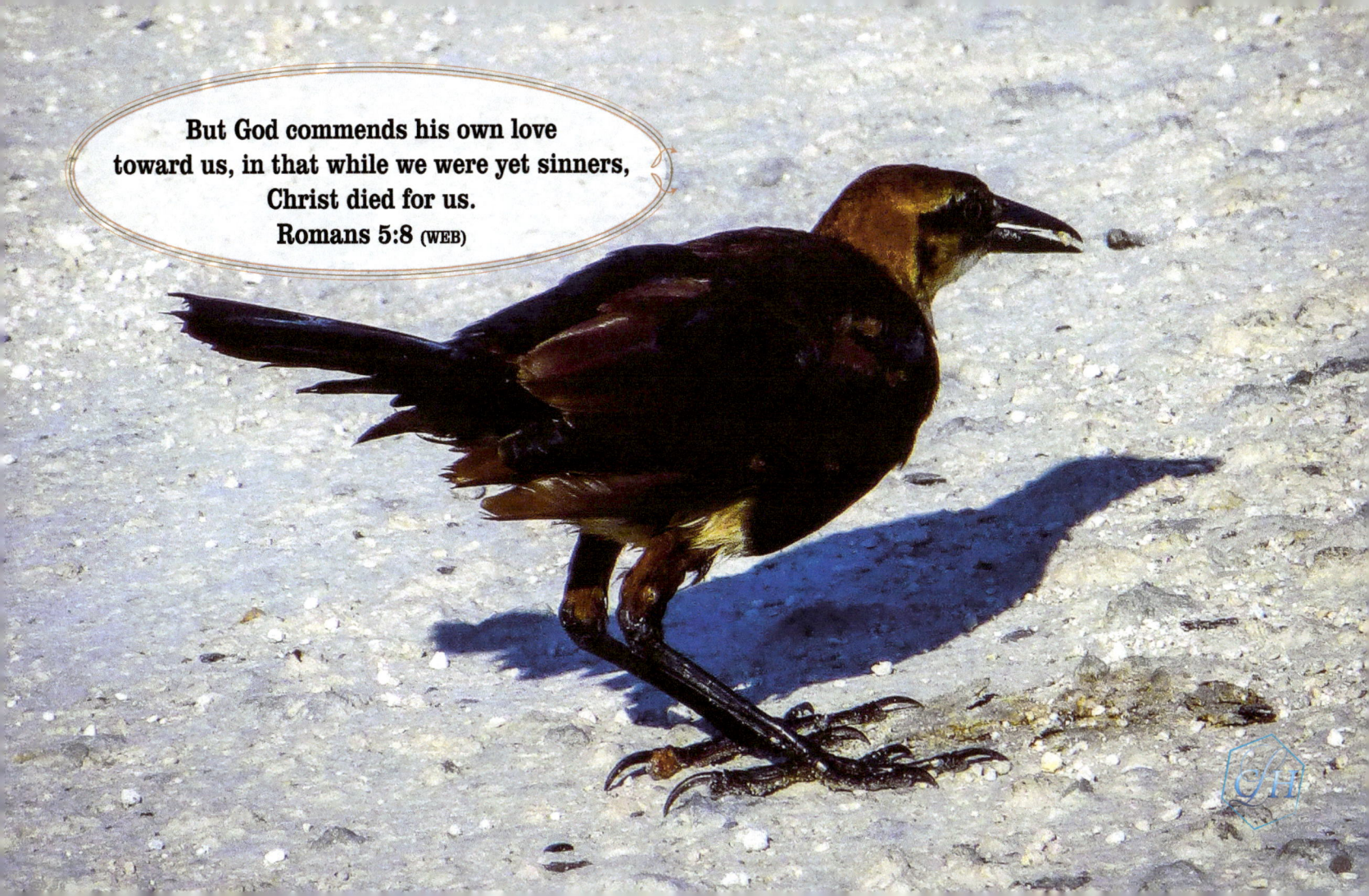

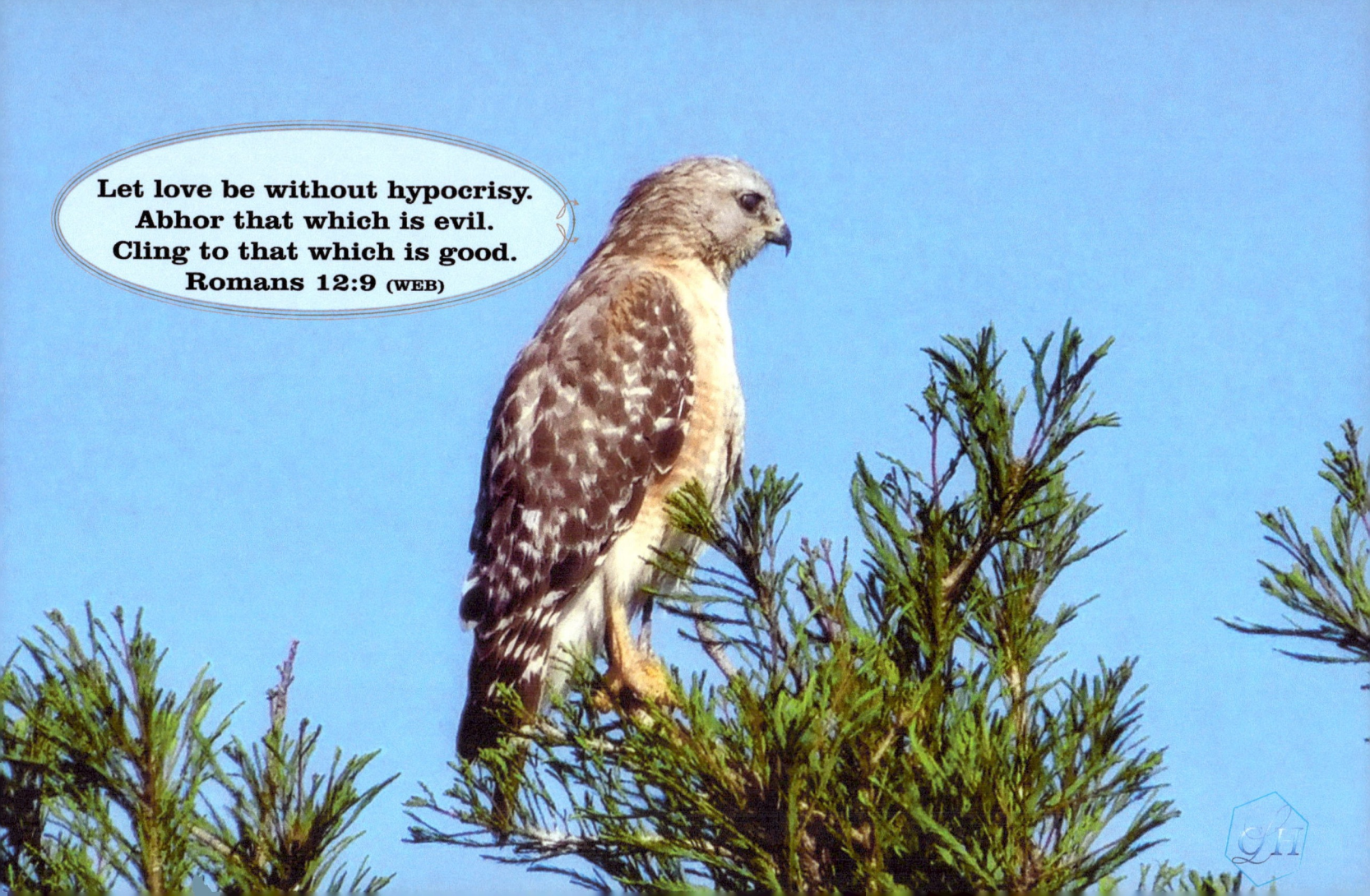

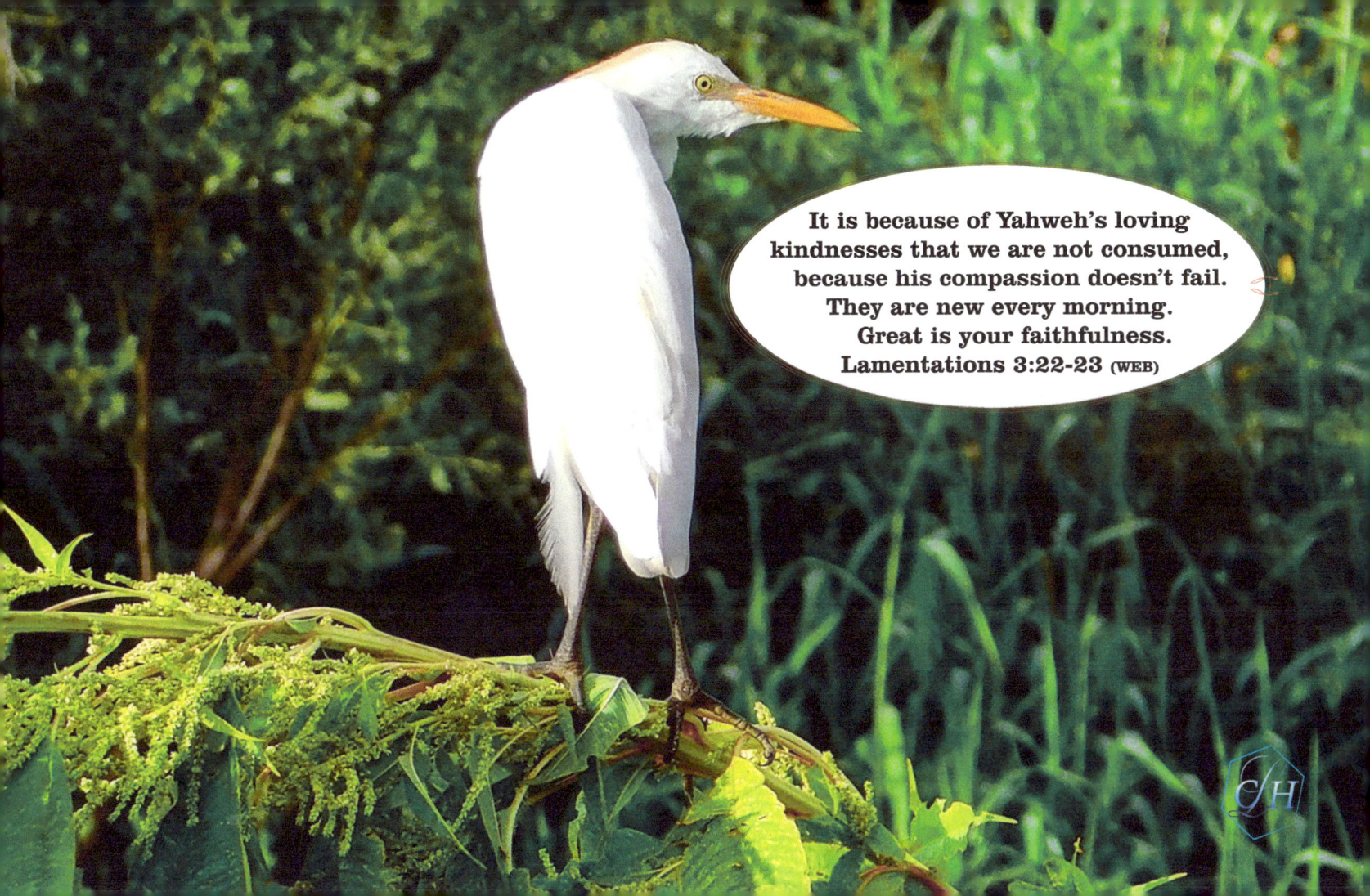

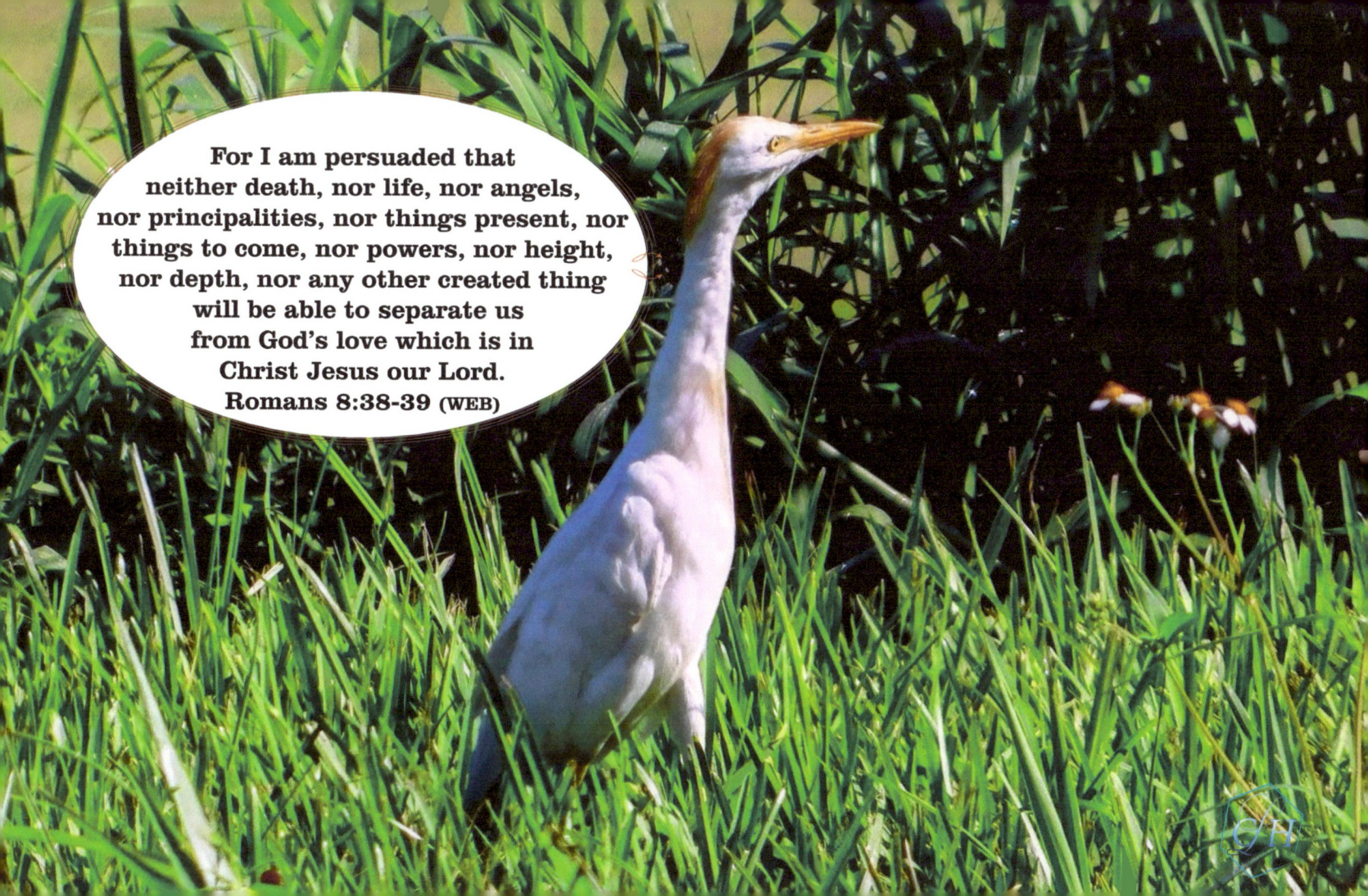

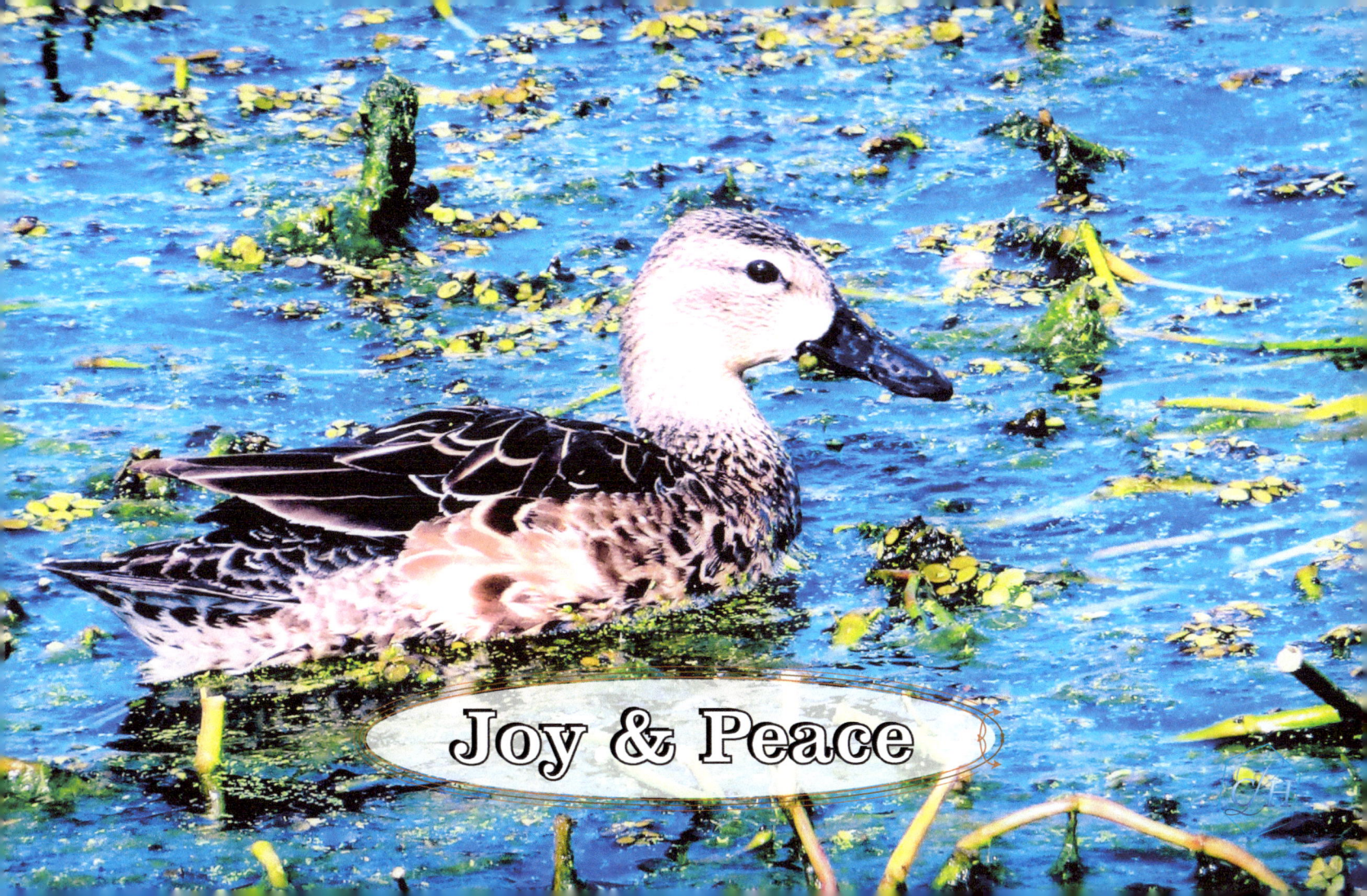

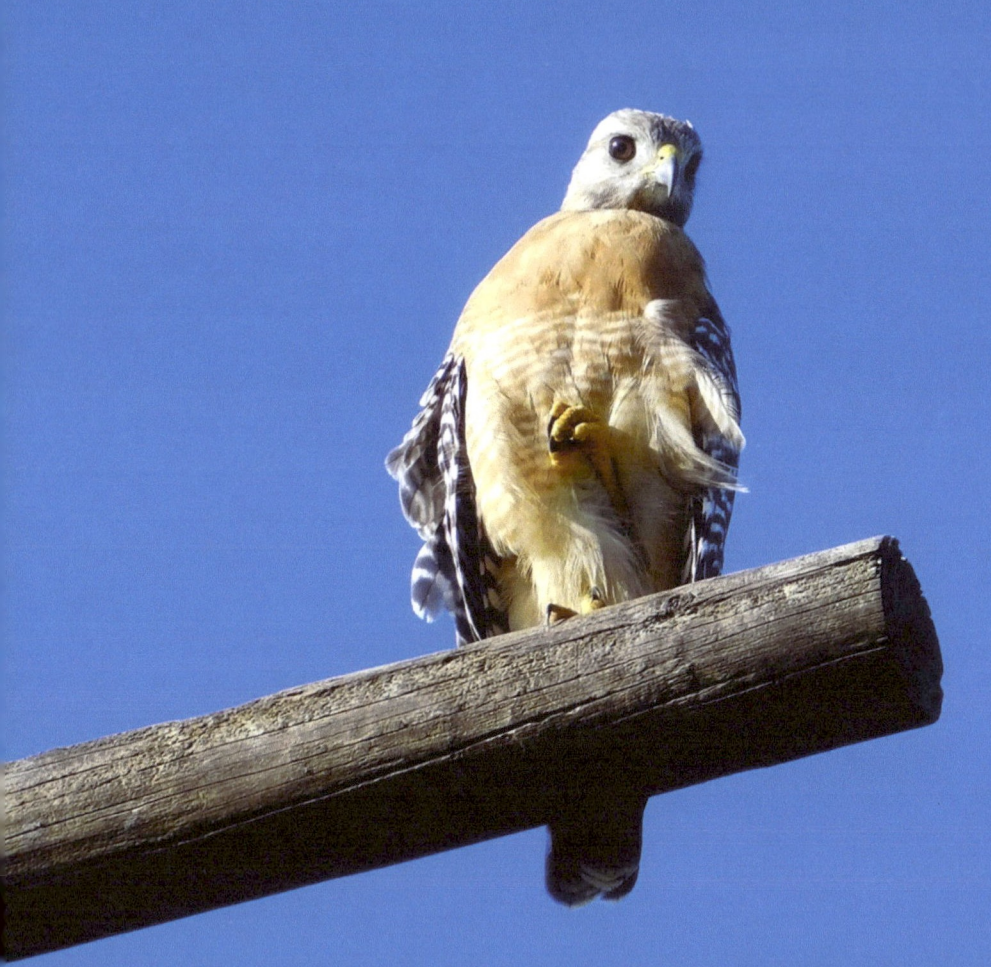

Psalms 29:11
Psalms 5:11
Philippians 4:4
Psalms 118:24
Psalms 16:11
Psalms 30:5
Psalms 16:9
Philippians 1:6
Psalms 130:5
Philippians 4:6-7
Psalms 34:8
Philippians 2:3-4
Psalms 94:18-19
Psalms 142:5
Psalms 119:57
Psalms 84:11
Psalms 37:4
Psalms 28:7
Psalms 27:4
Psalms 30:11

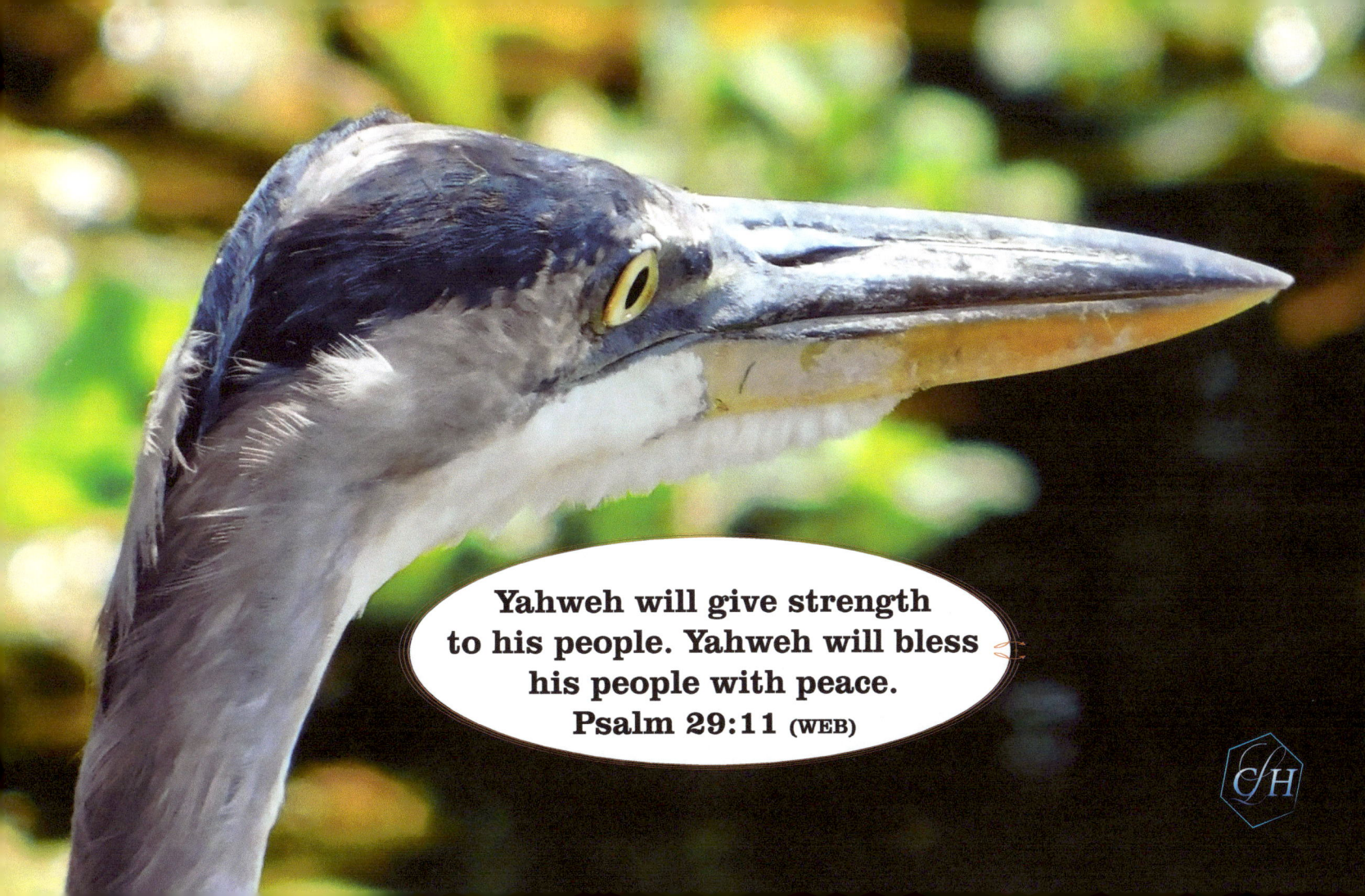

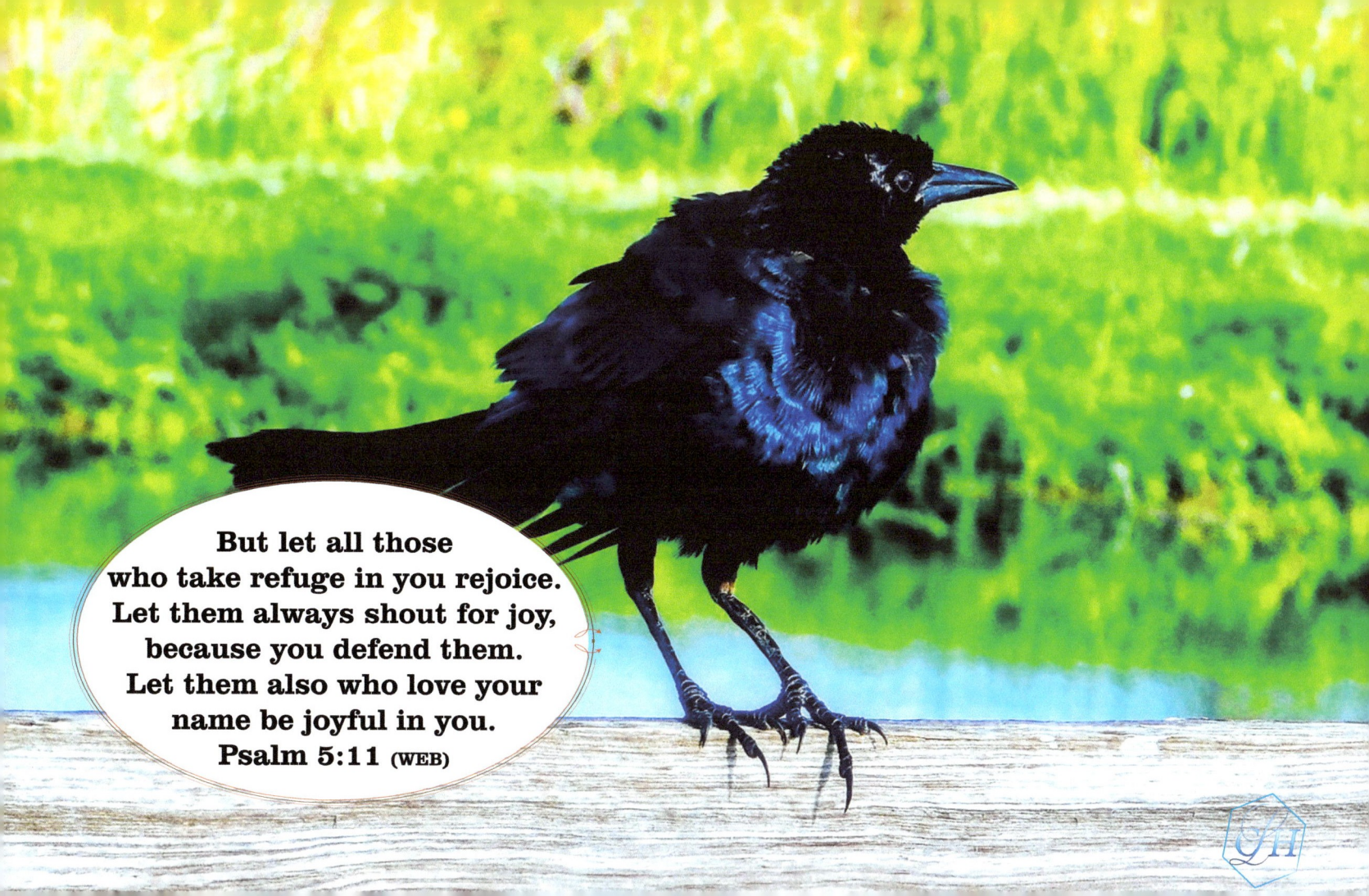

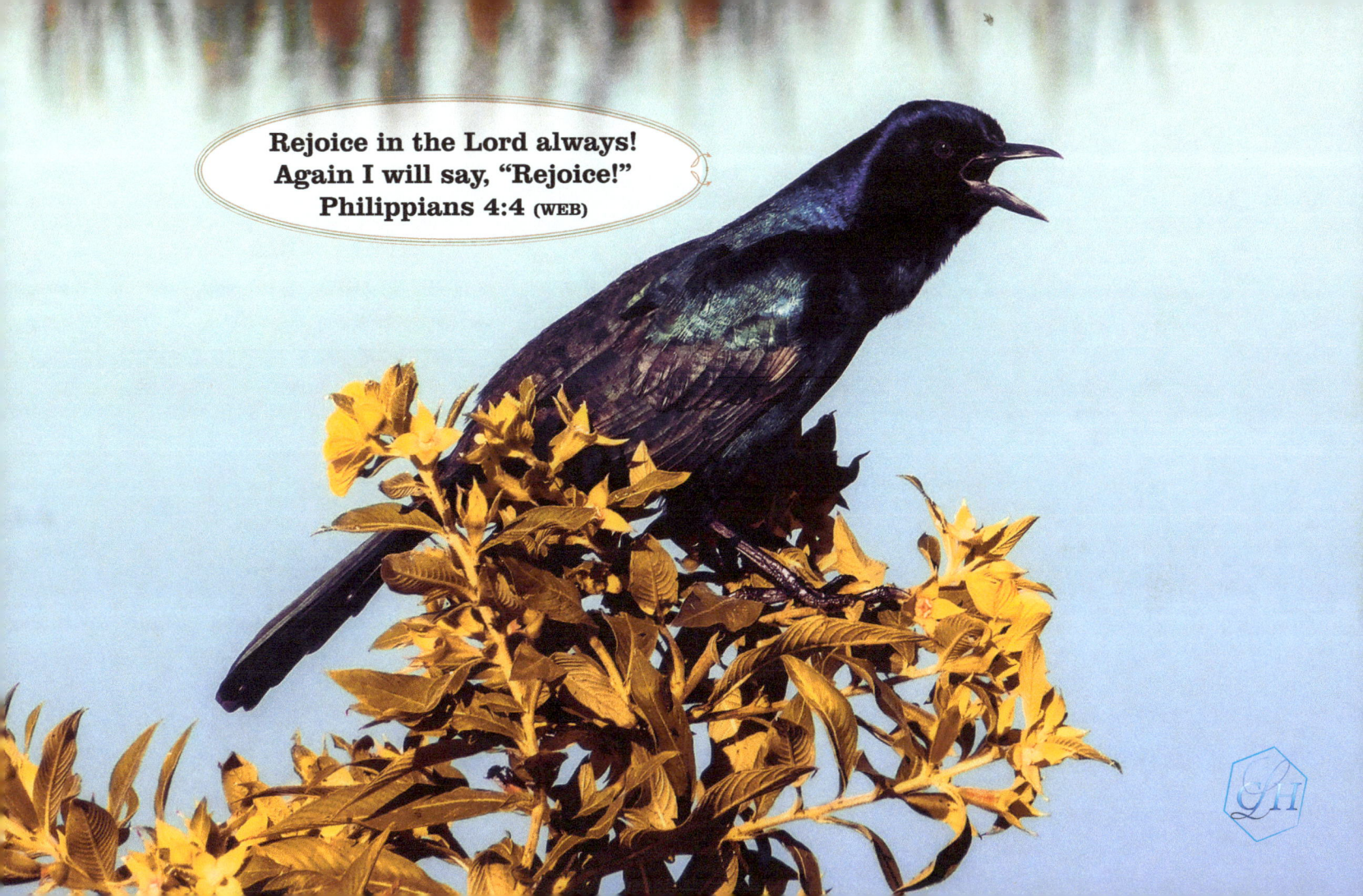

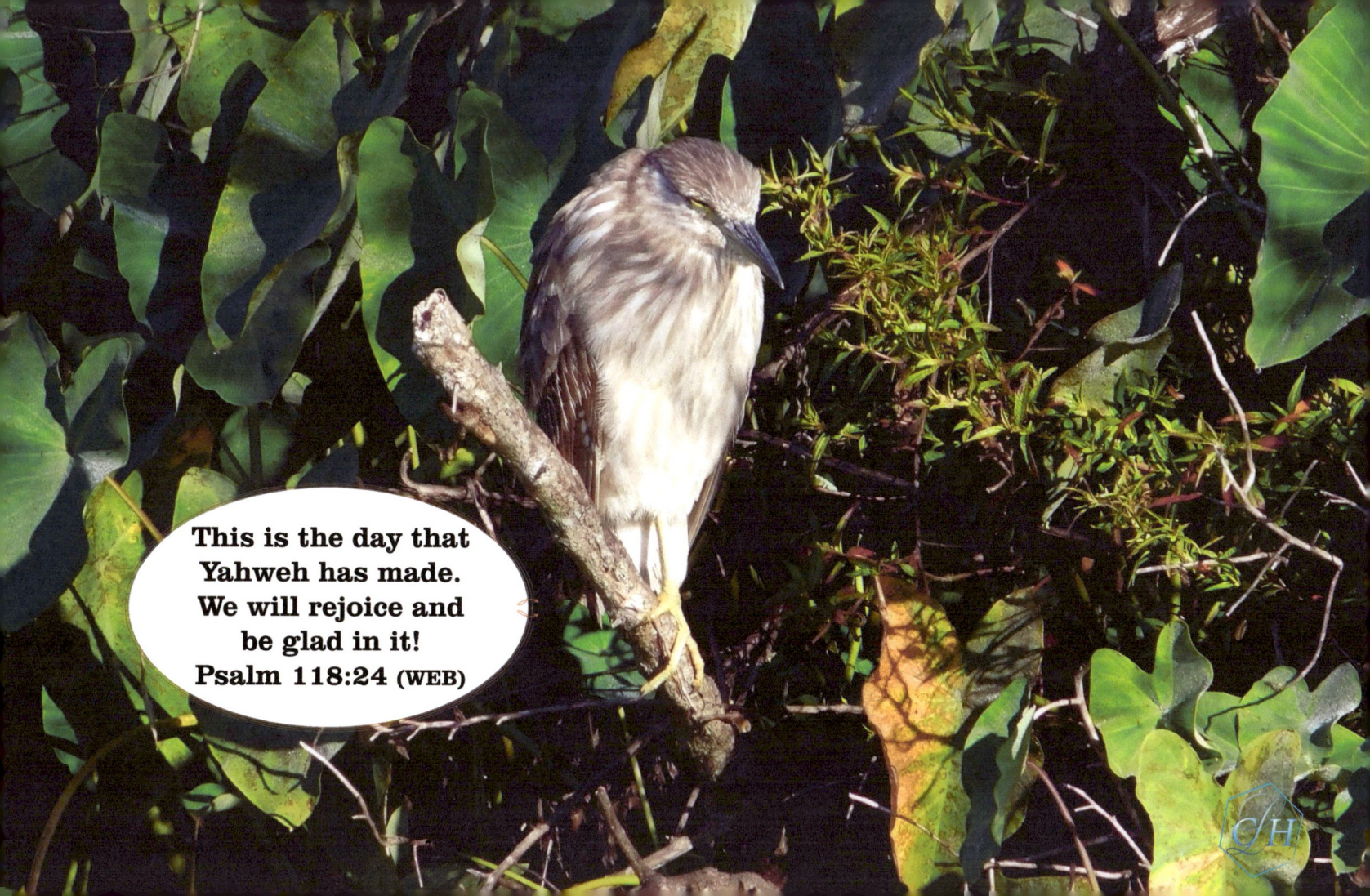

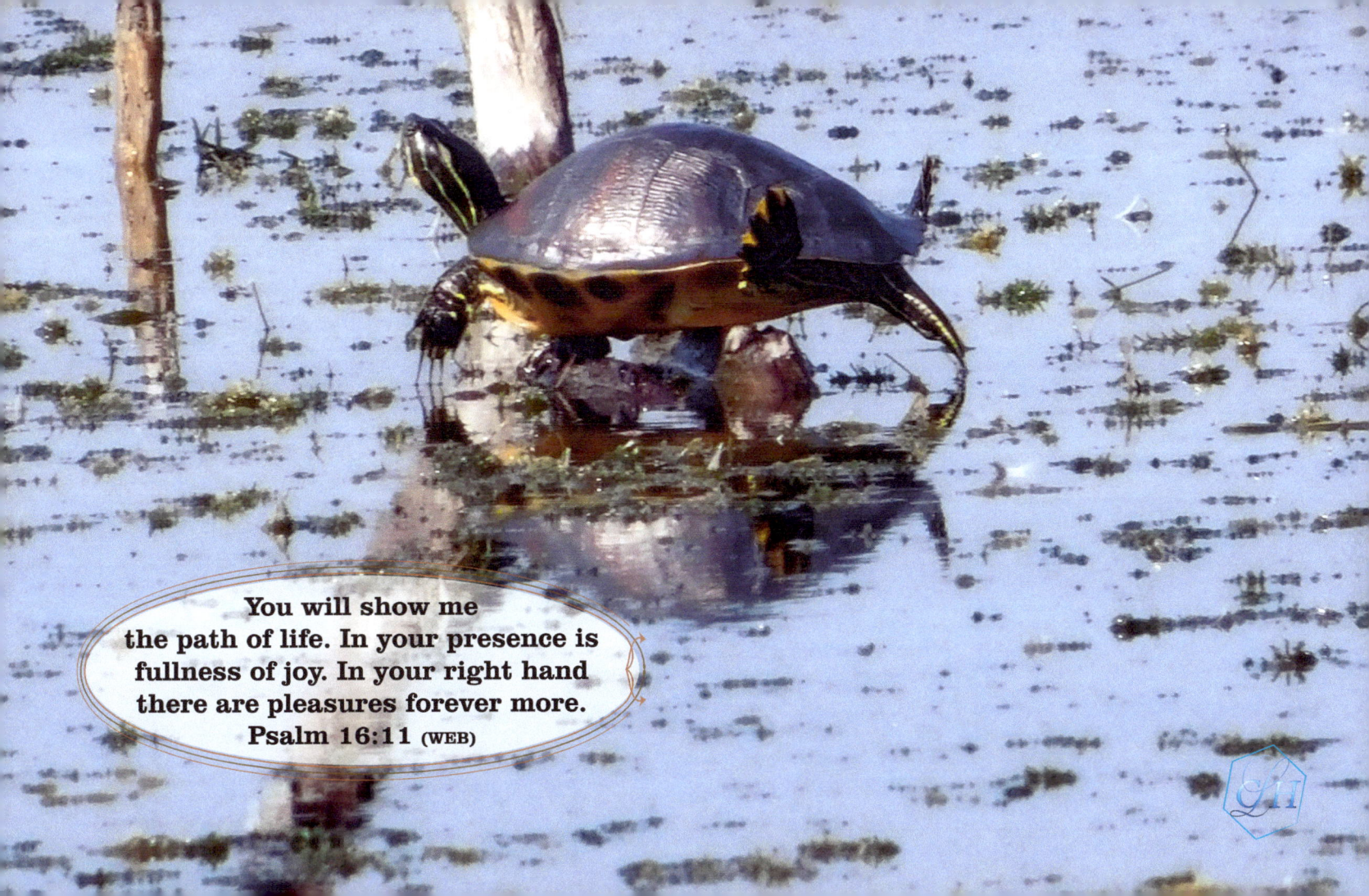

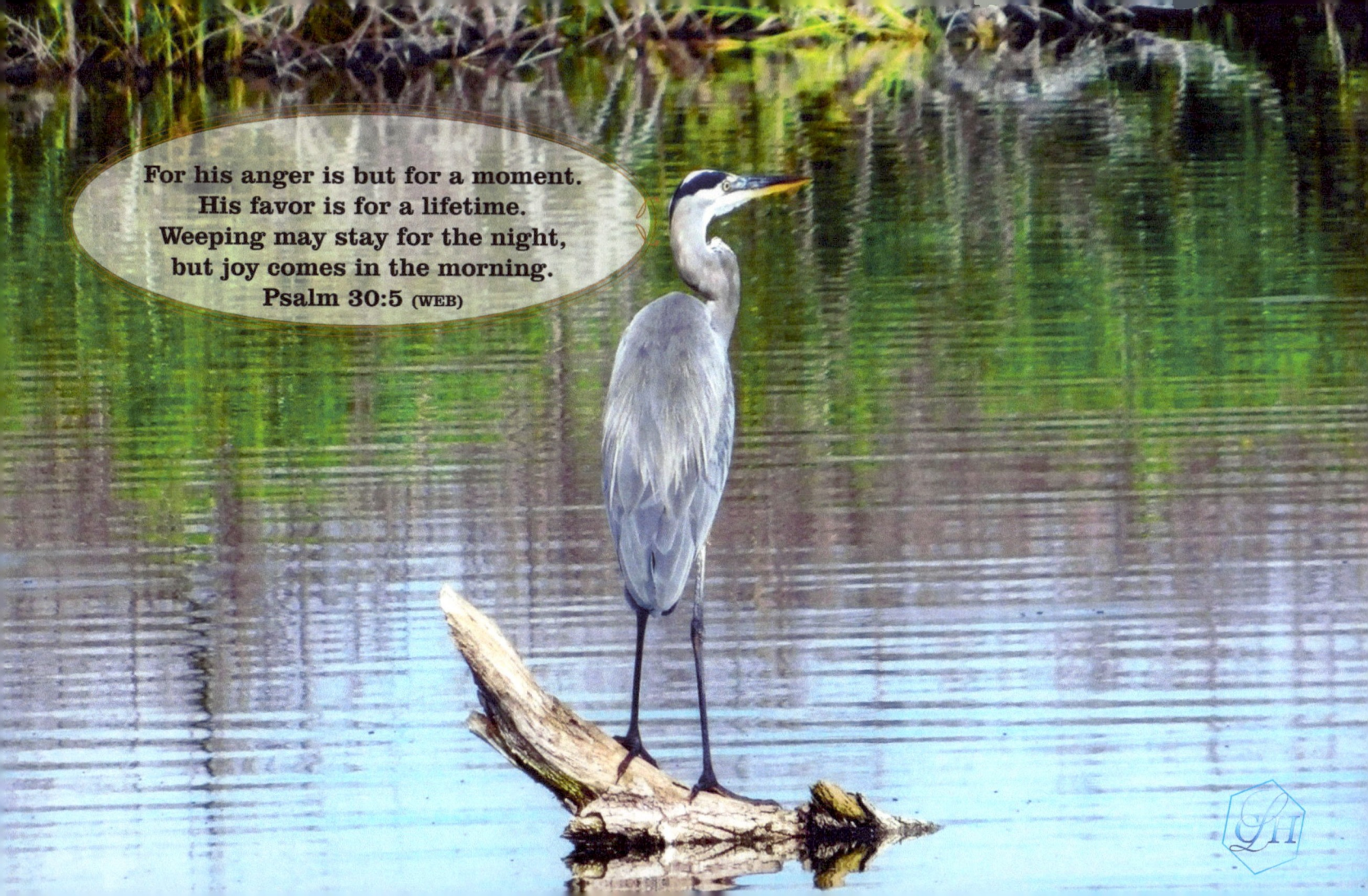

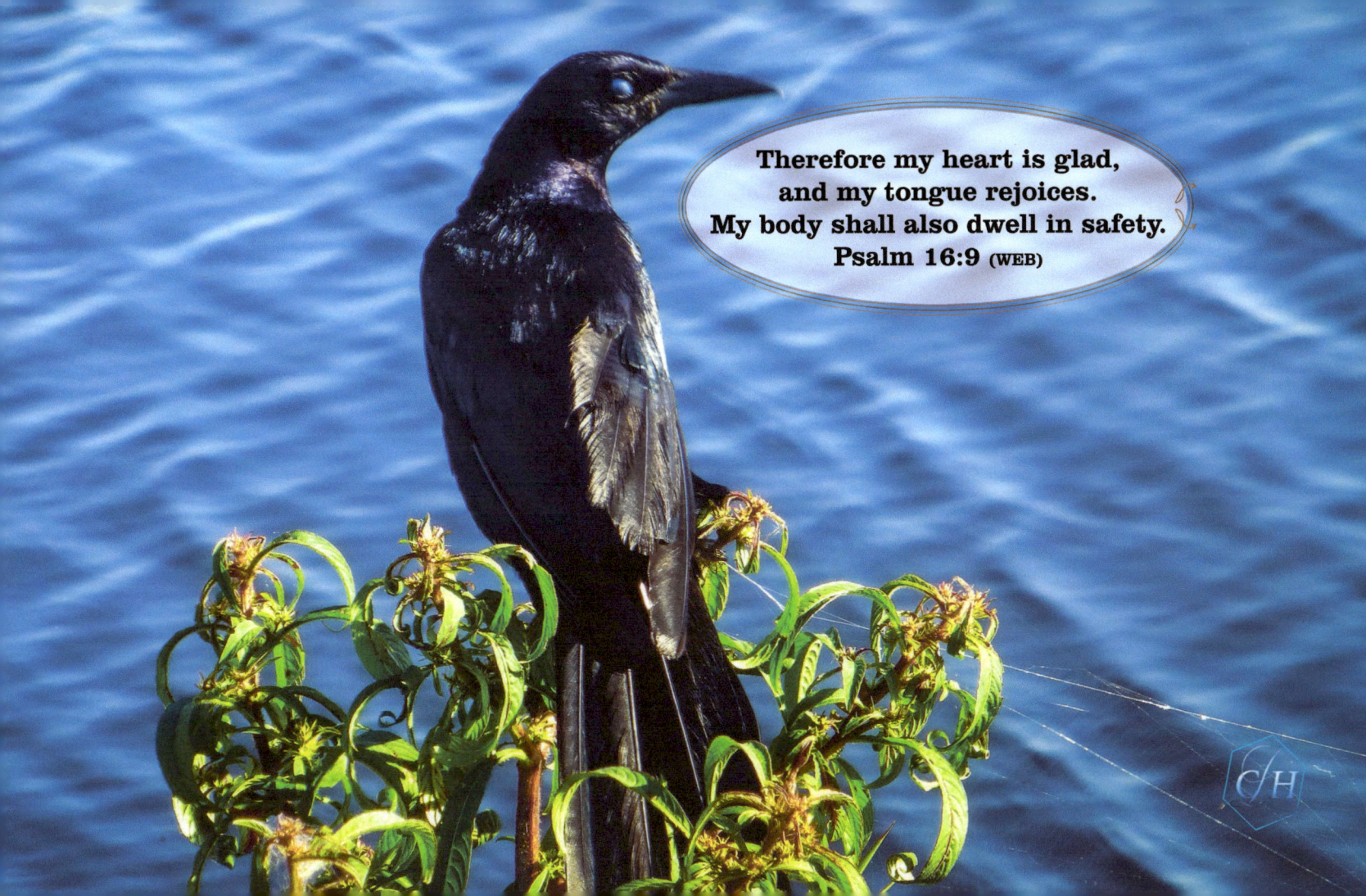

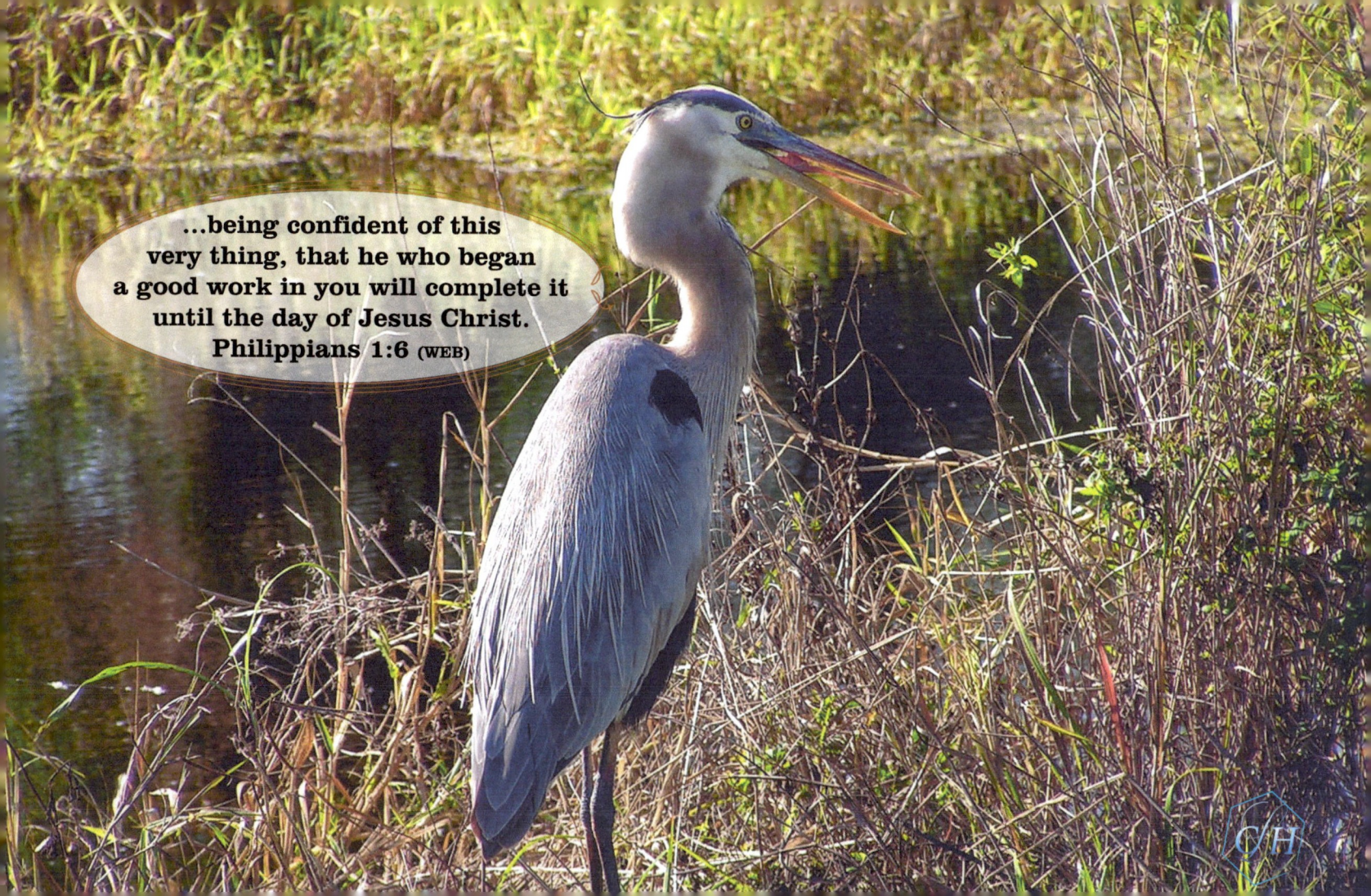

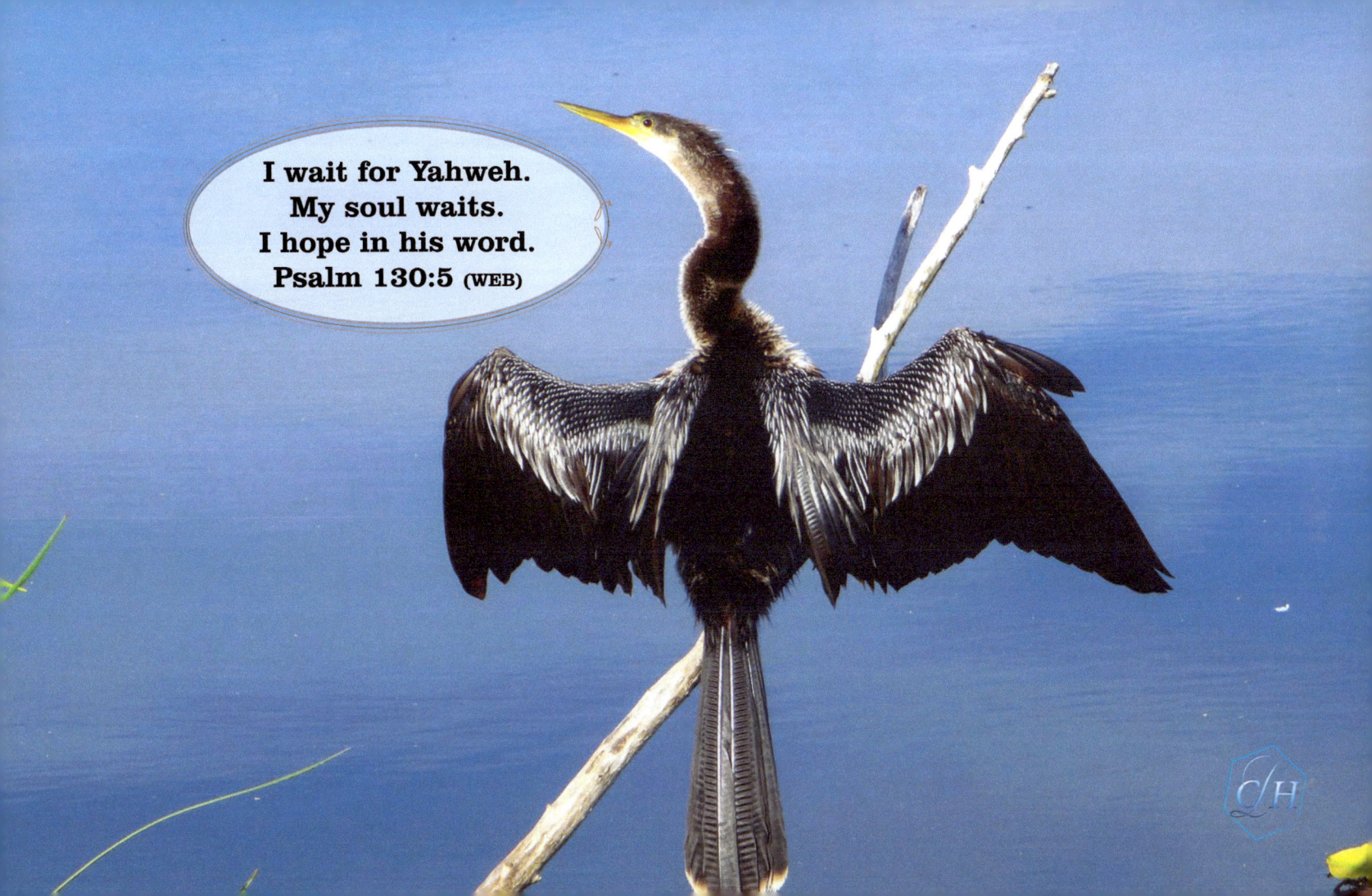

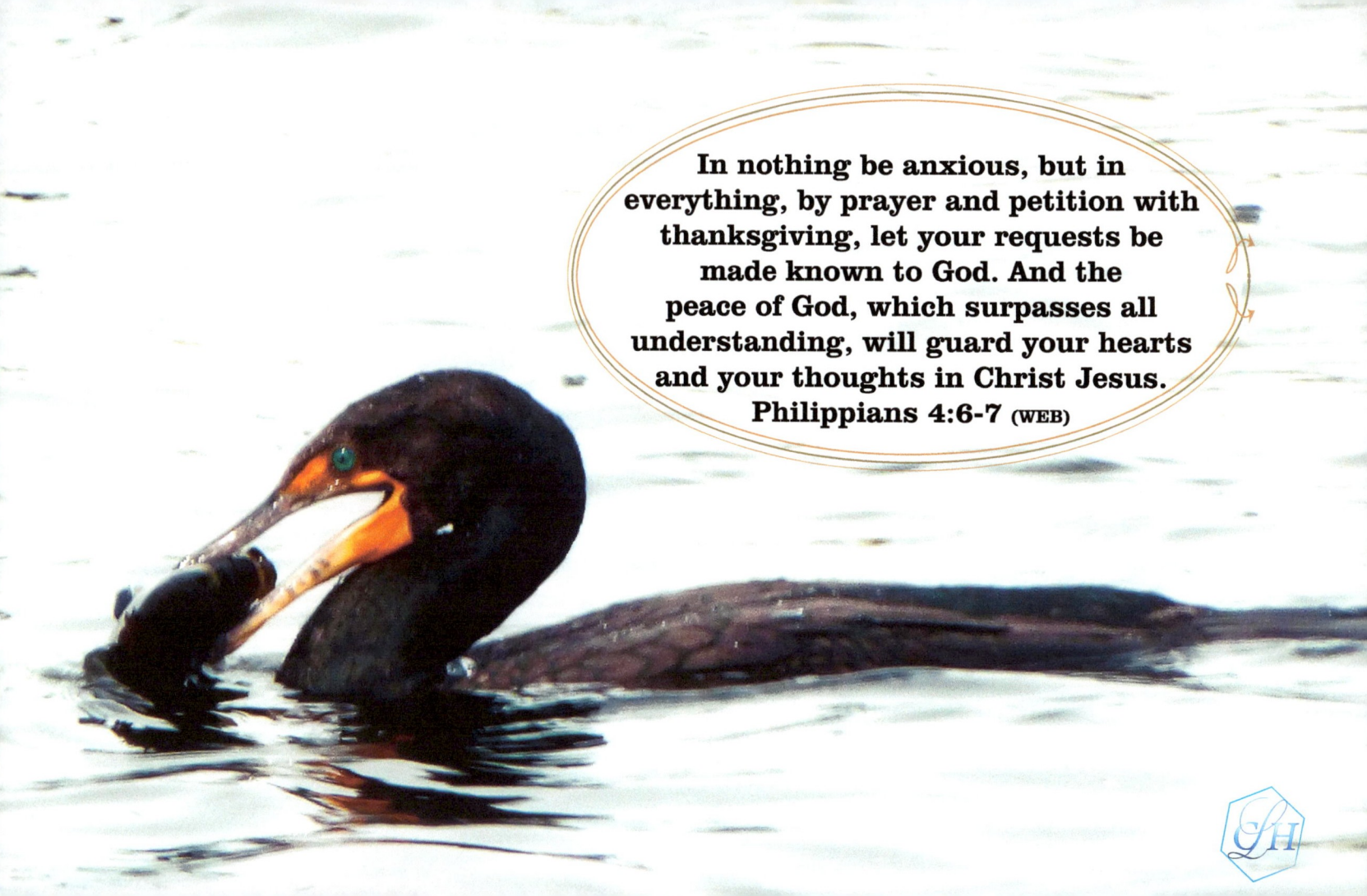

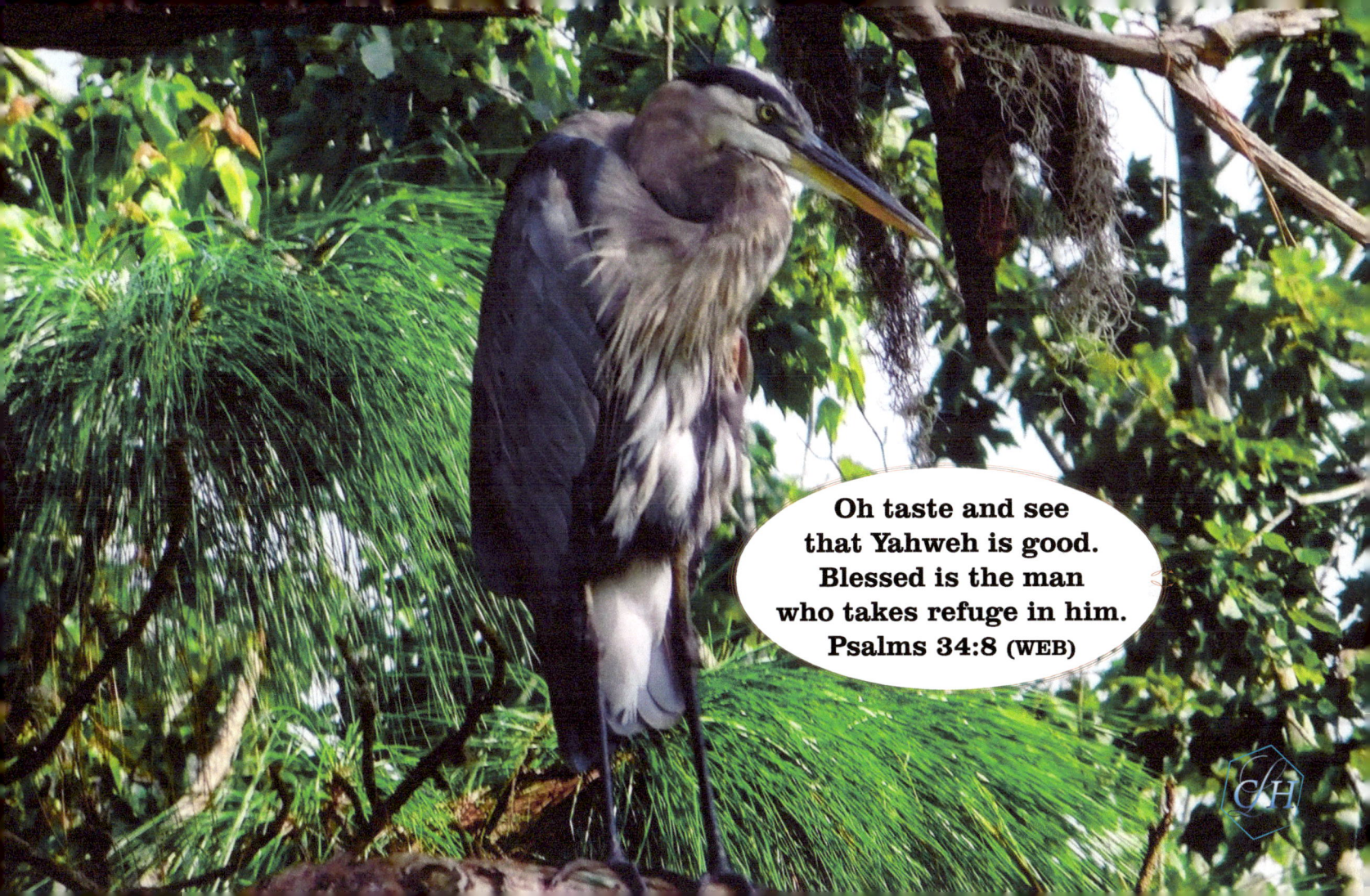

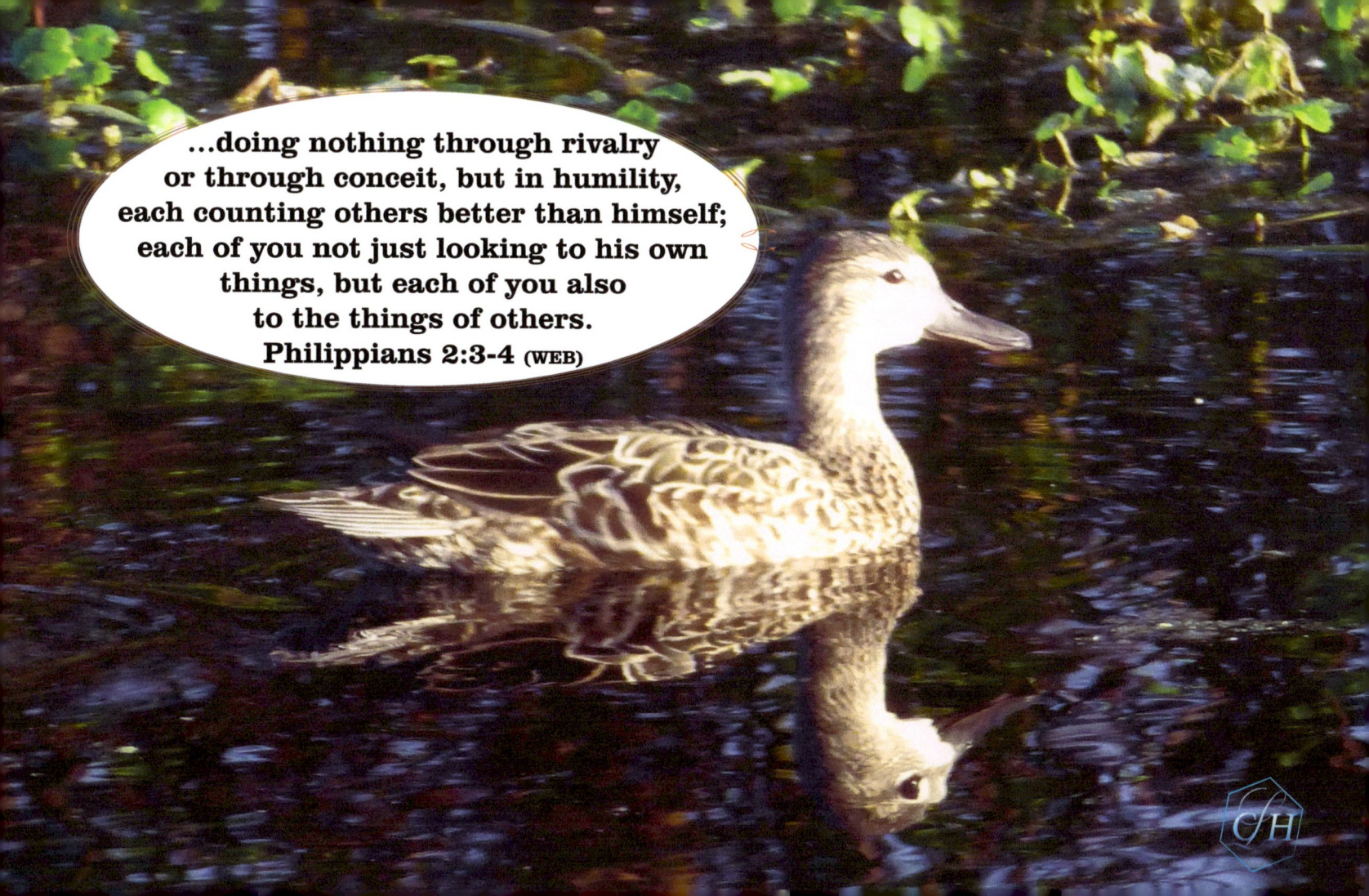

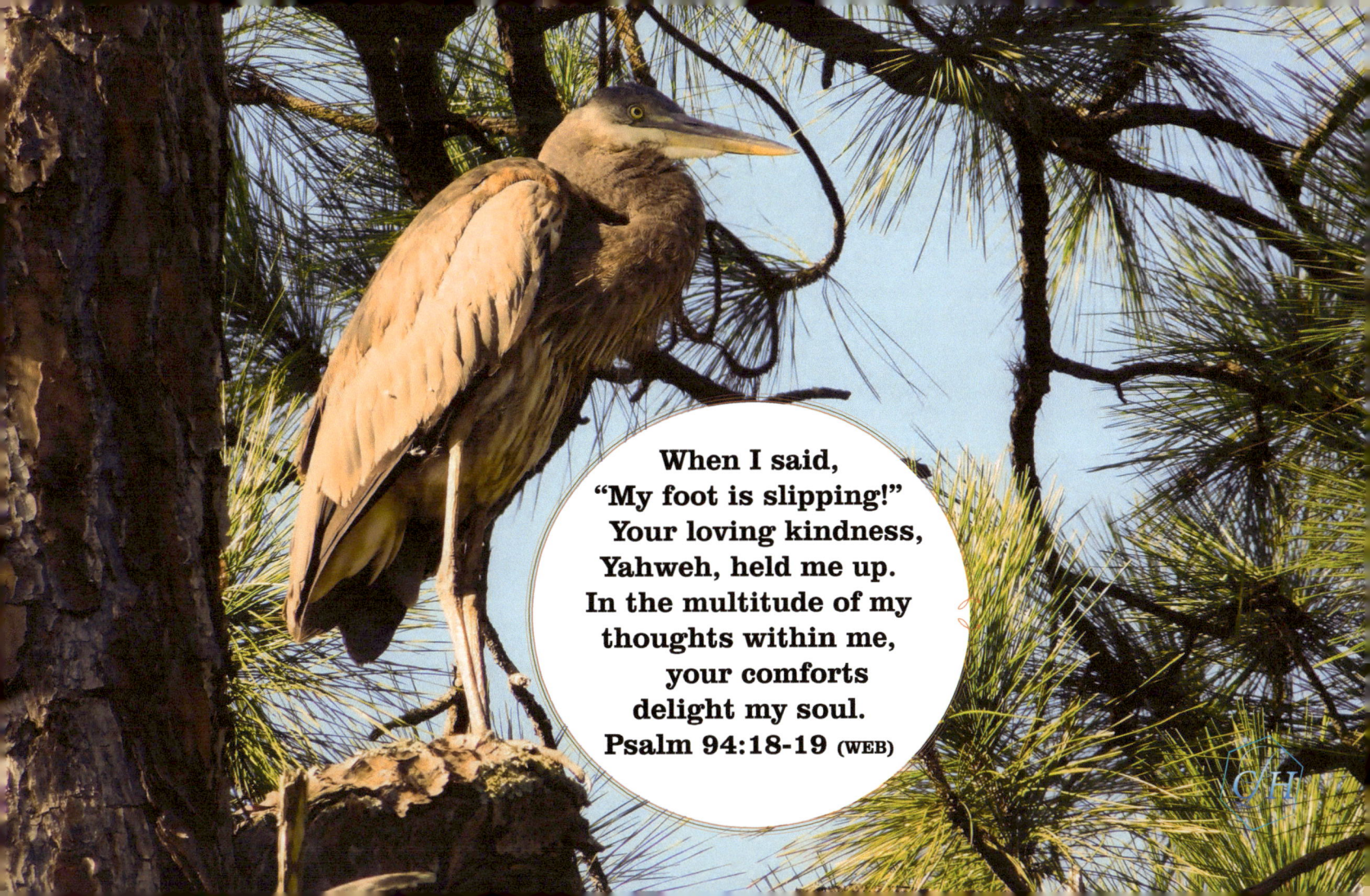

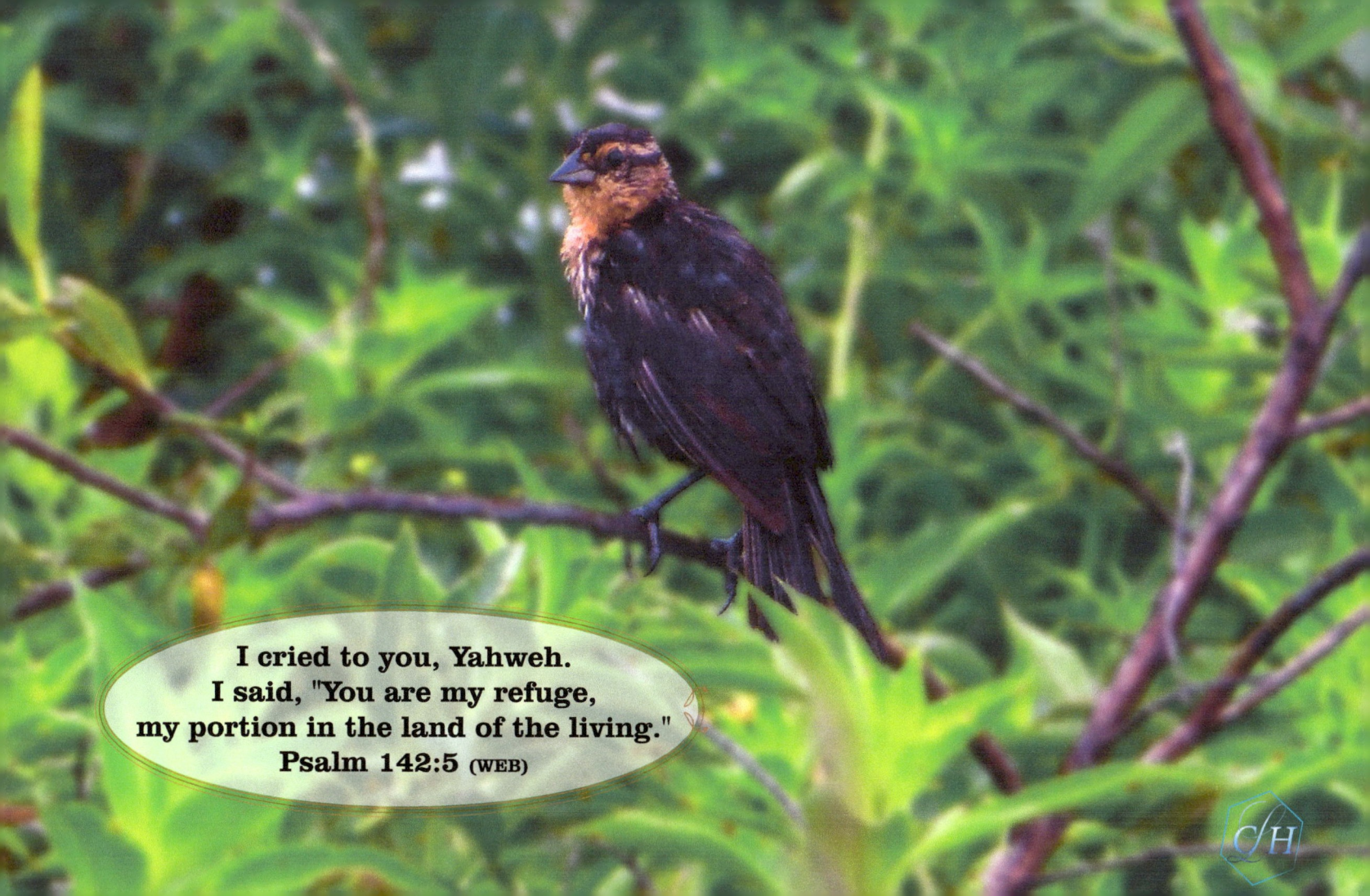

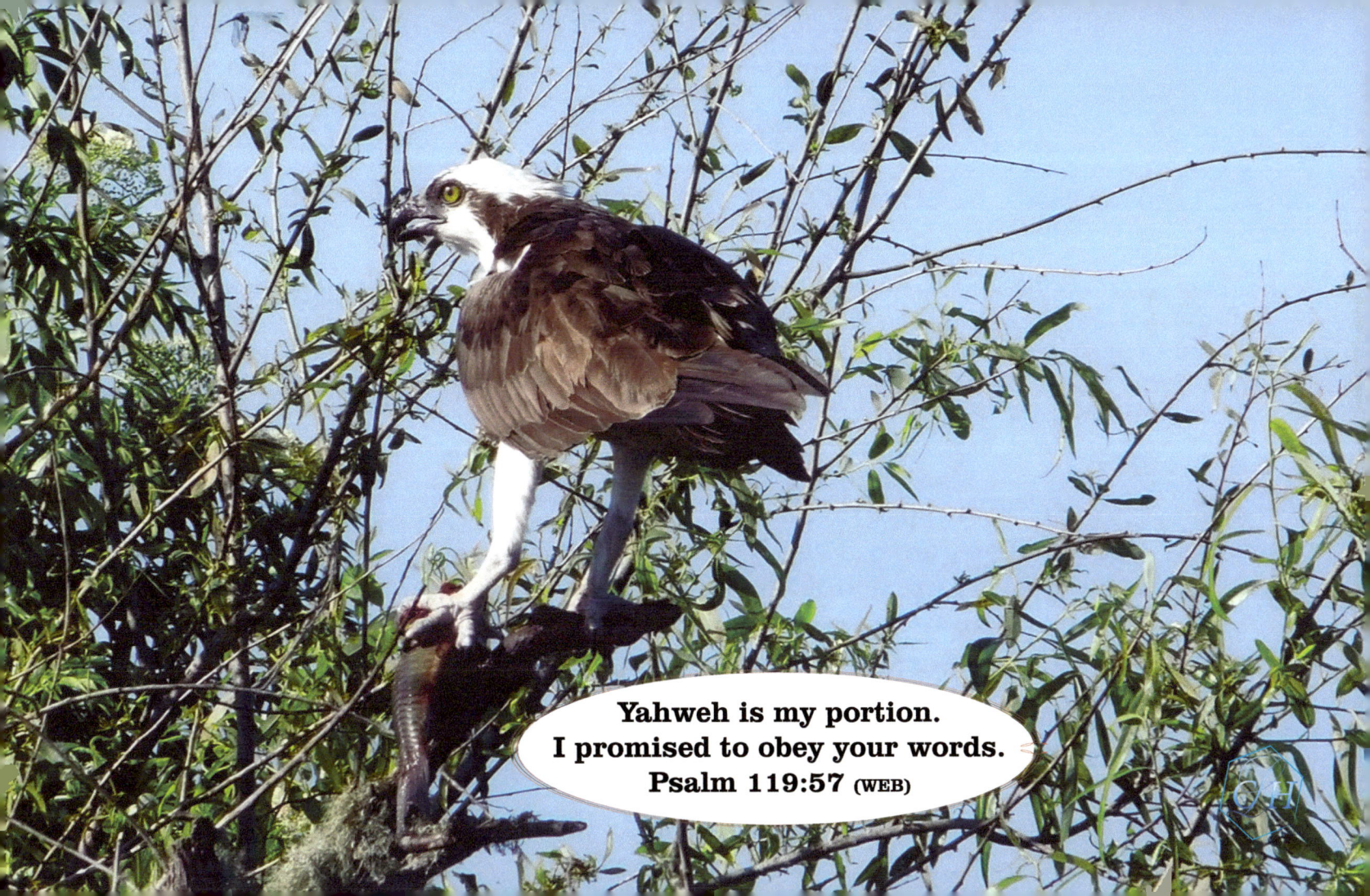

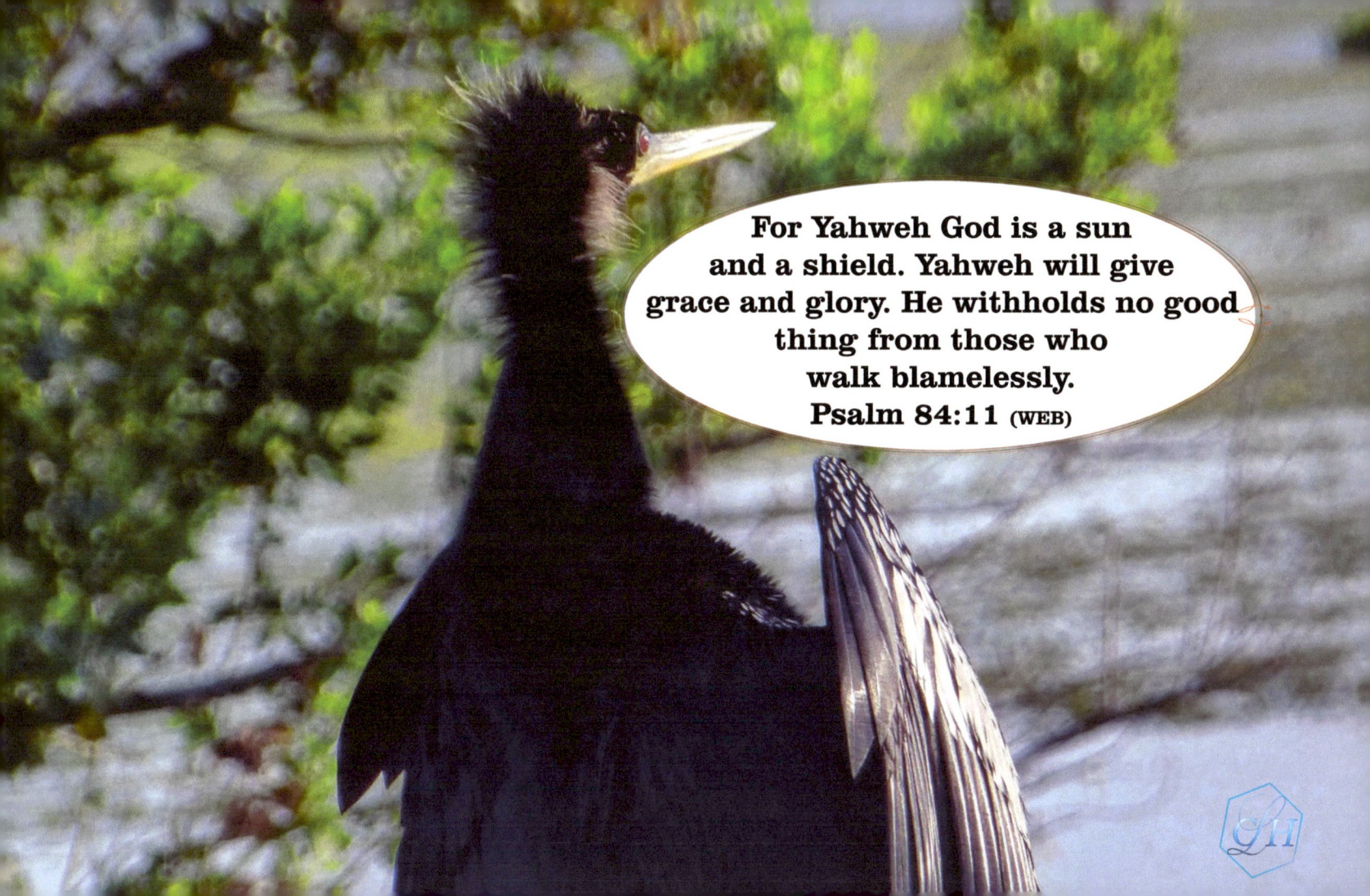

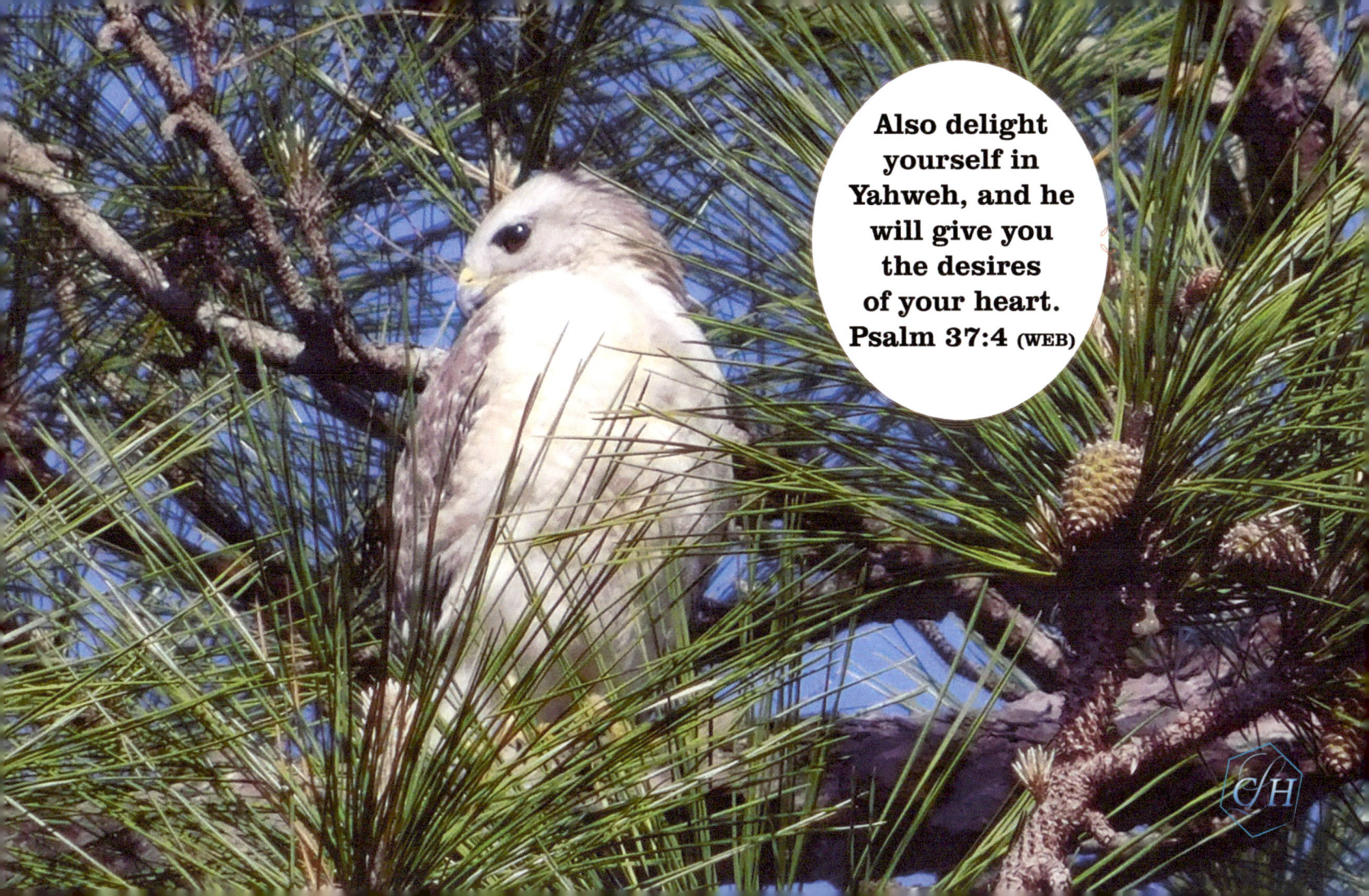

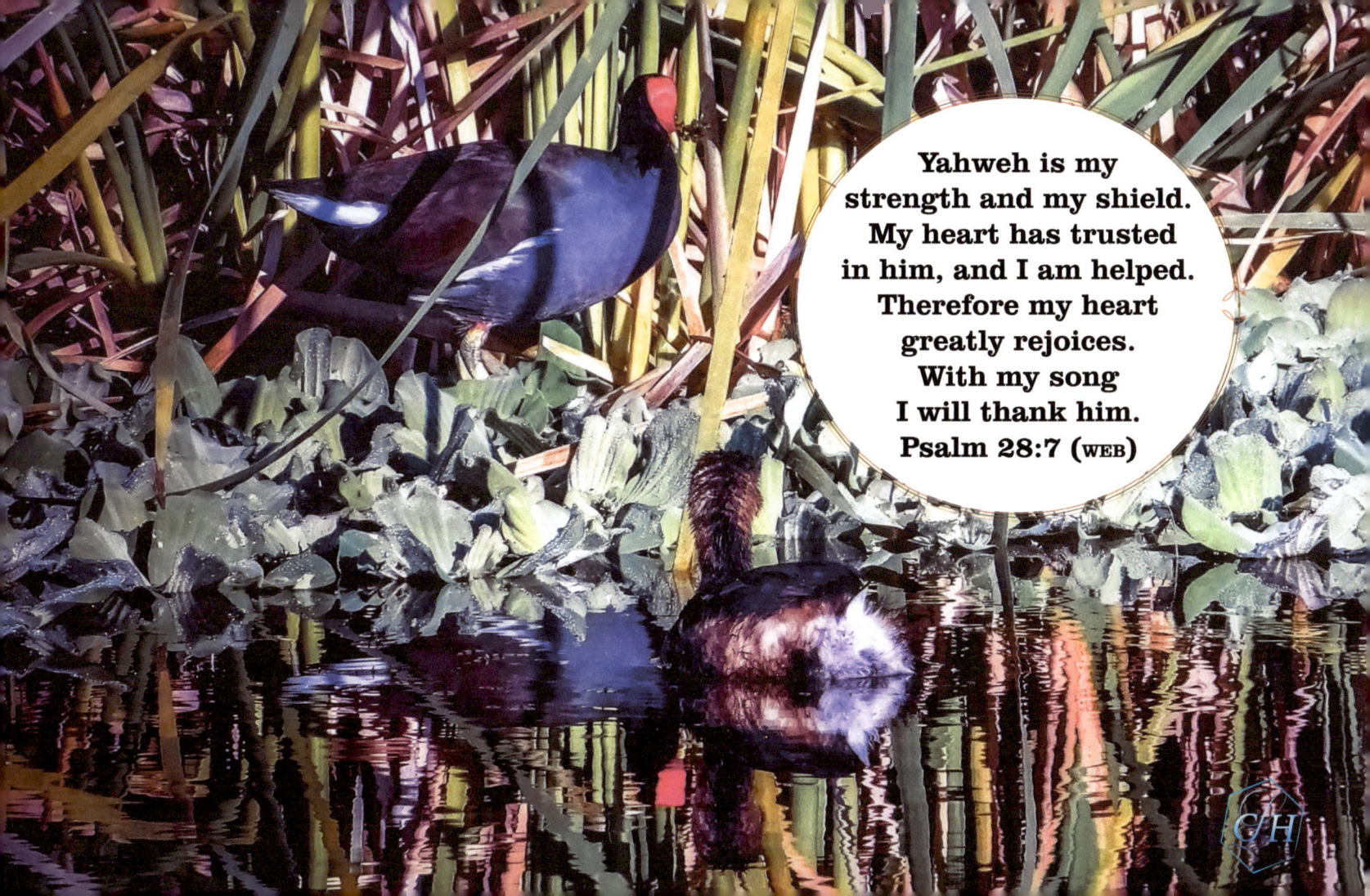

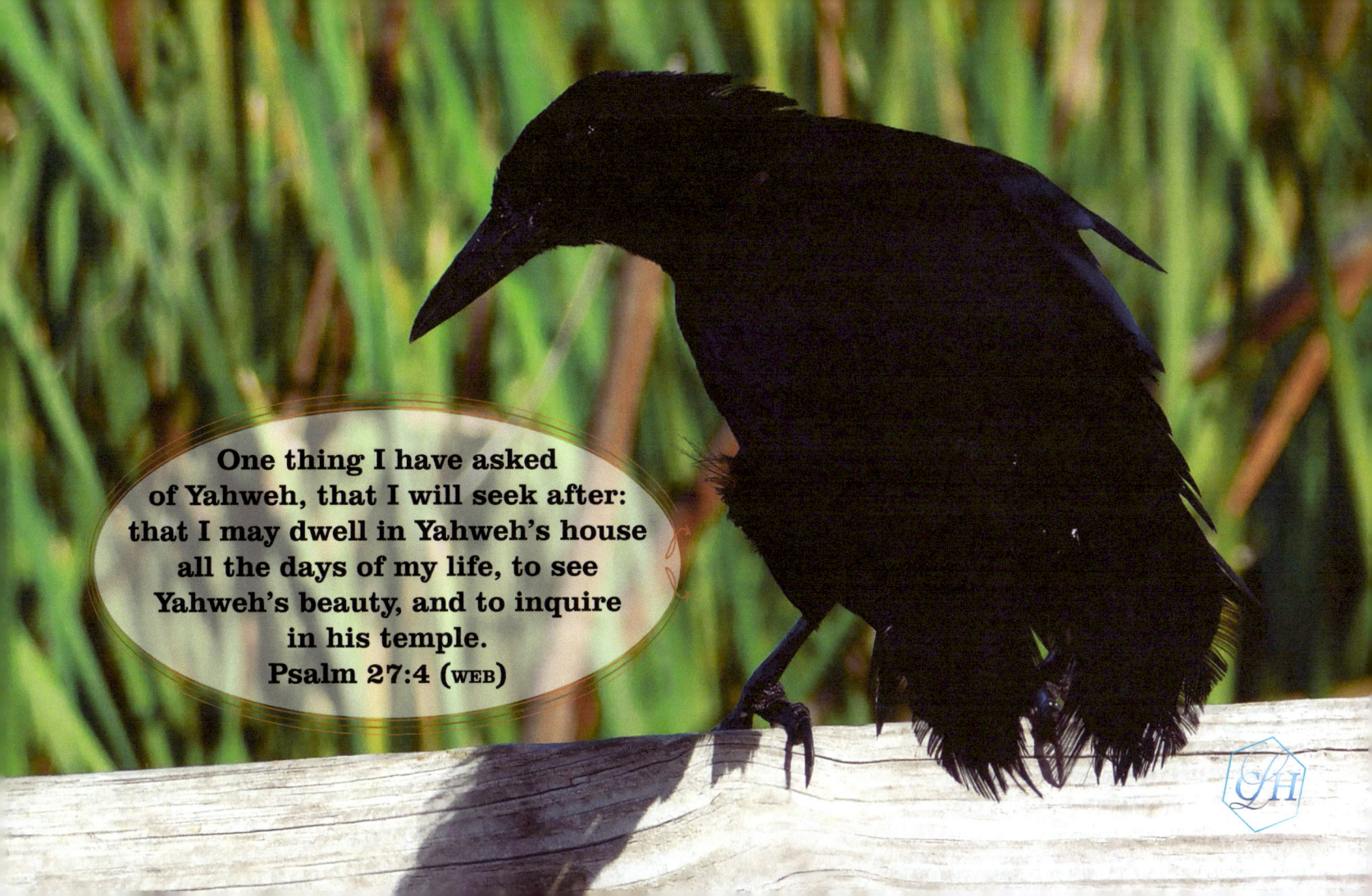

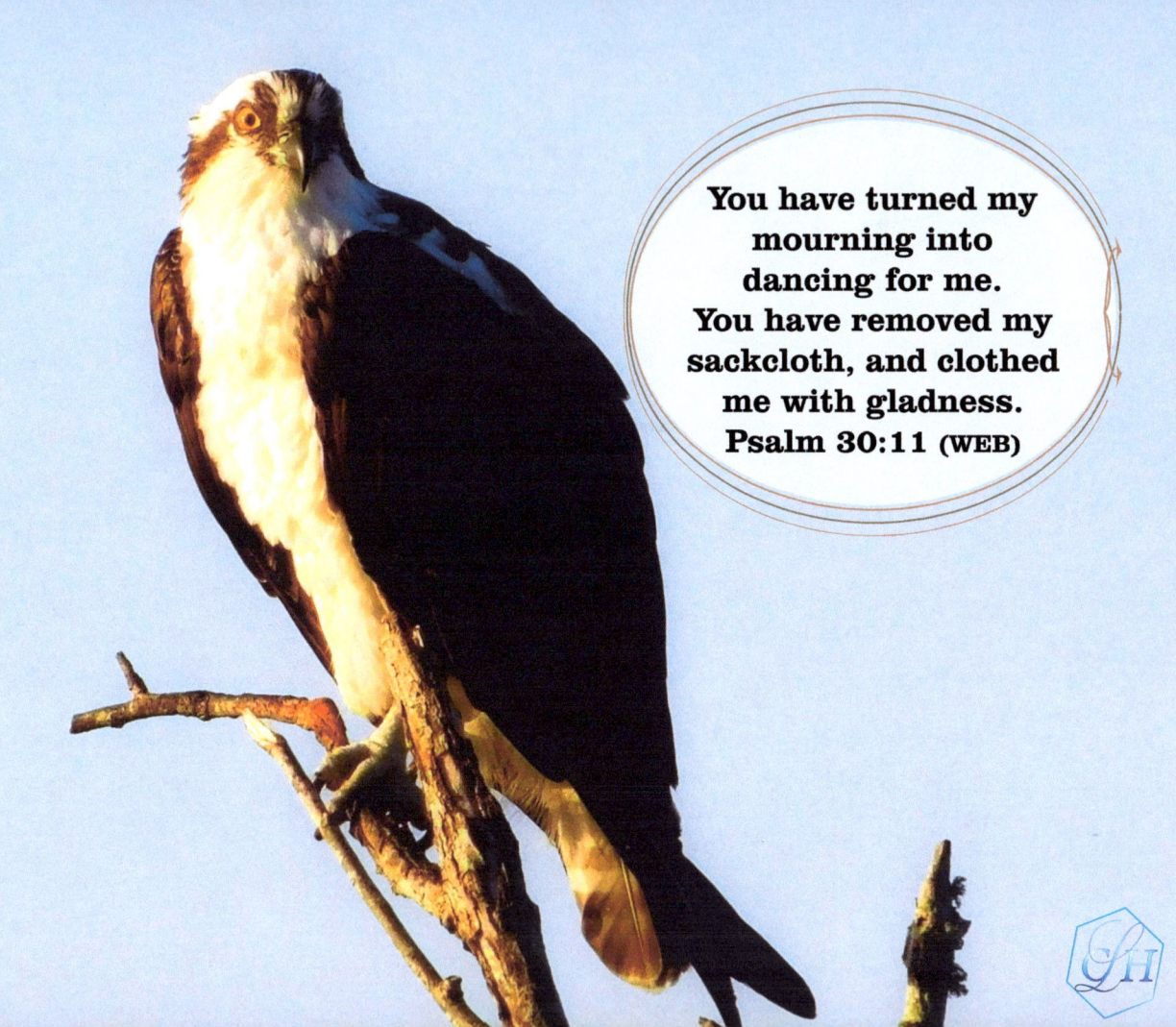

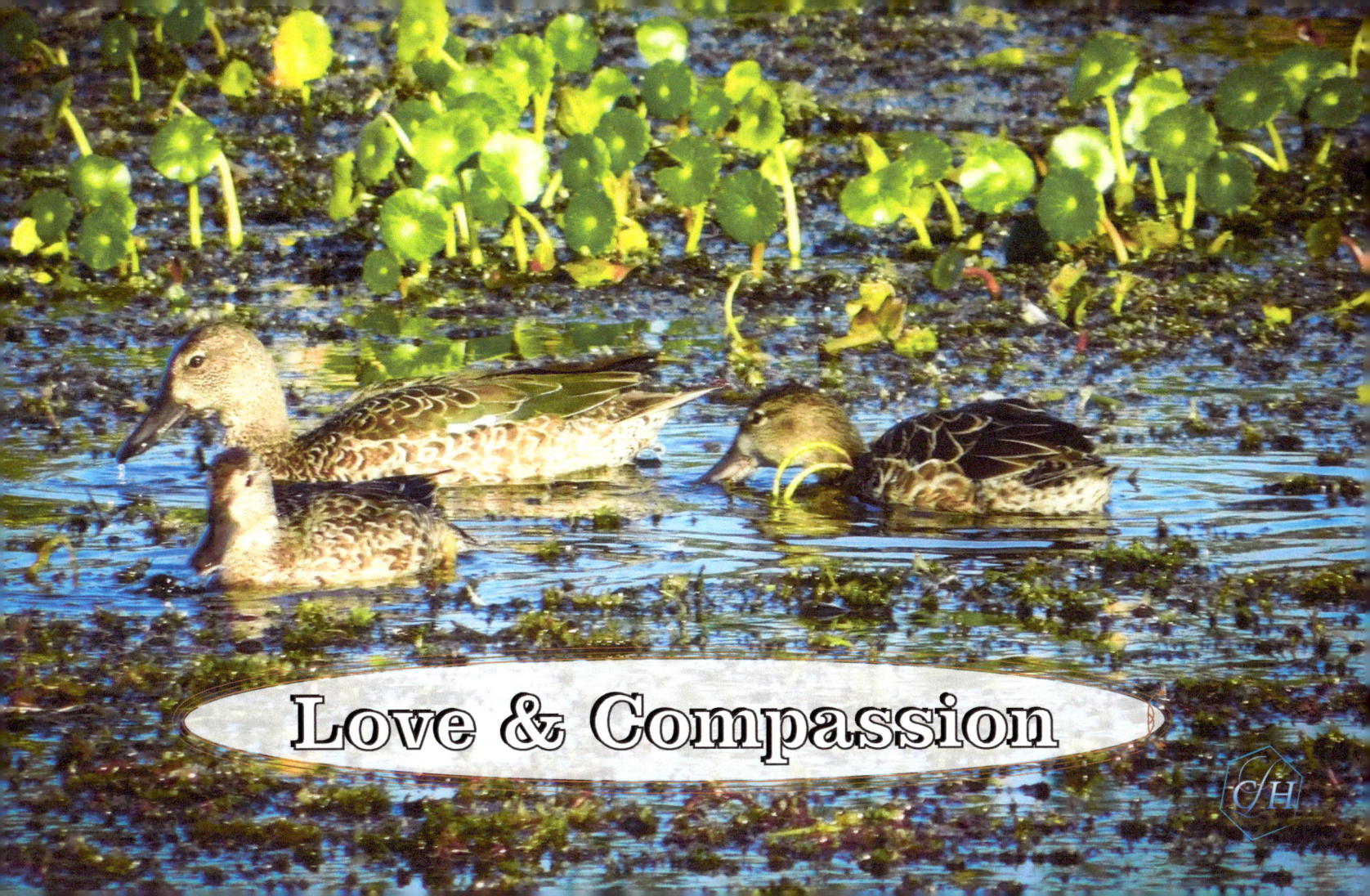

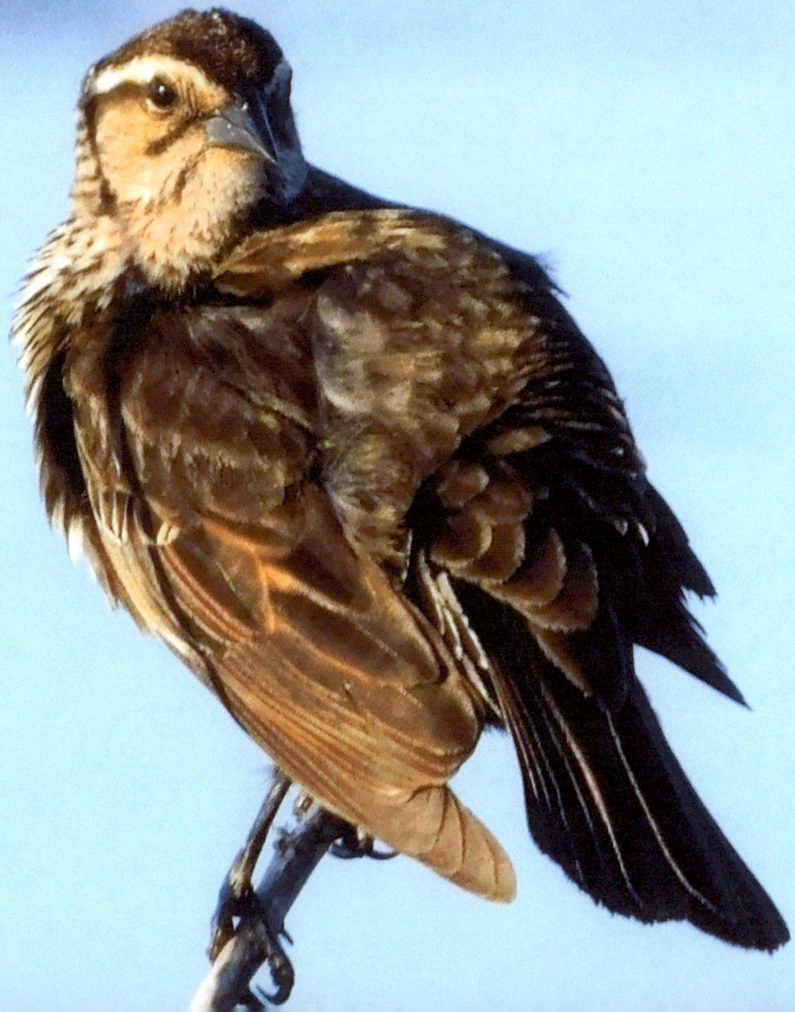

1 Corinthians 10:13
Mark 12:30
John 16:33
Ephesians 2:8-9
Mark 11:22-24
John 14:27
Isaiah 43:1
John 16:22
John 16:24
John 15:11
John 15:13
1 Corinthians 13:4-8
1 John 4:16
1 John 3:1
1 Corinthians 16:14
John 3:16
John 13:34-35
1 Corinthians 13:13
Mark 12:29-31
1 John 3:21-22

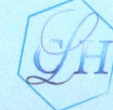

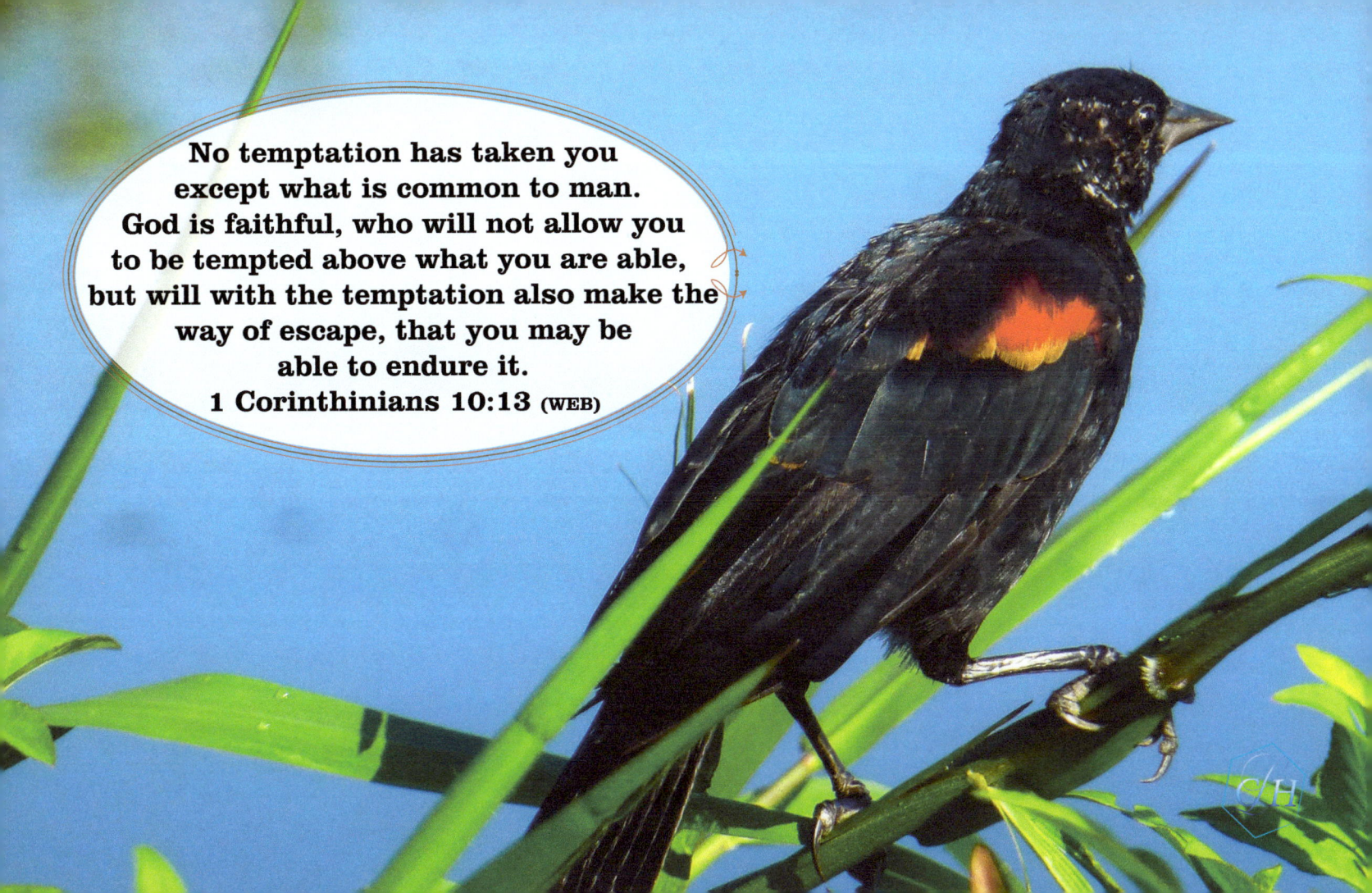

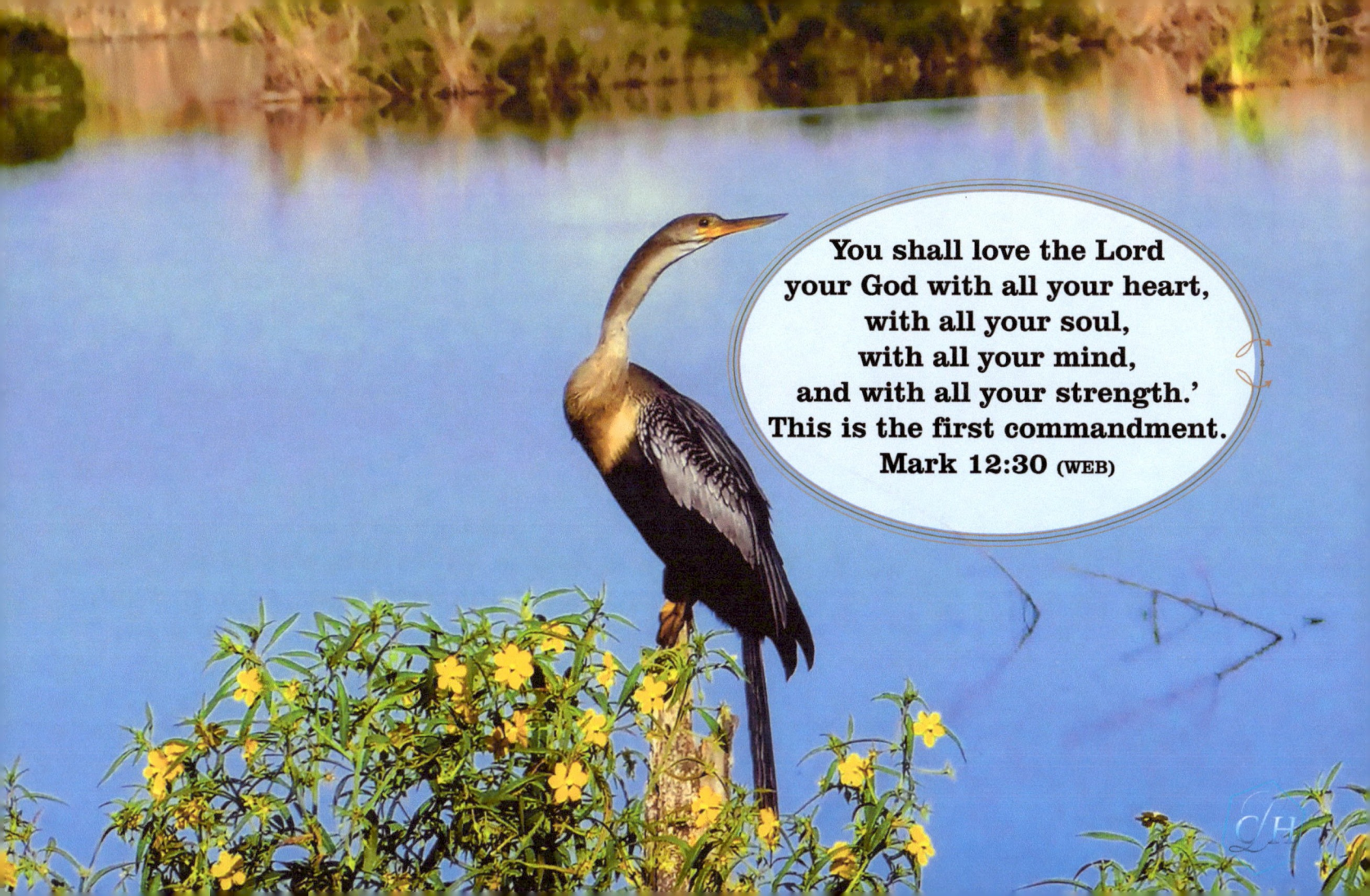

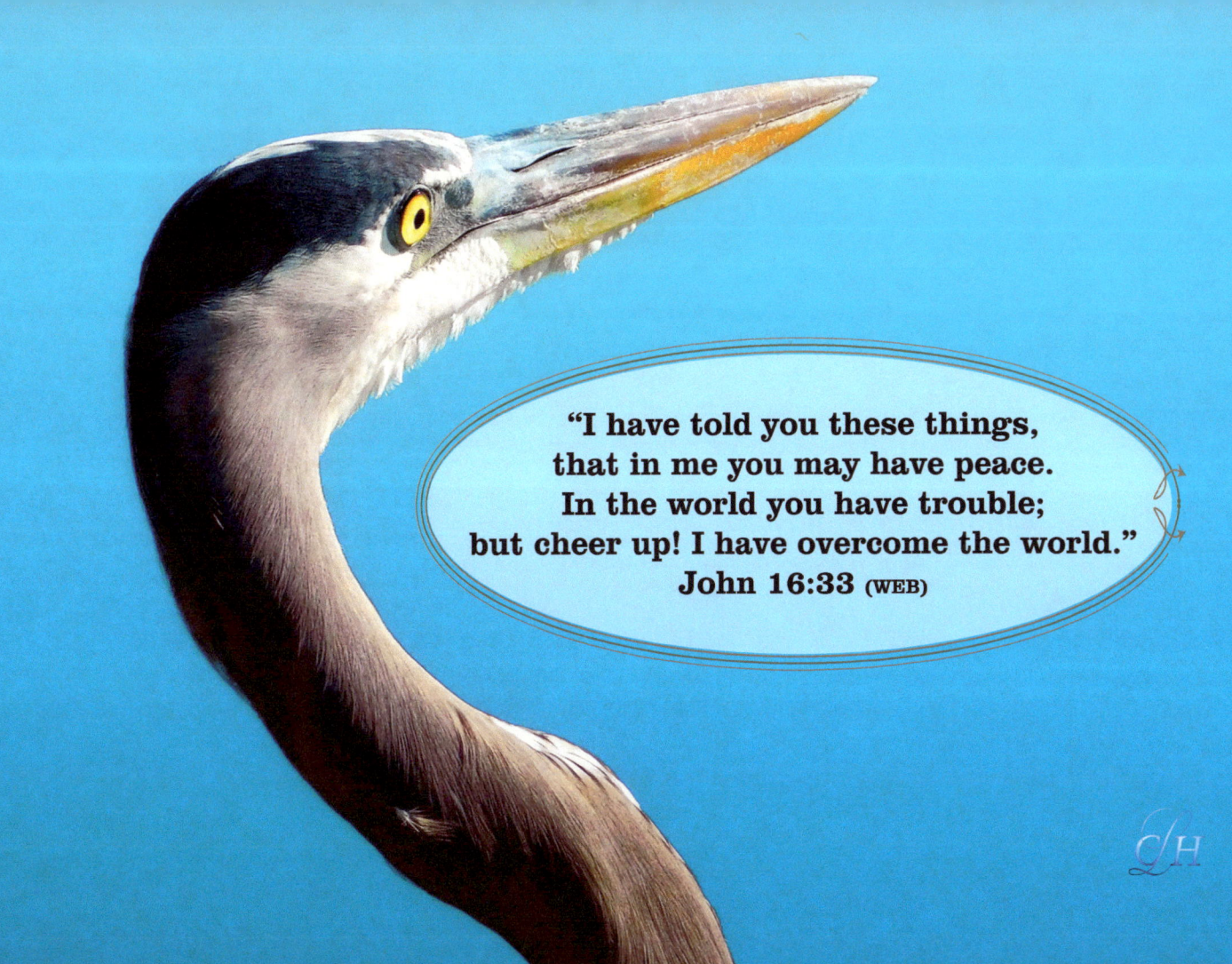

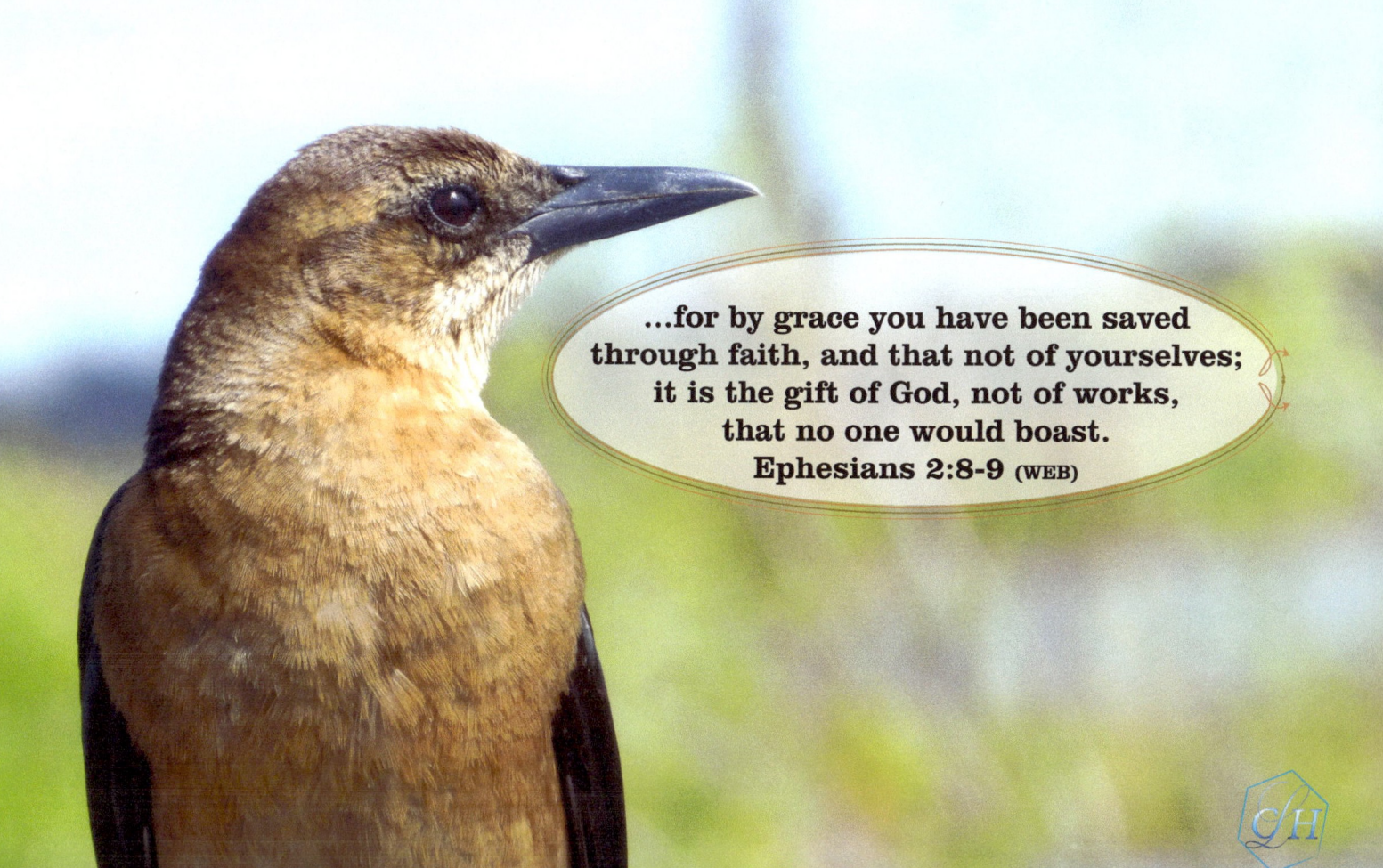

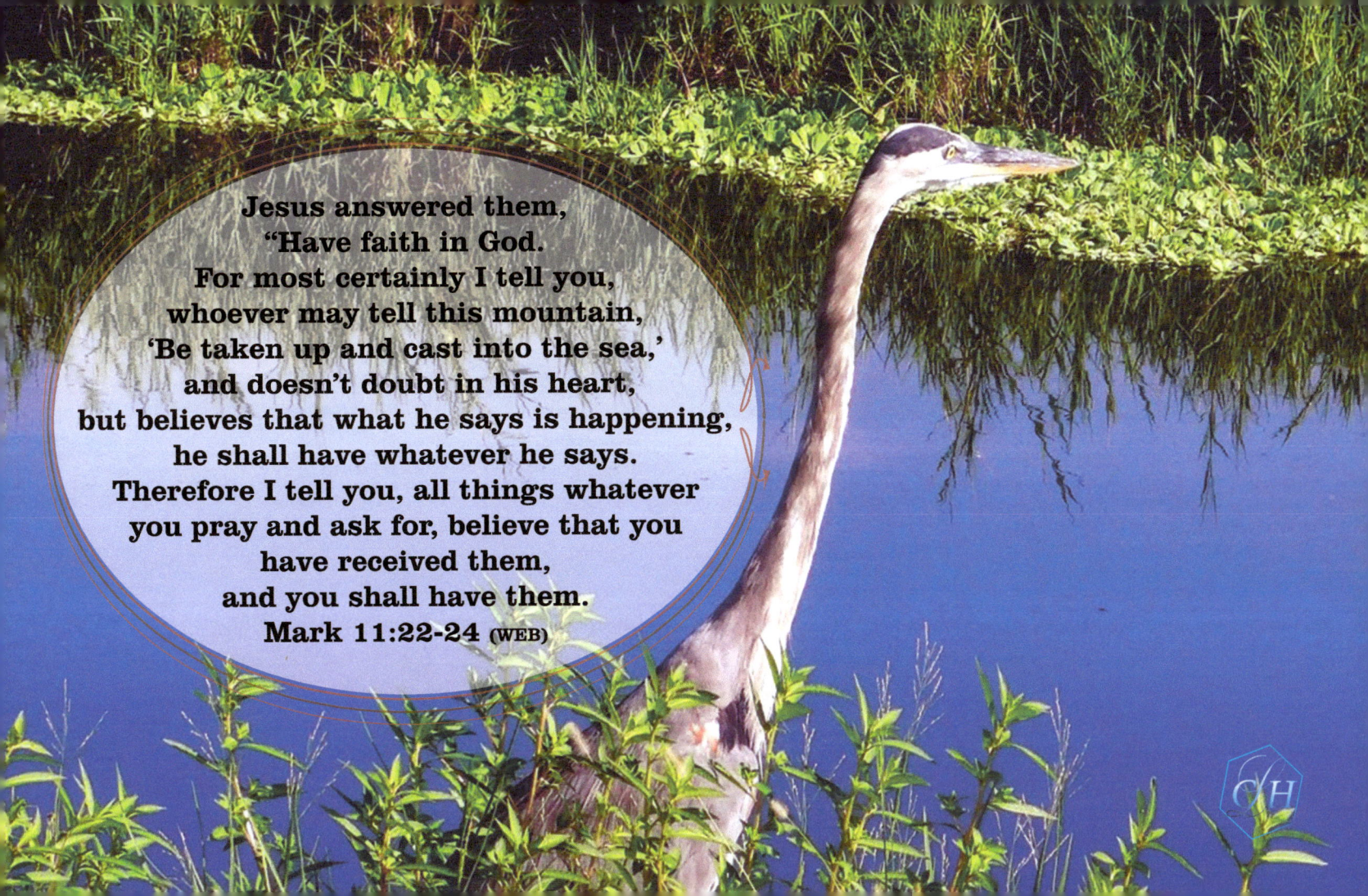

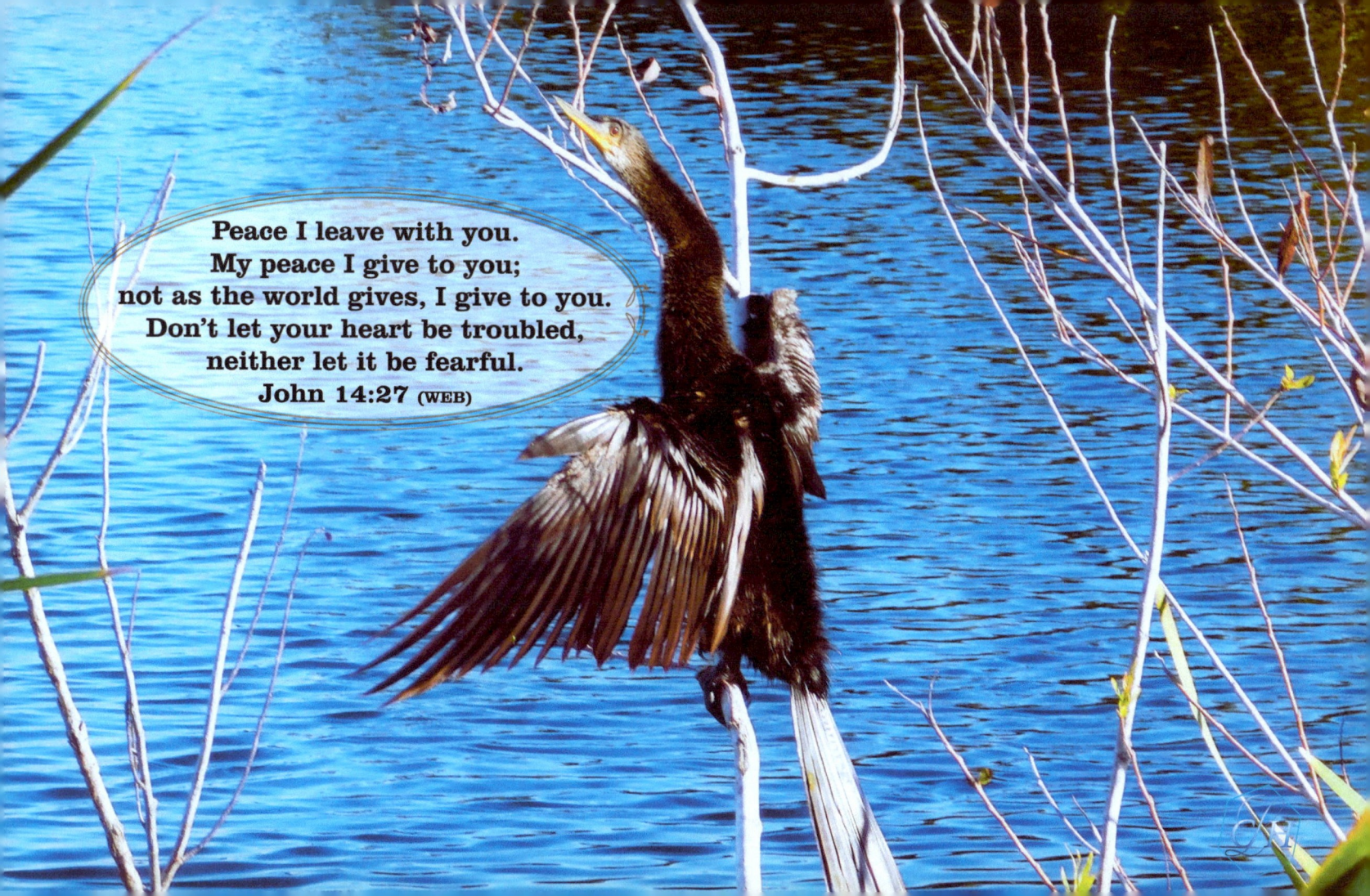

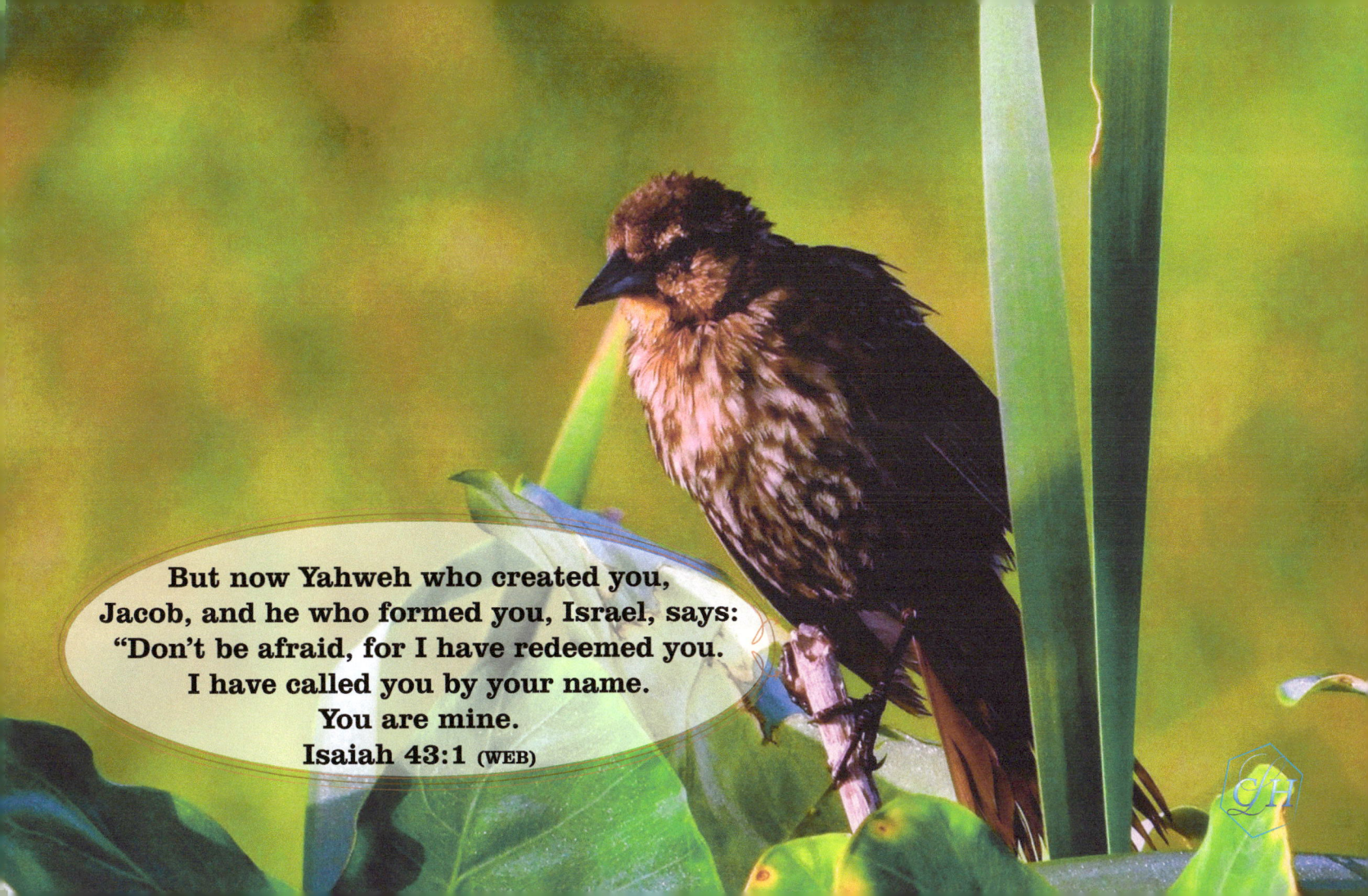

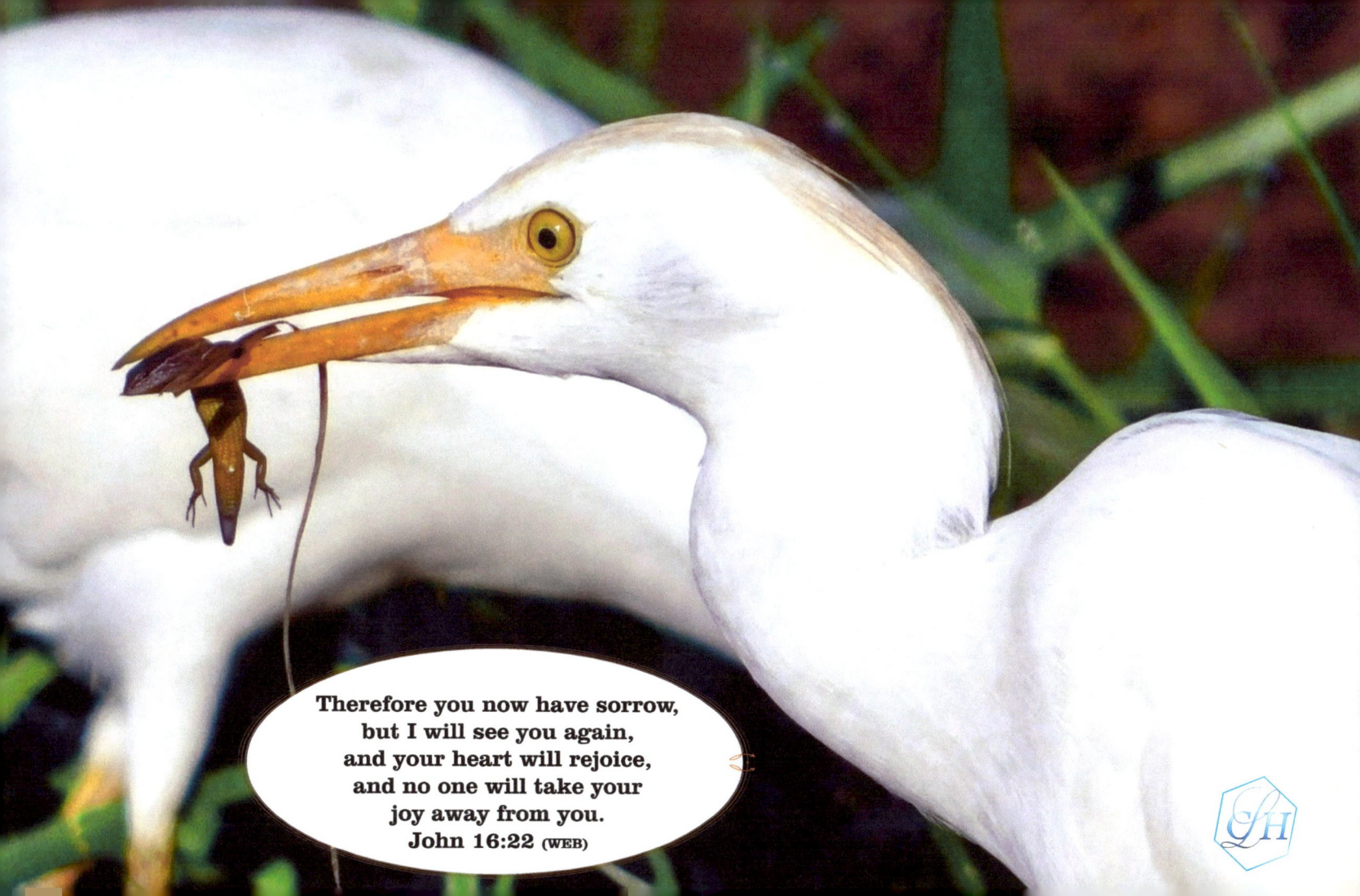

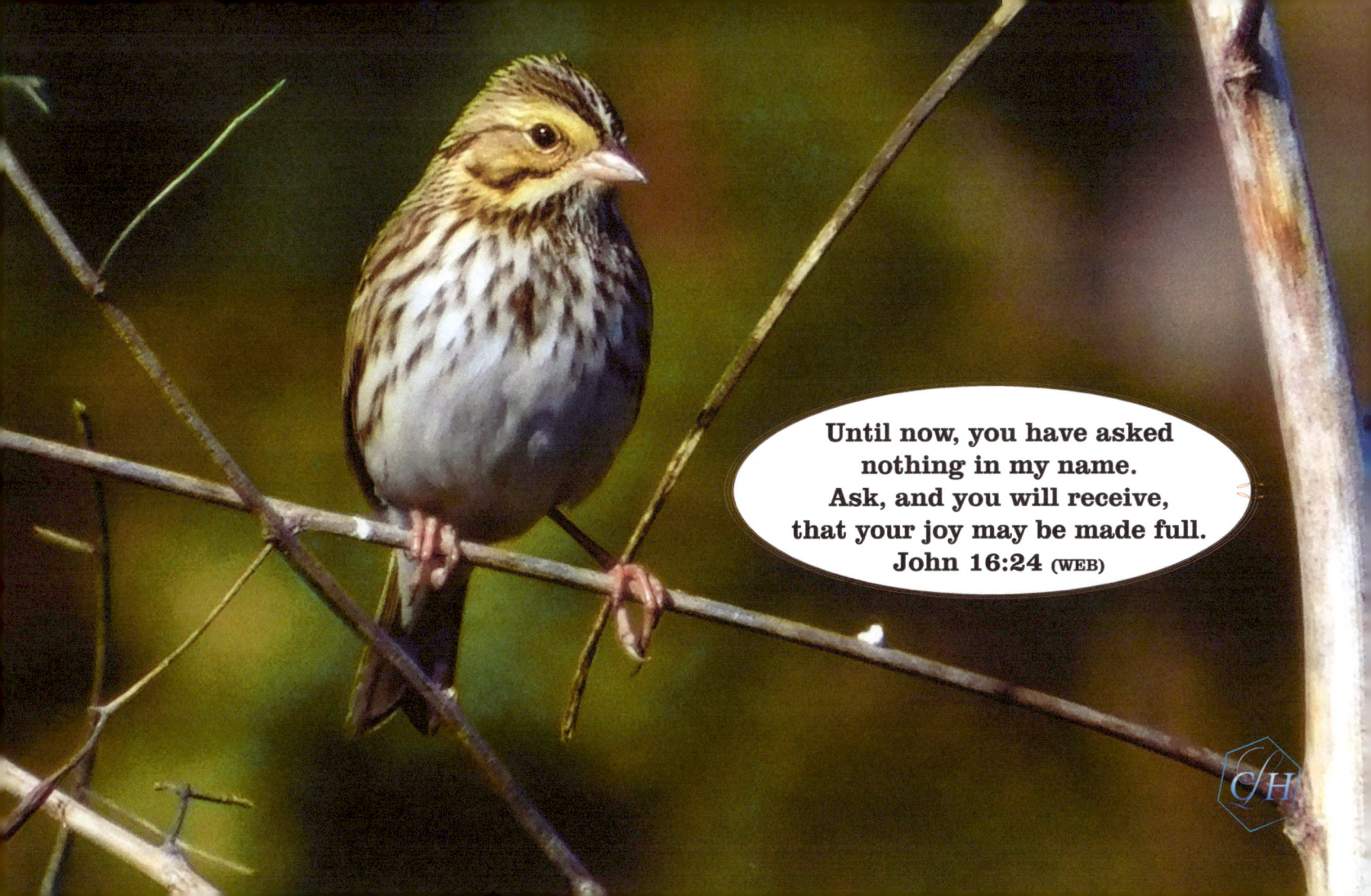

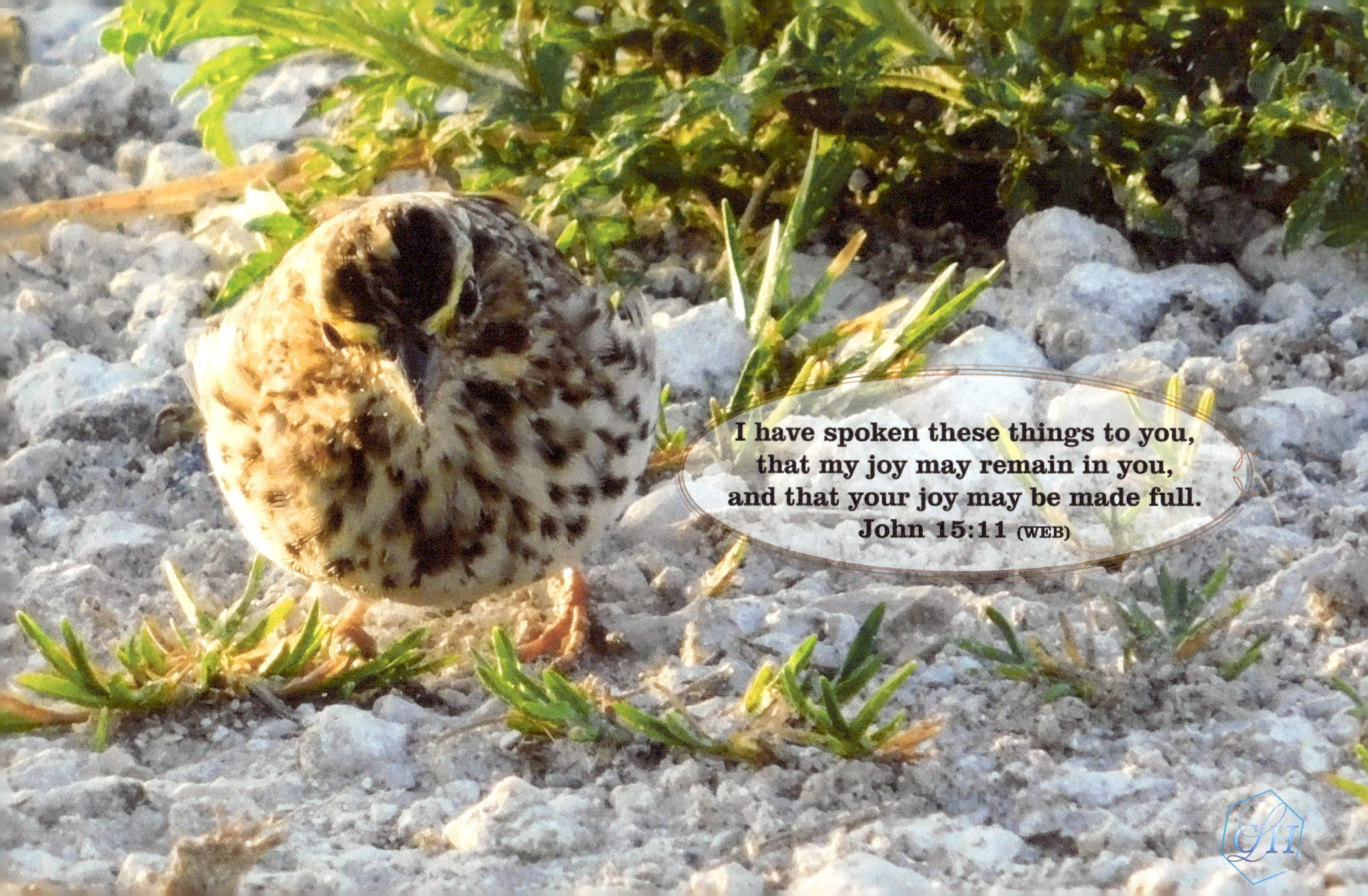

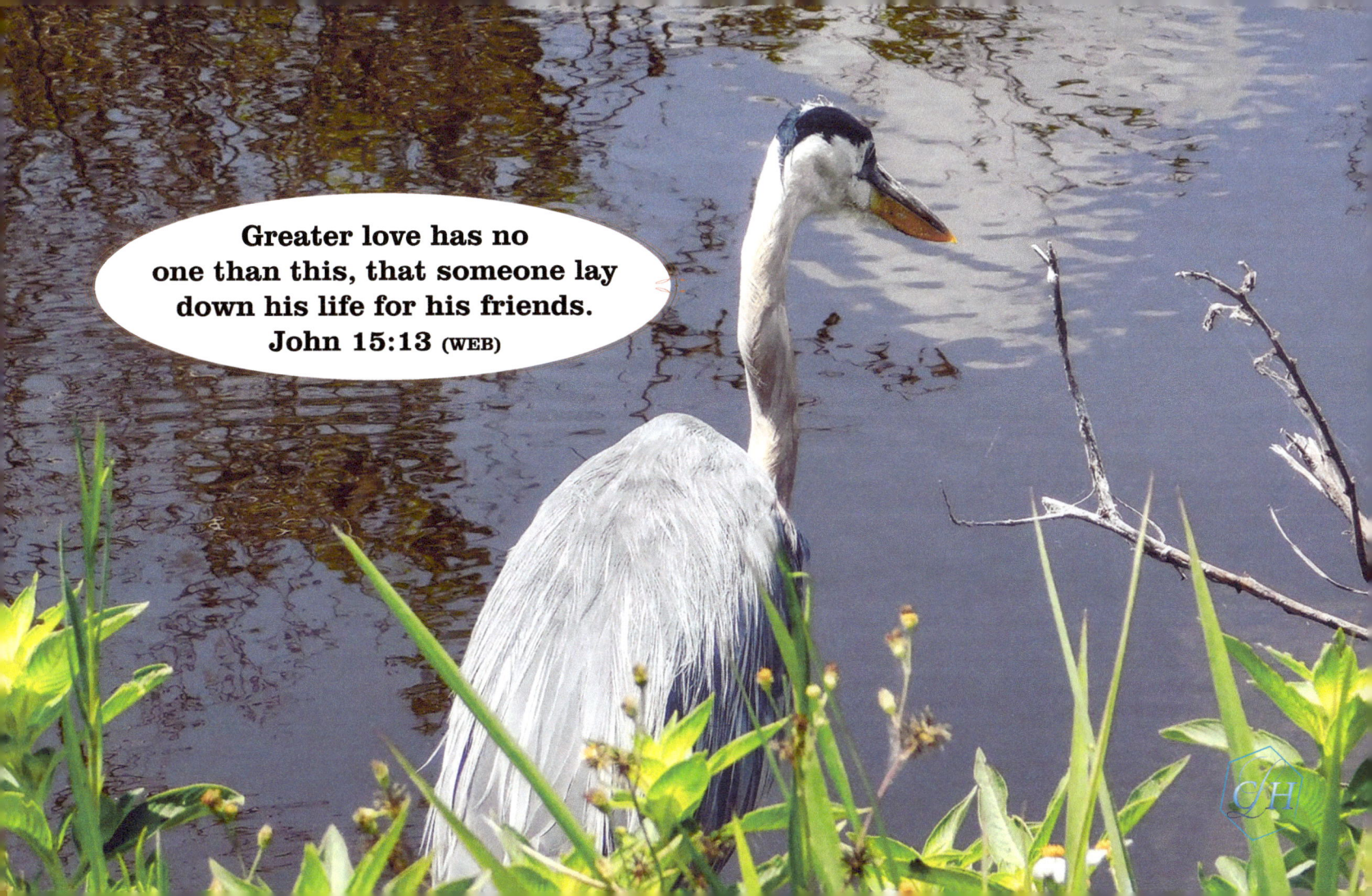

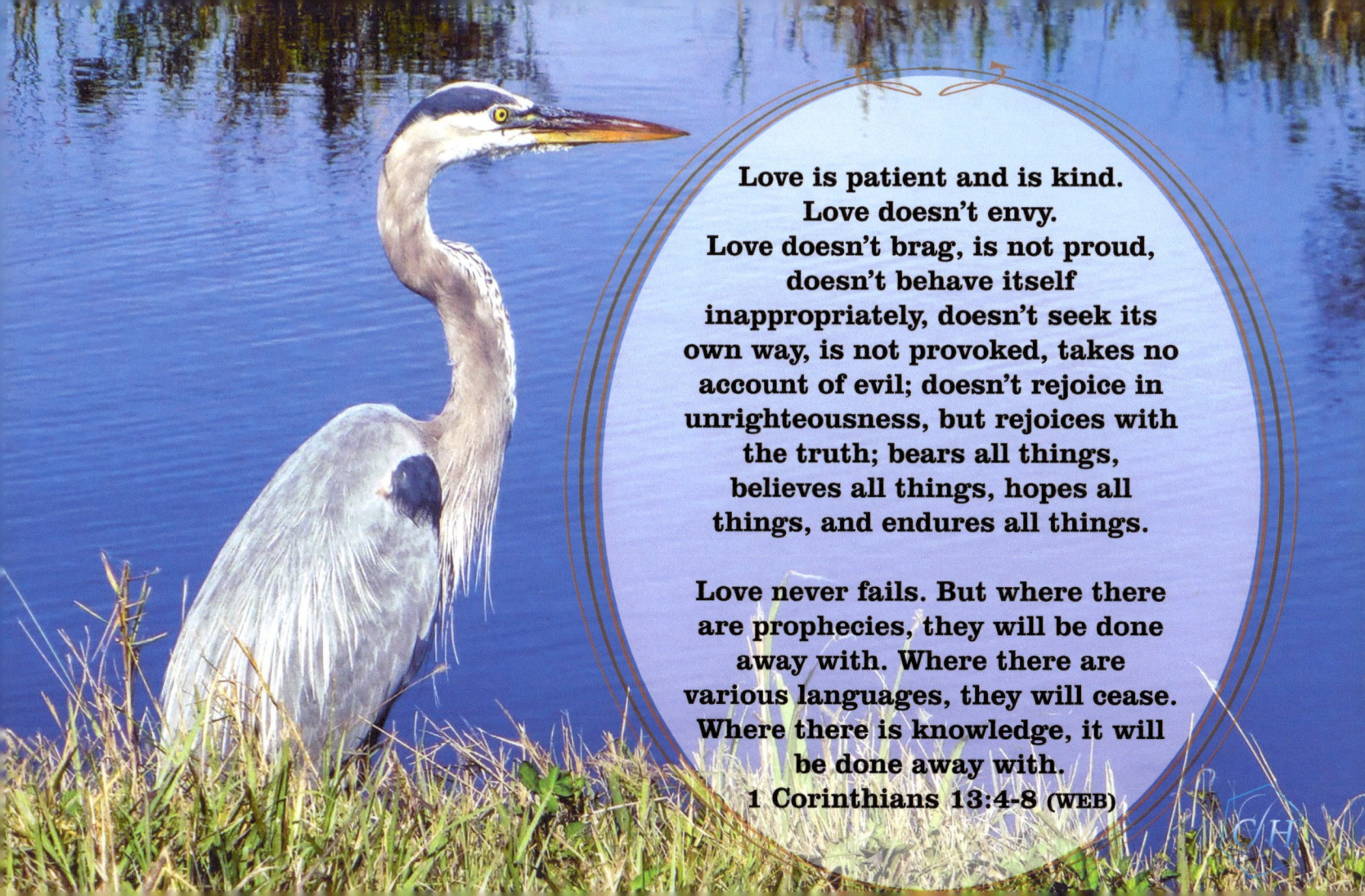

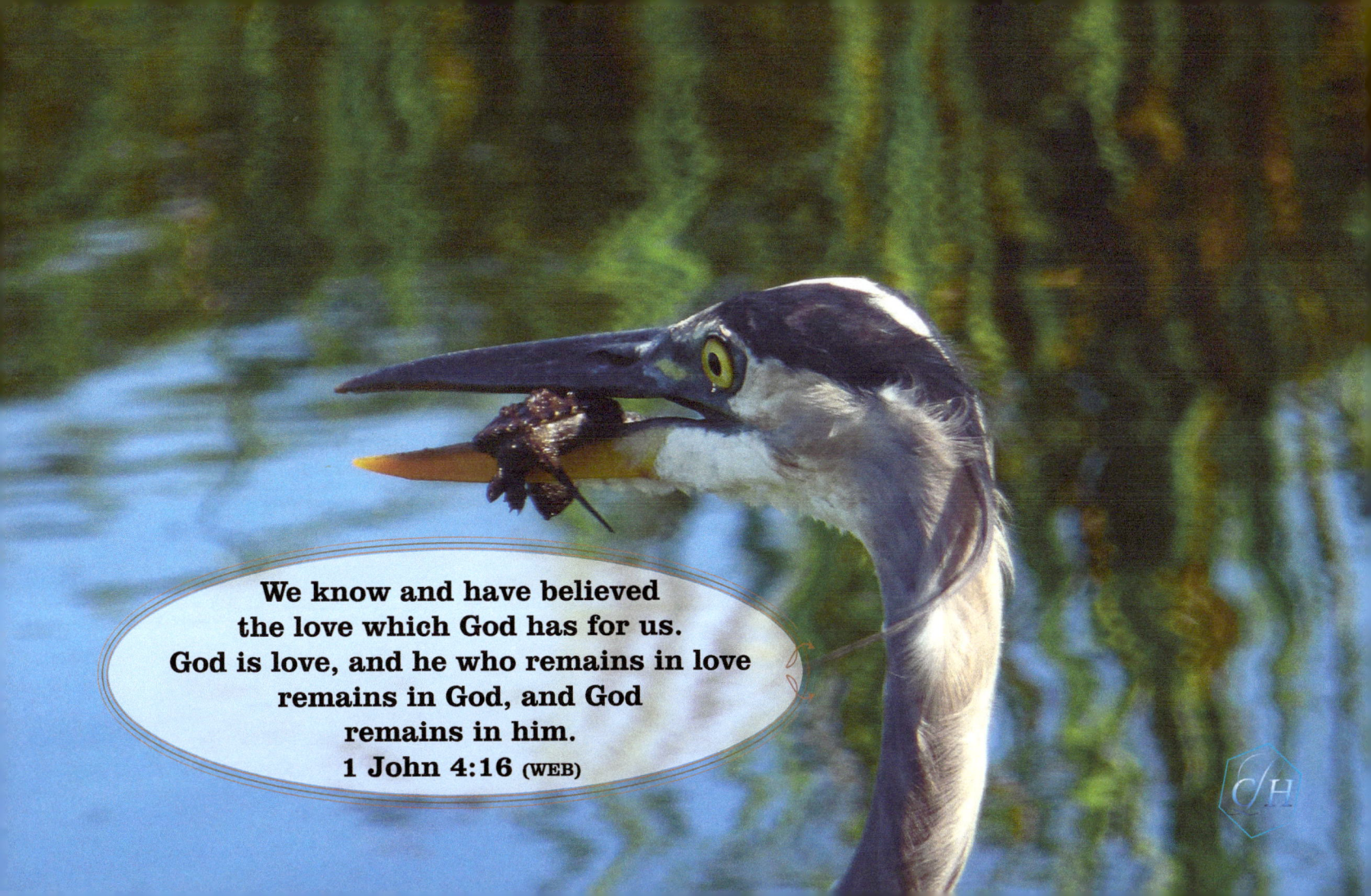

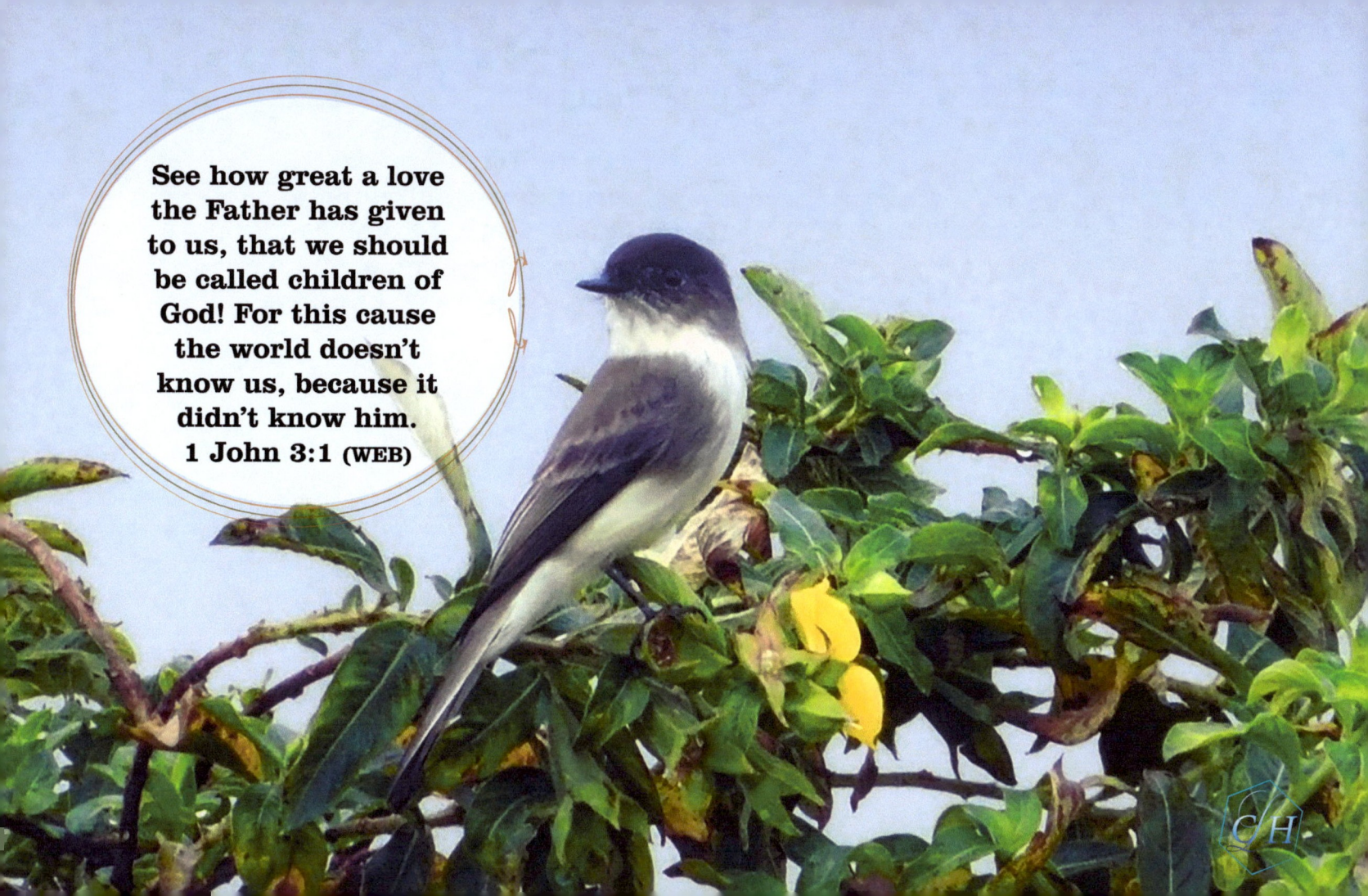

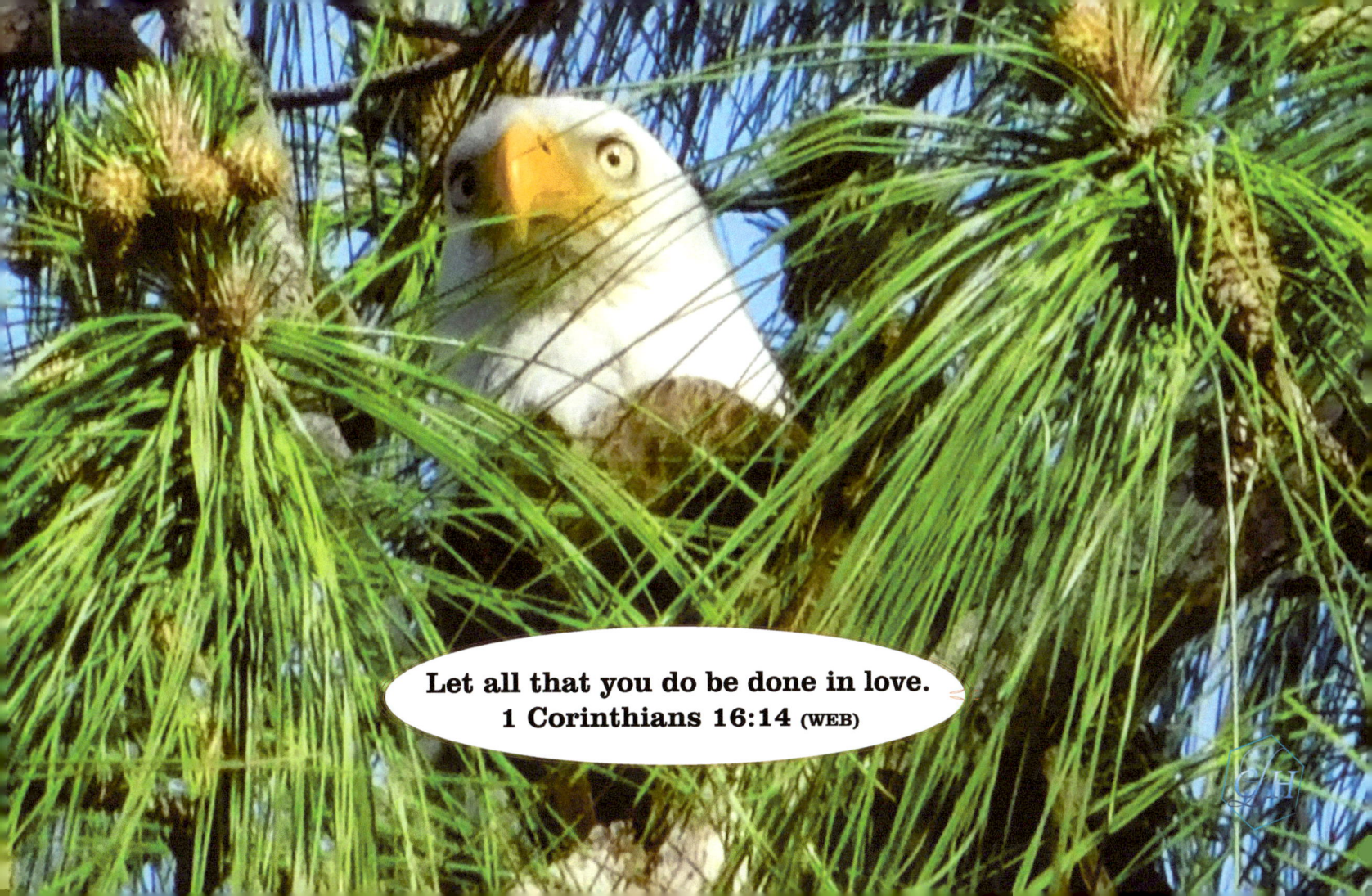

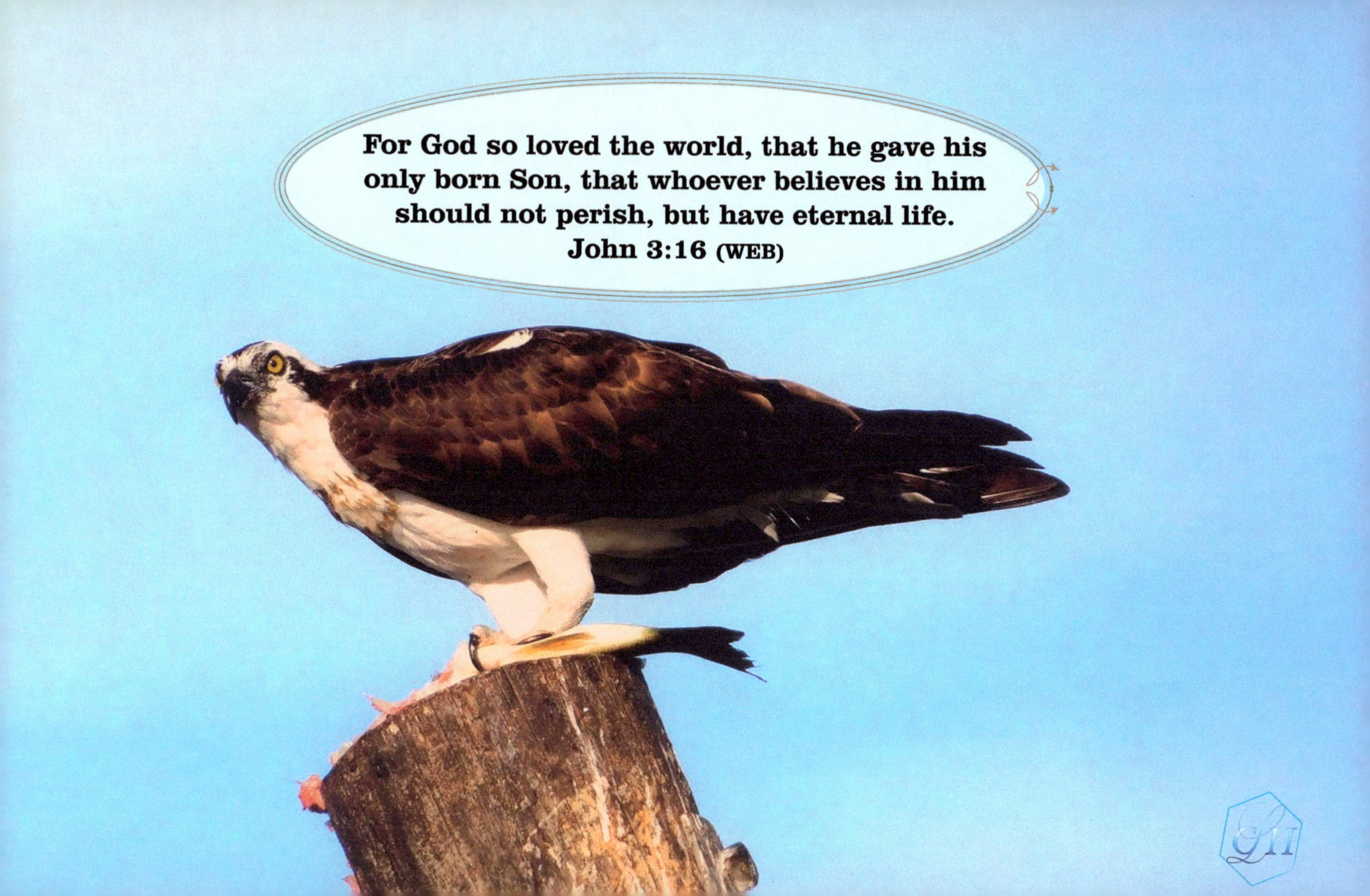

For God so loved the world, that he gave his only born Son, that whoever believes in him should not perish, but have eternal life.
John 3:16 (WEB)

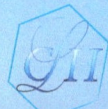

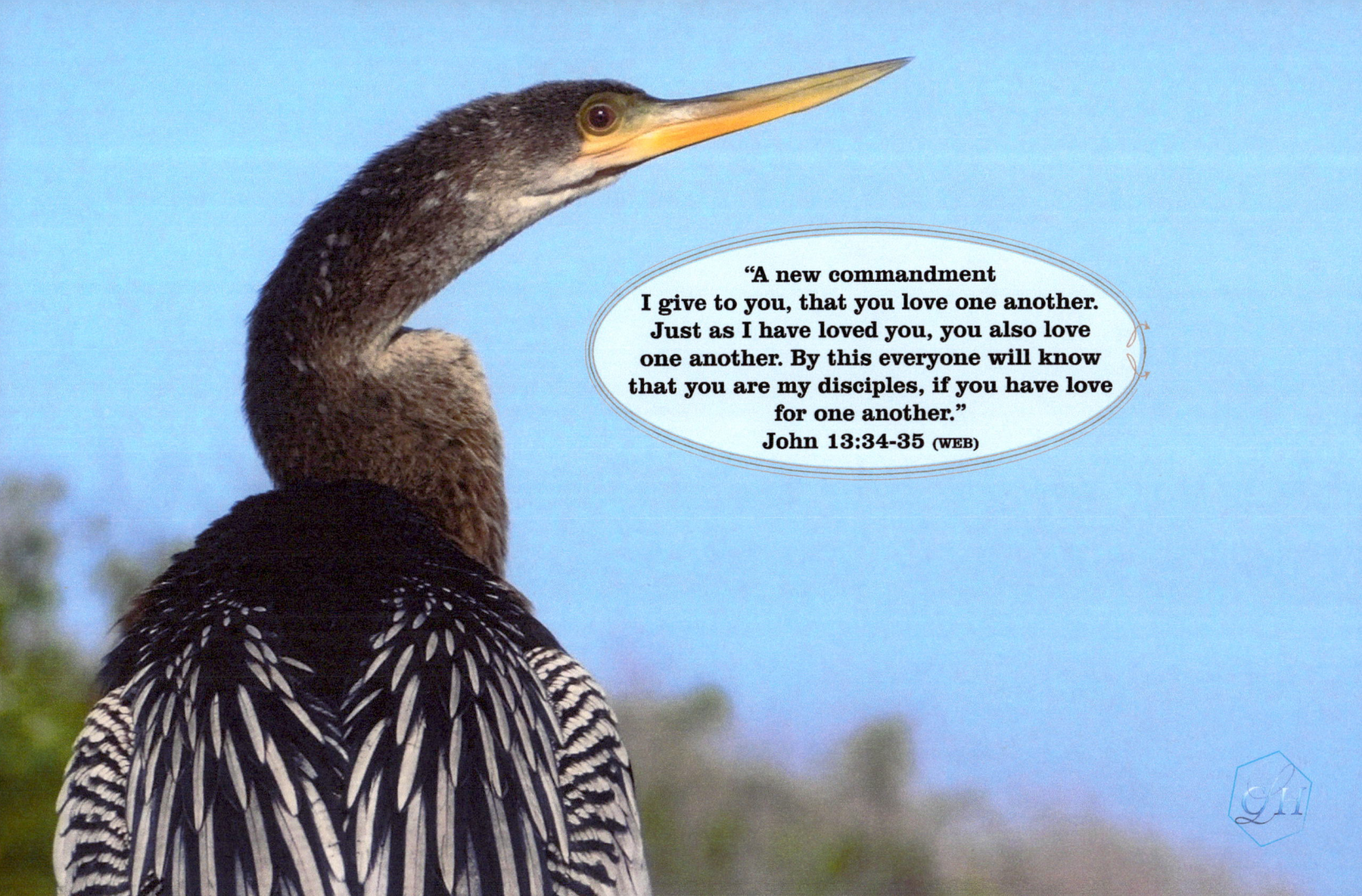

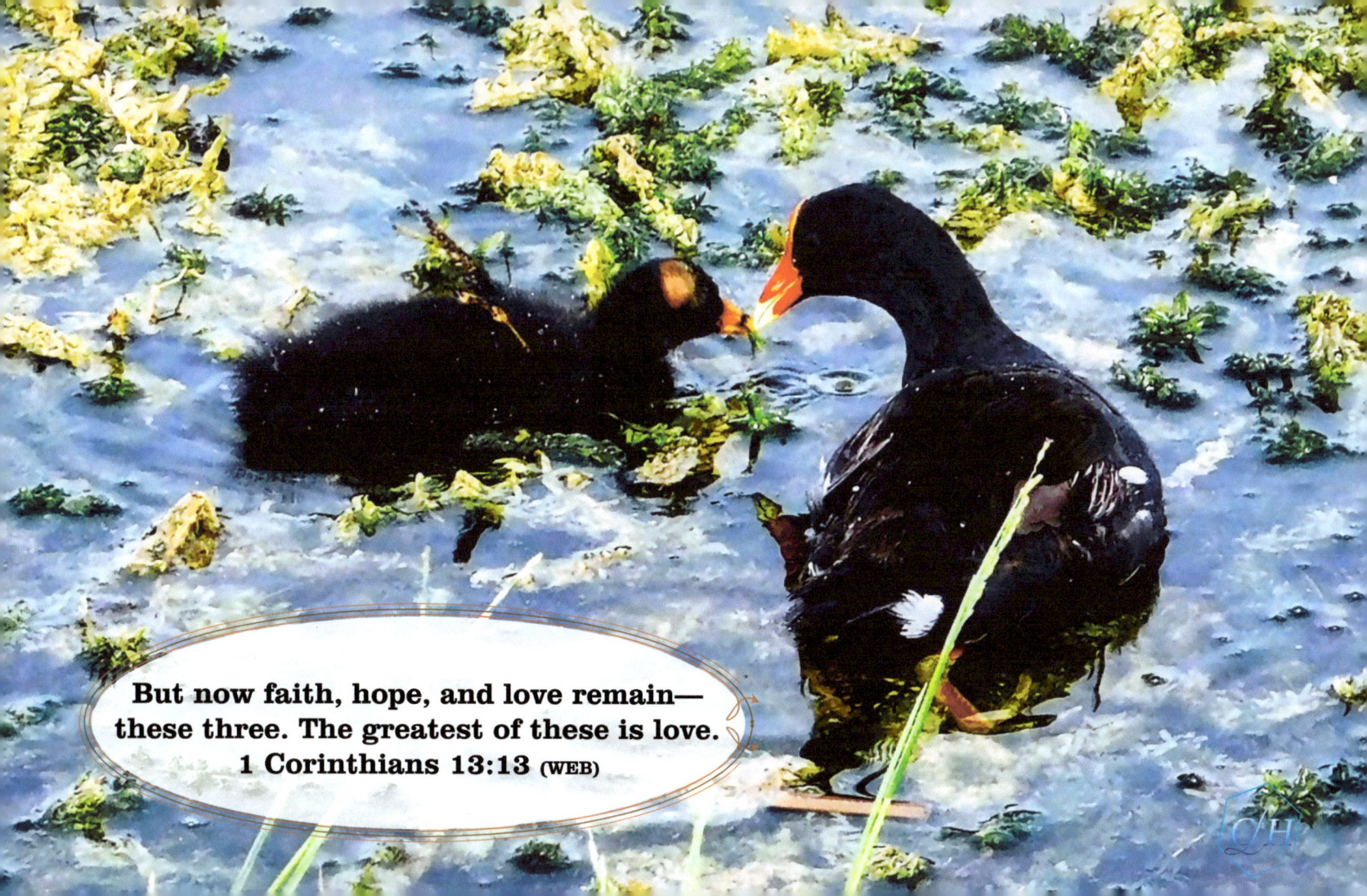

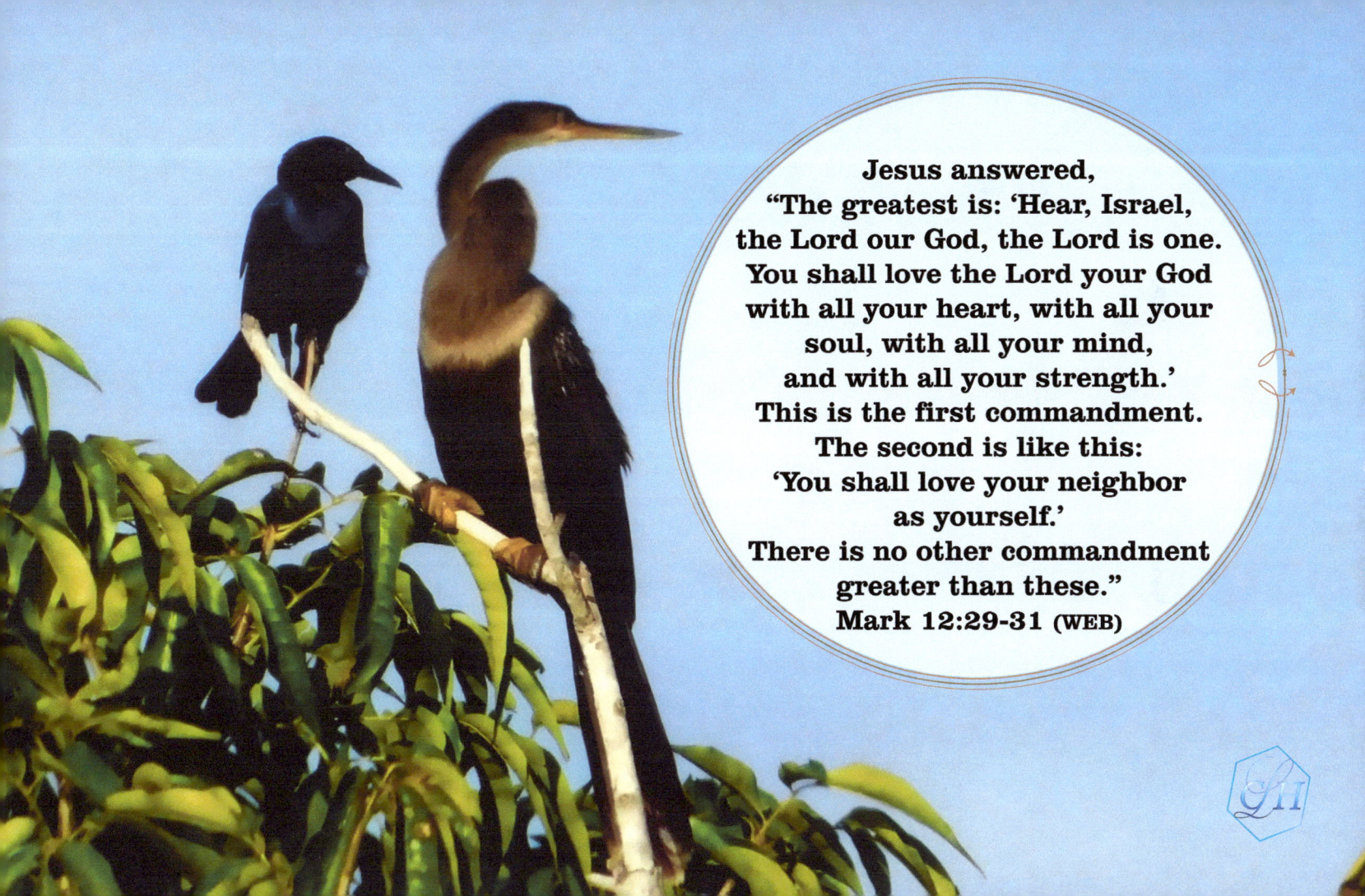

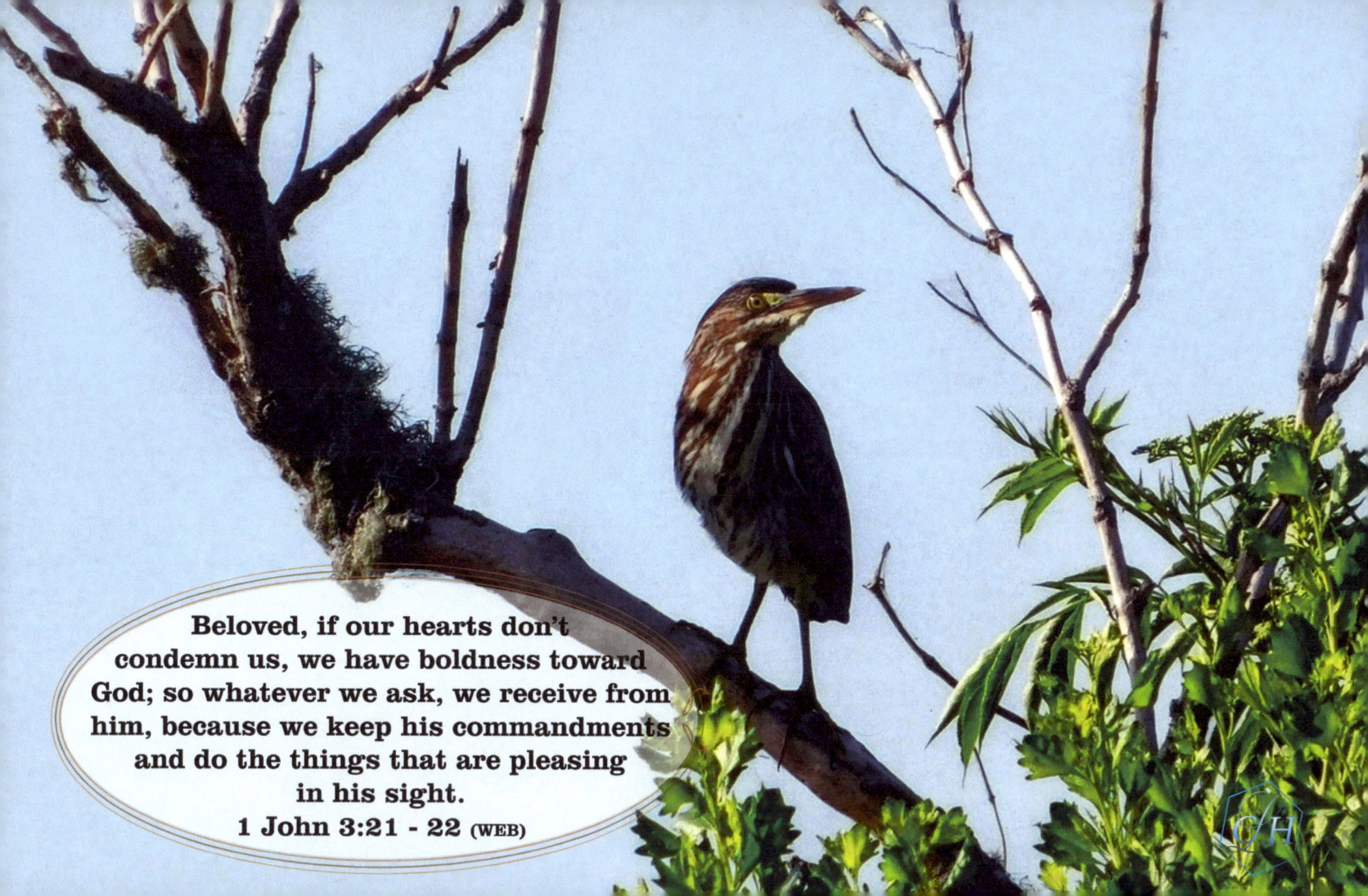

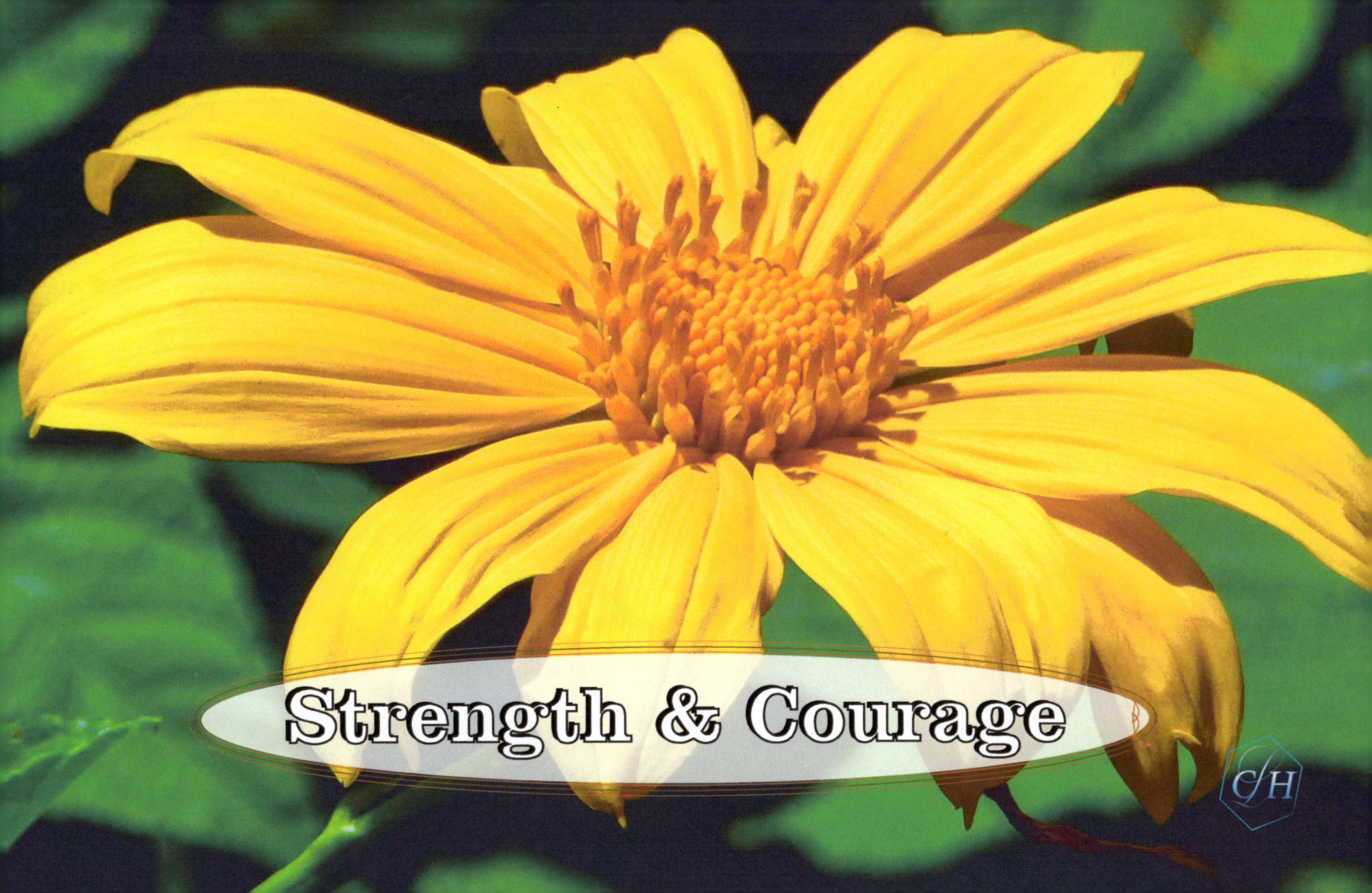

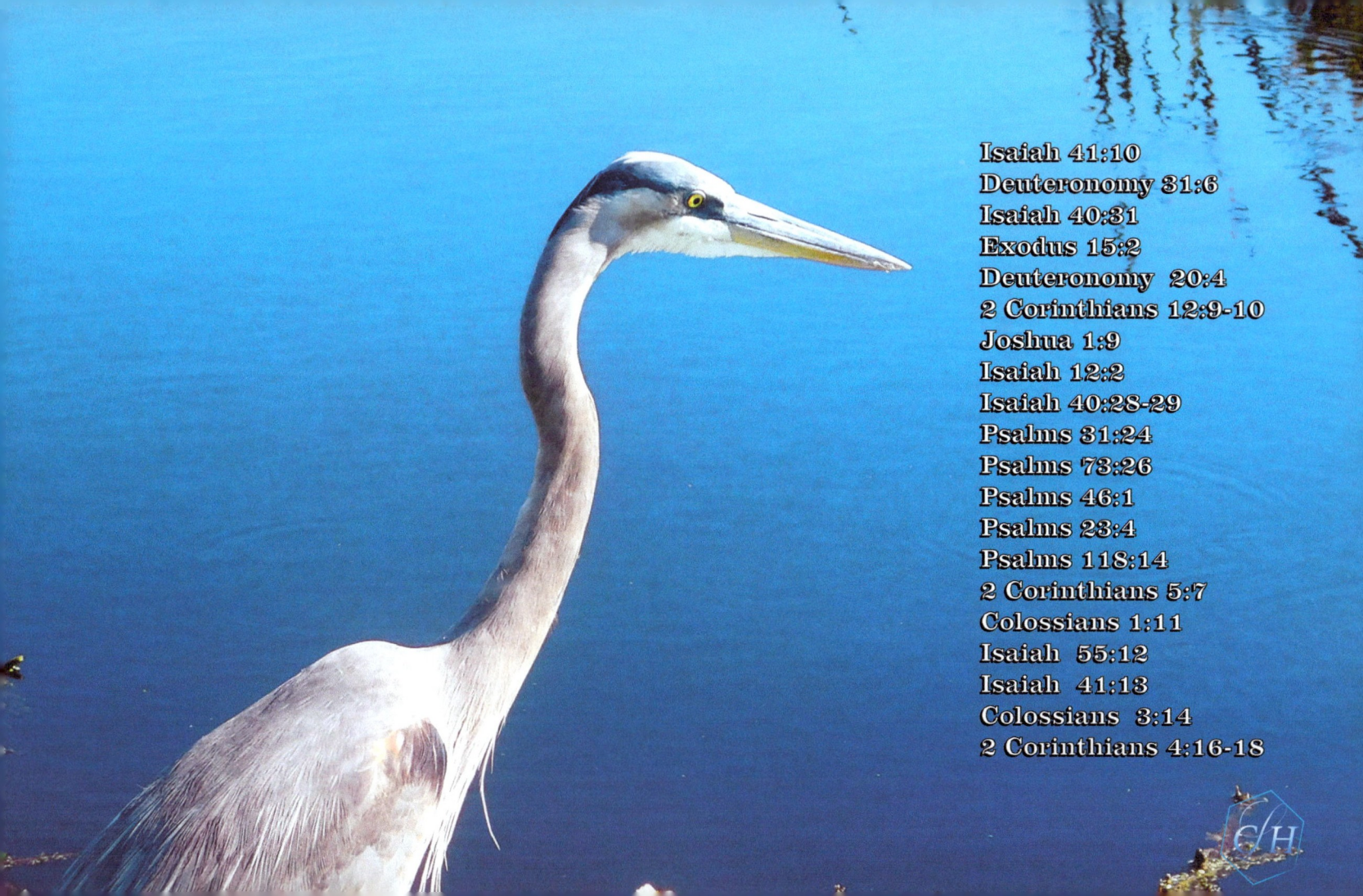

Isaiah 41:10
Deuteronomy 31:6
Isaiah 40:31
Exodus 15:2
Deuteronomy 20:4
2 Corinthians 12:9-10
Joshua 1:9
Isaiah 12:2
Isaiah 40:28-29
Psalms 31:24
Psalms 73:26
Psalms 46:1
Psalms 23:4
Psalms 118:14
2 Corinthians 5:7
Colossians 1:11
Isaiah 55:12
Isaiah 41:13
Colossians 3:14
2 Corinthians 4:16-18

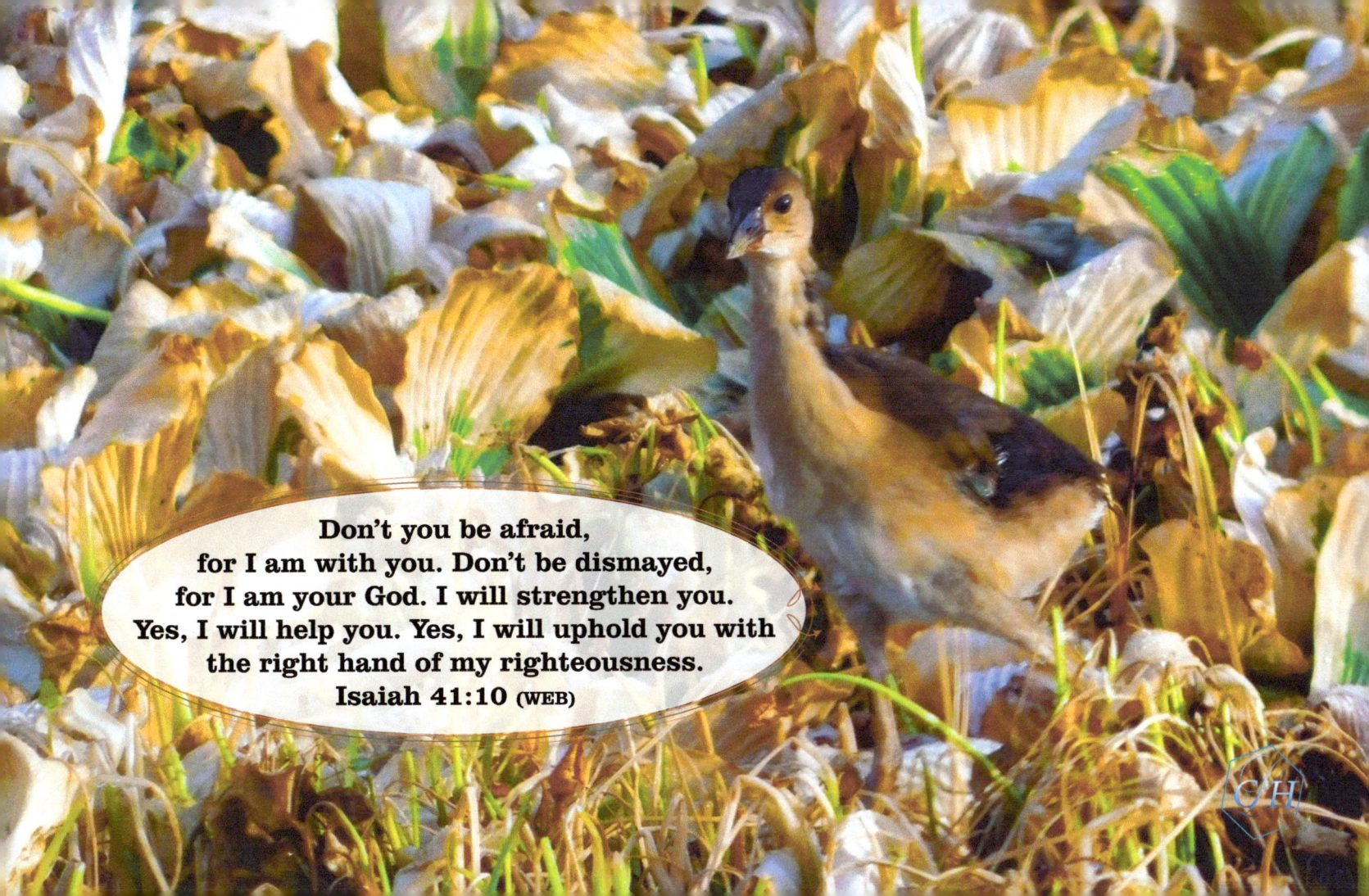

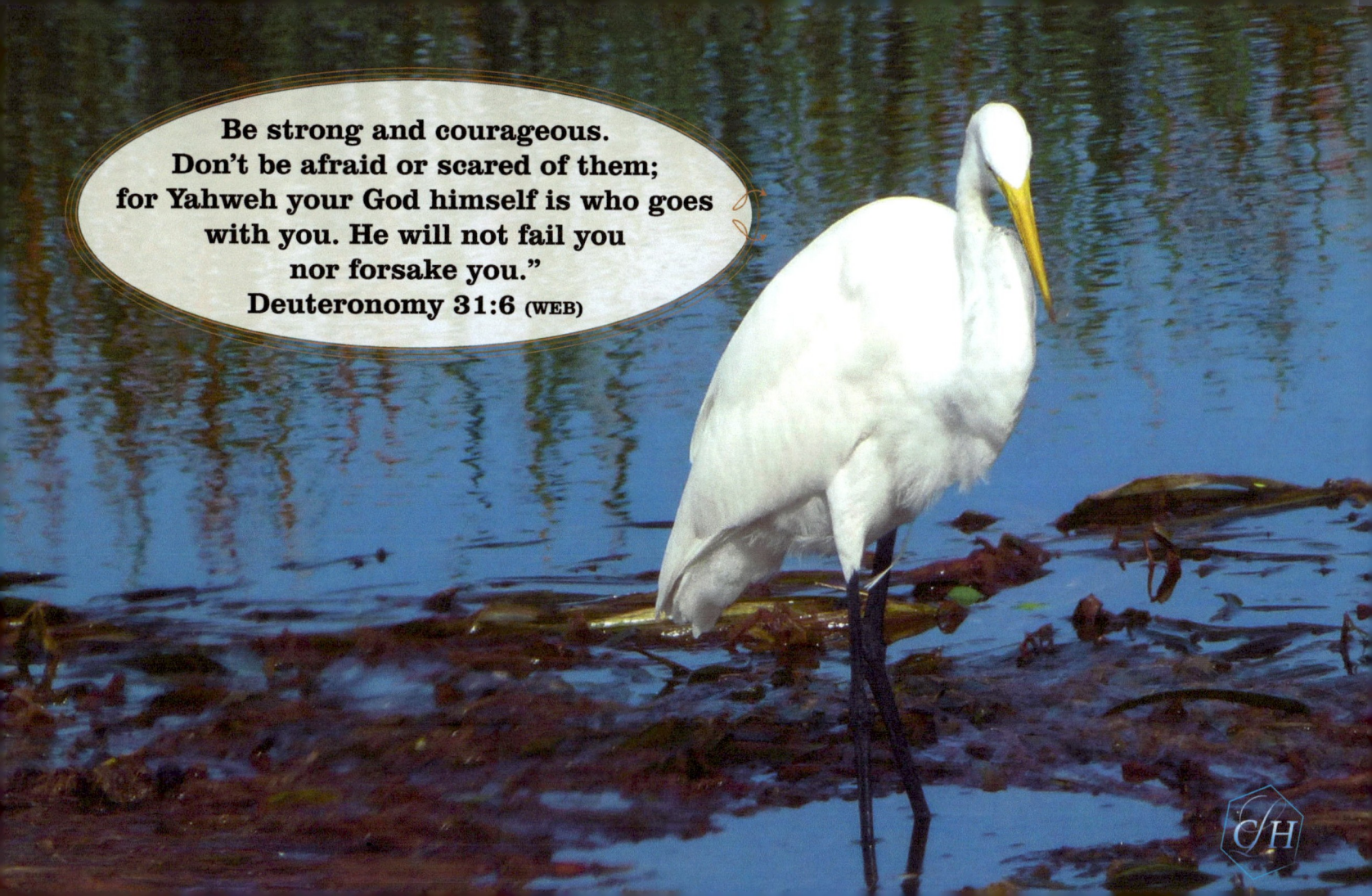

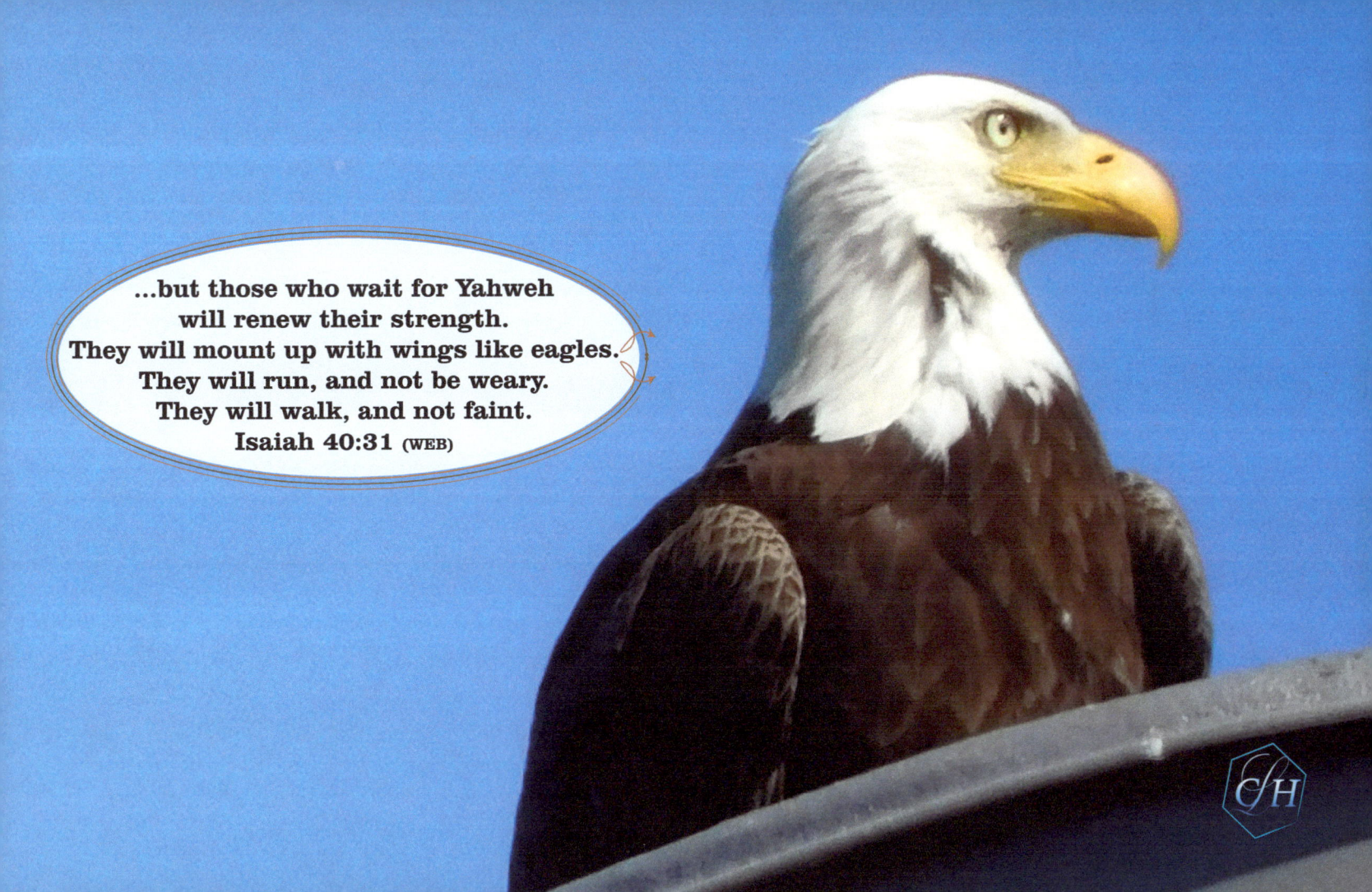

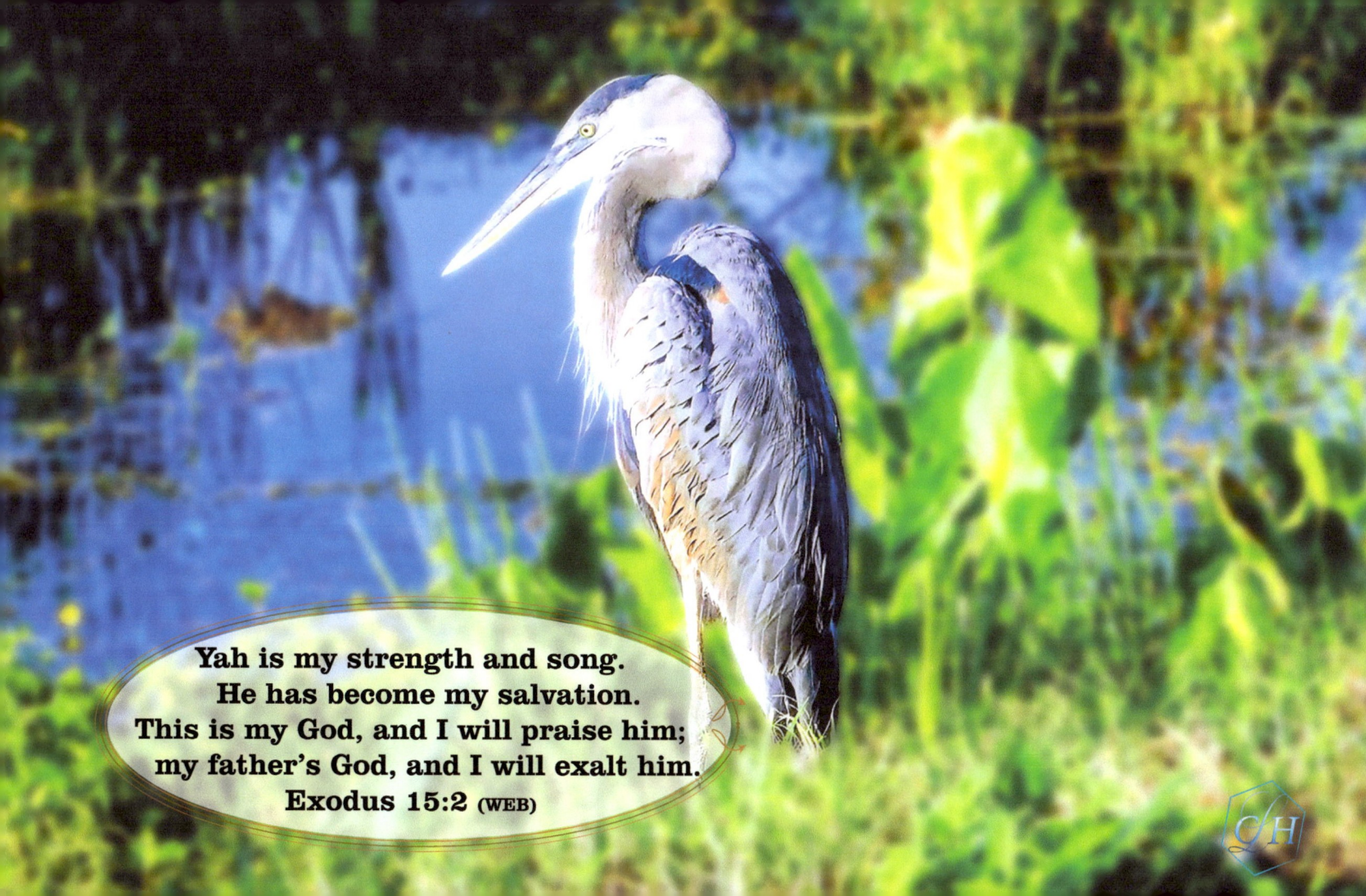

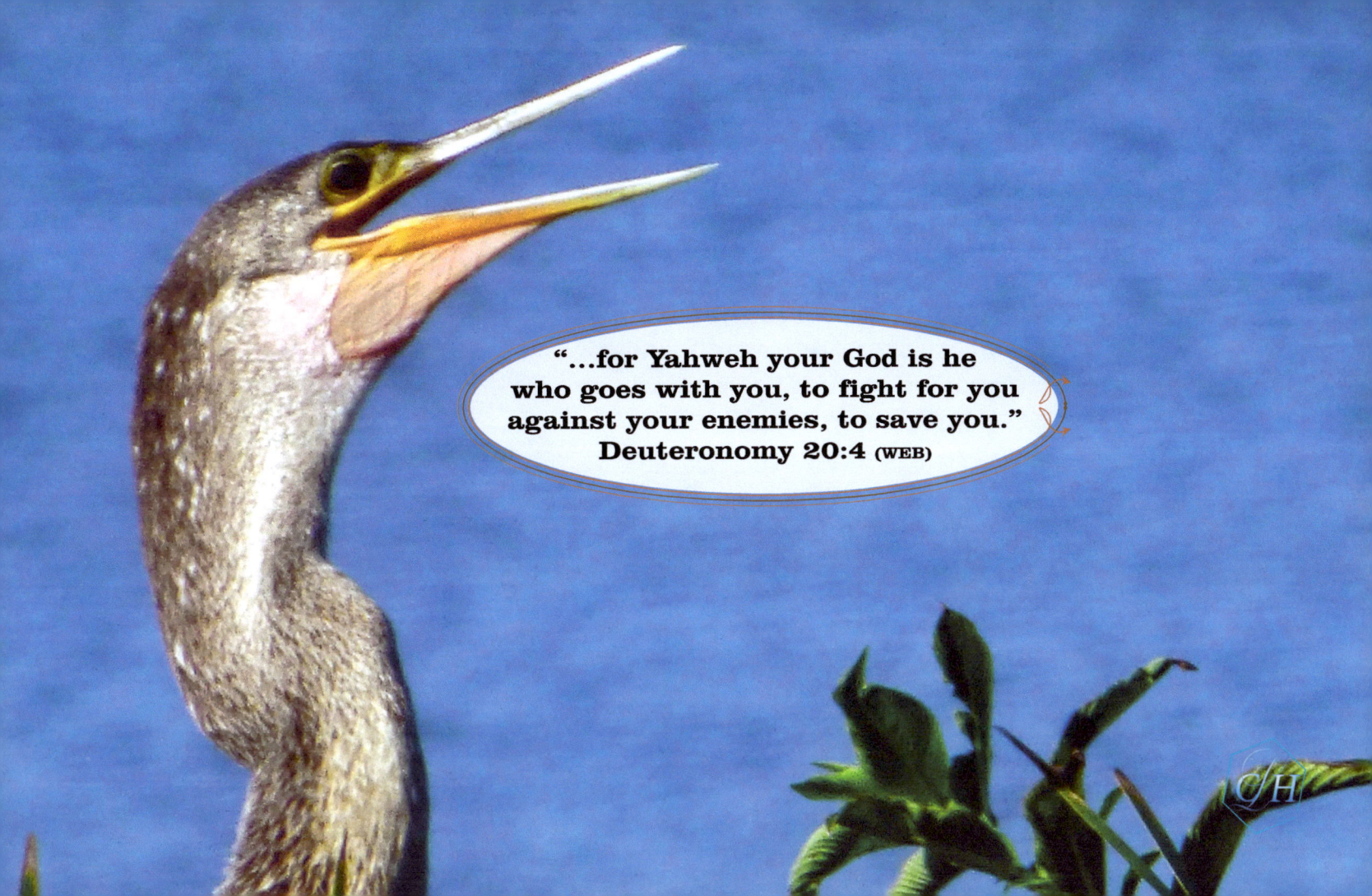

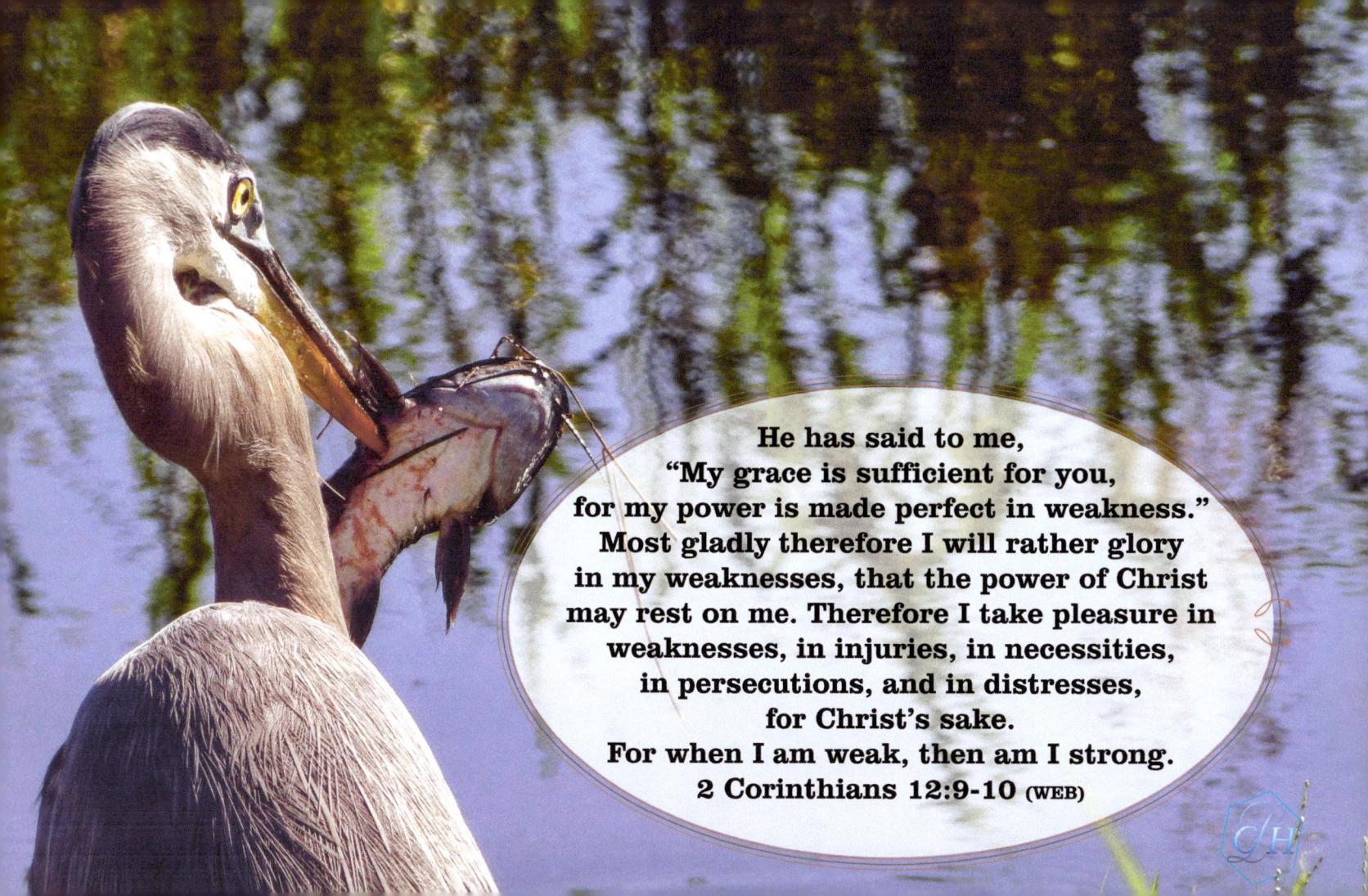

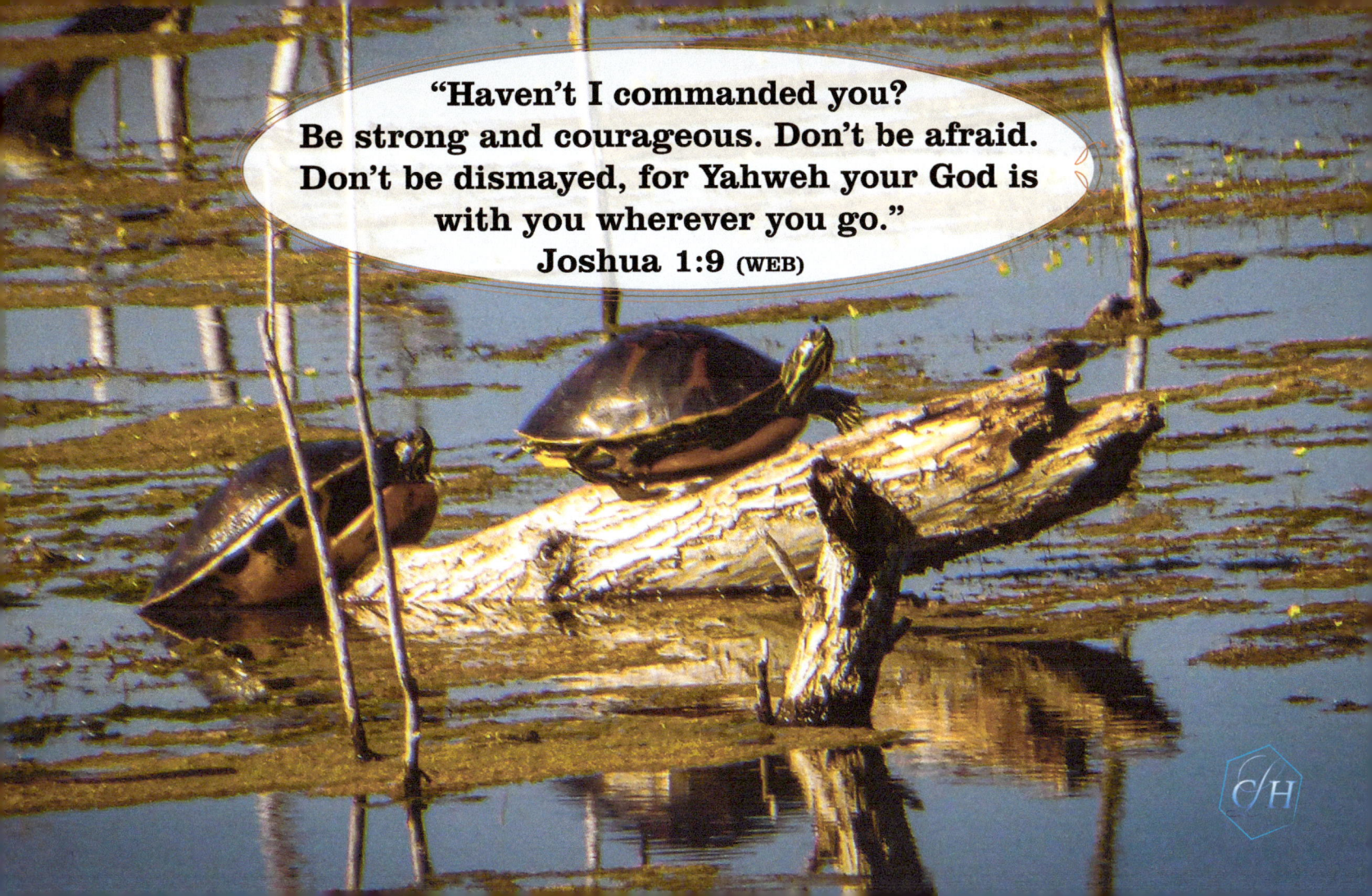

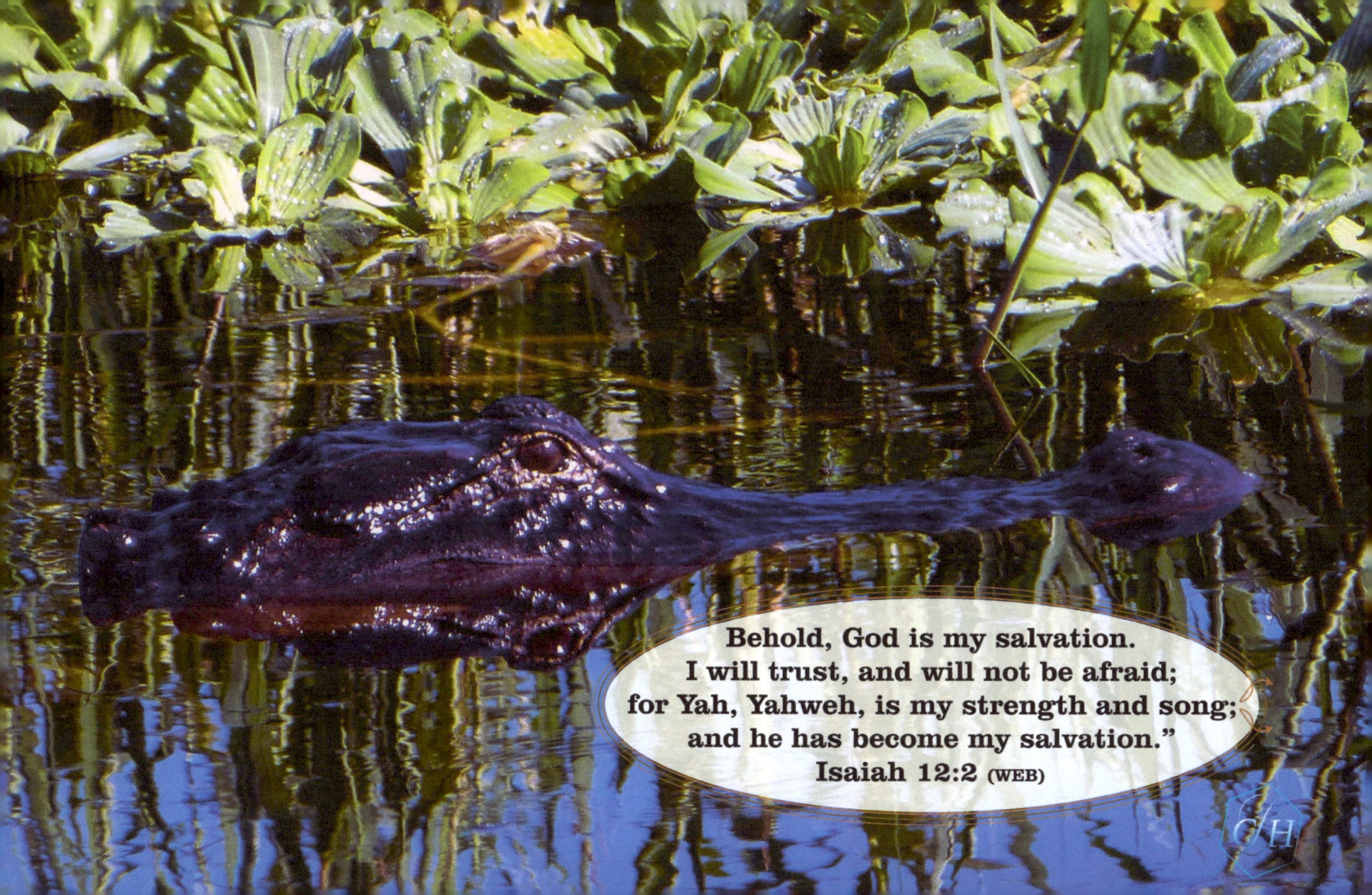

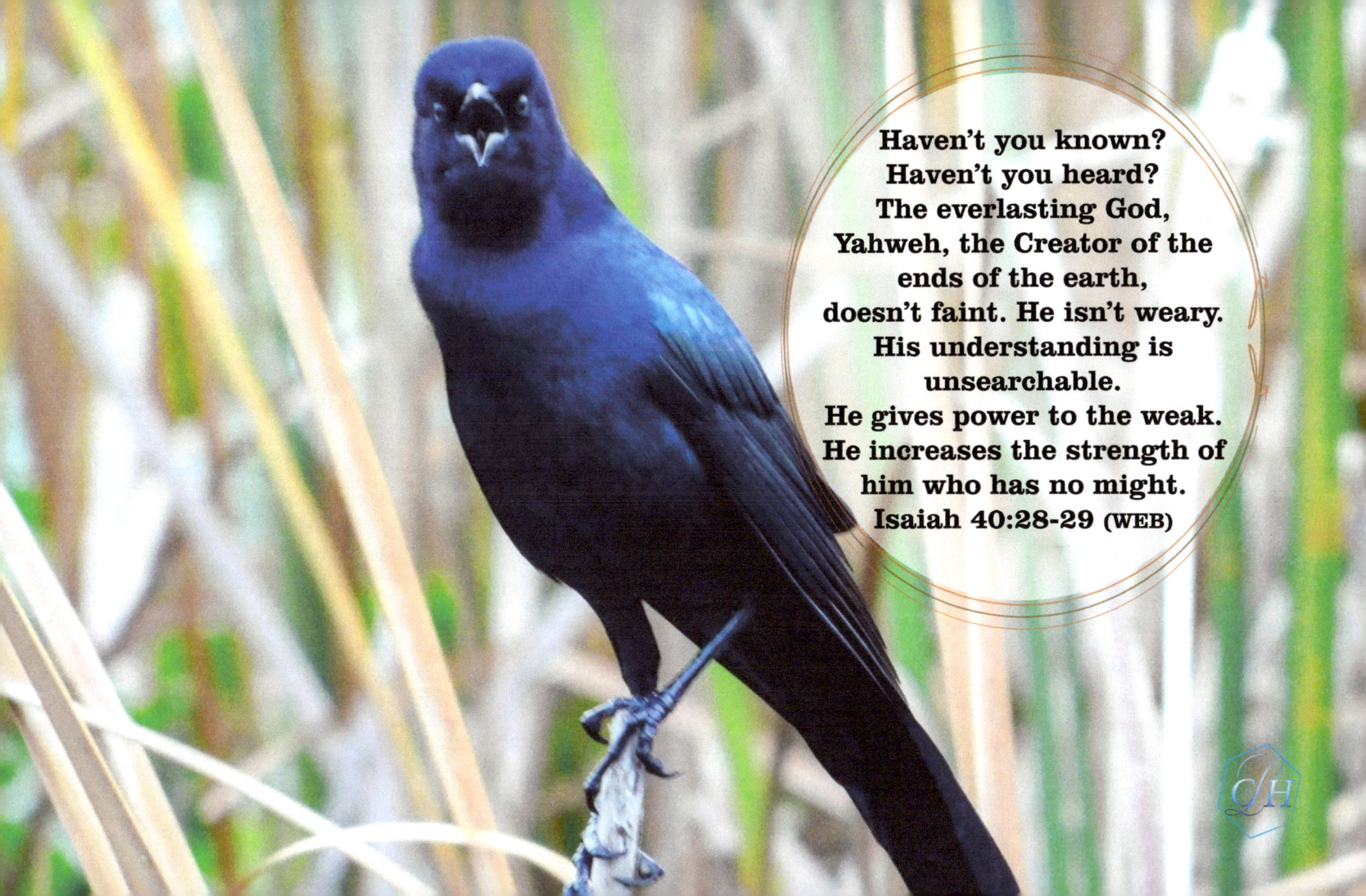

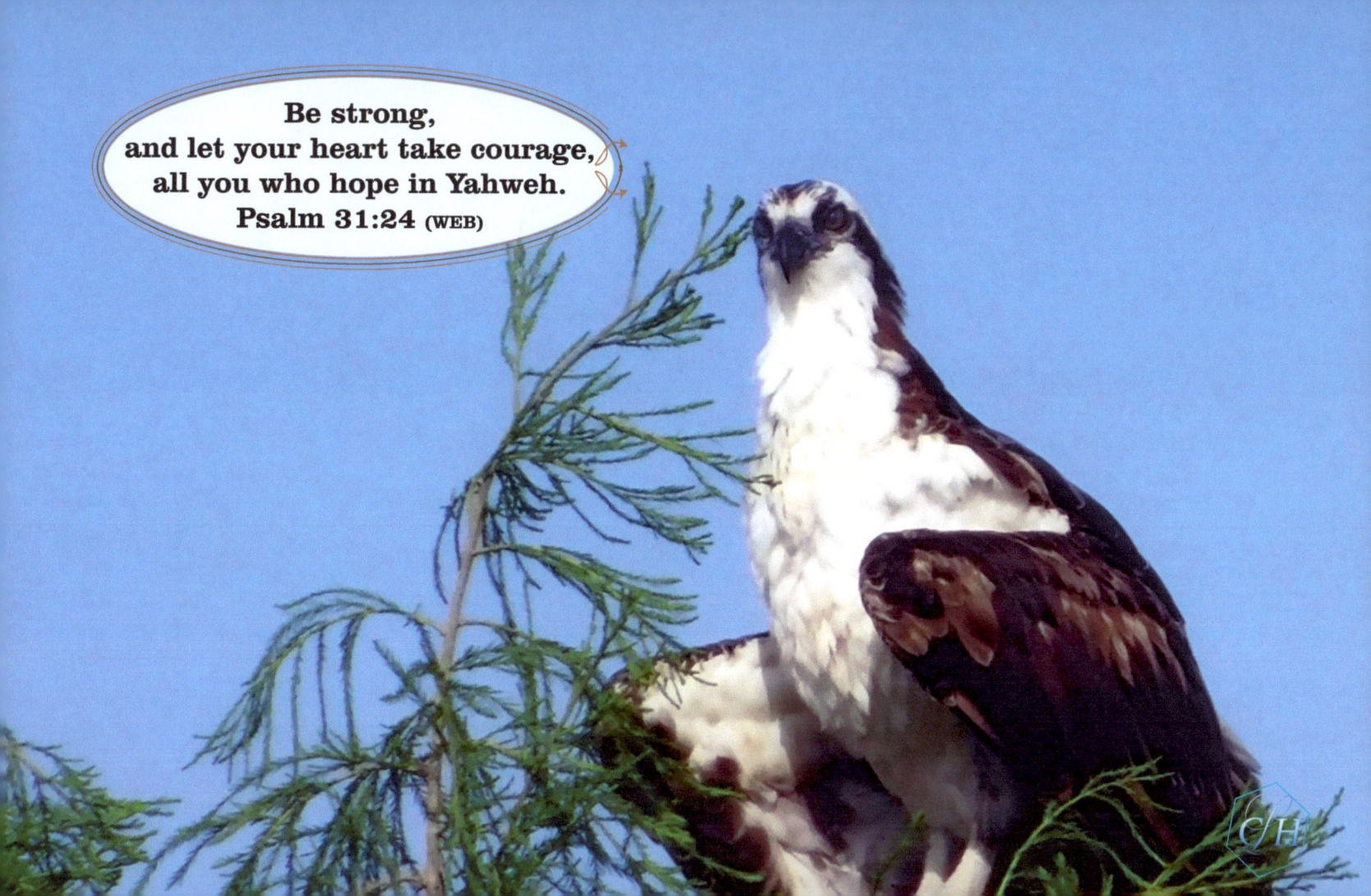

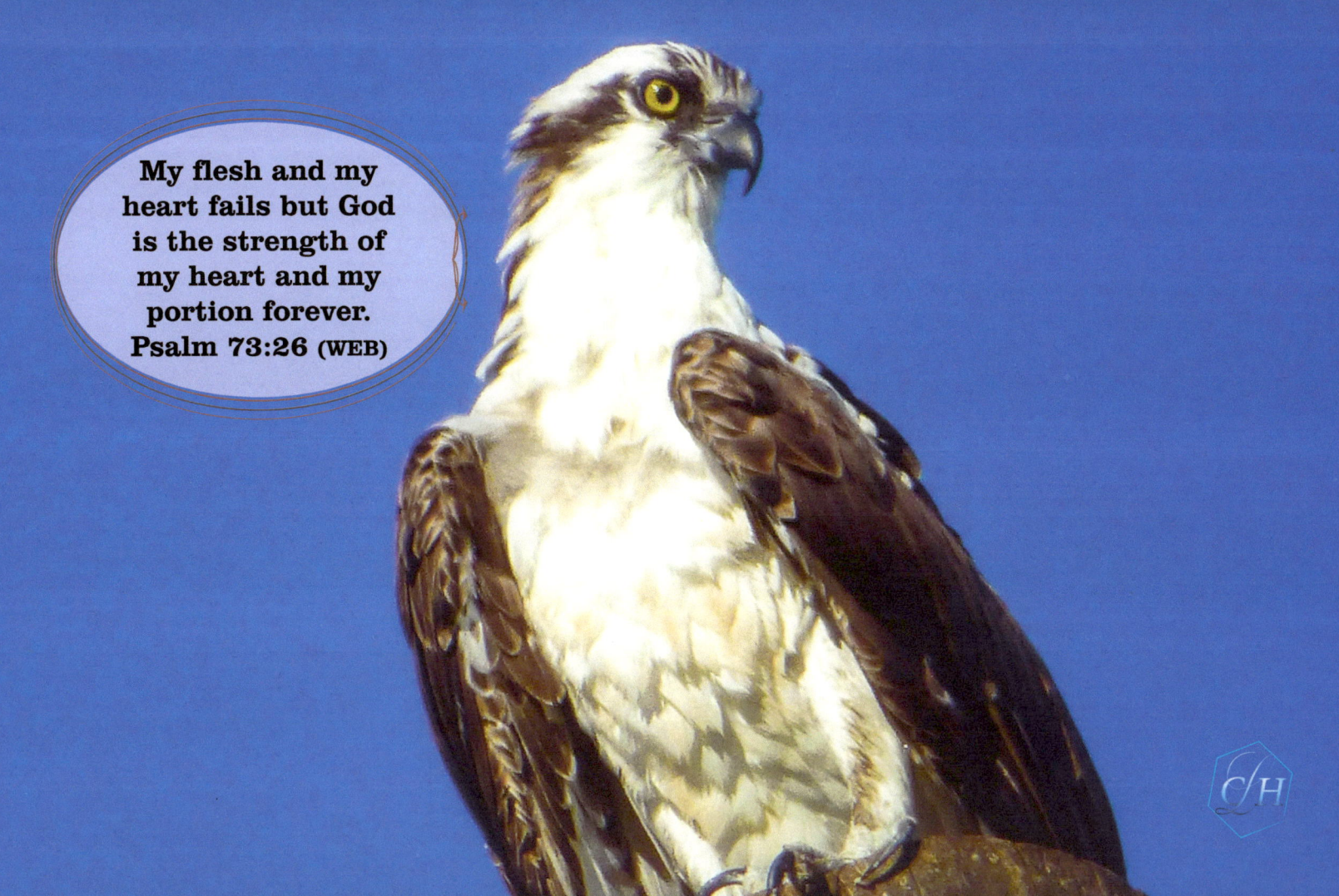

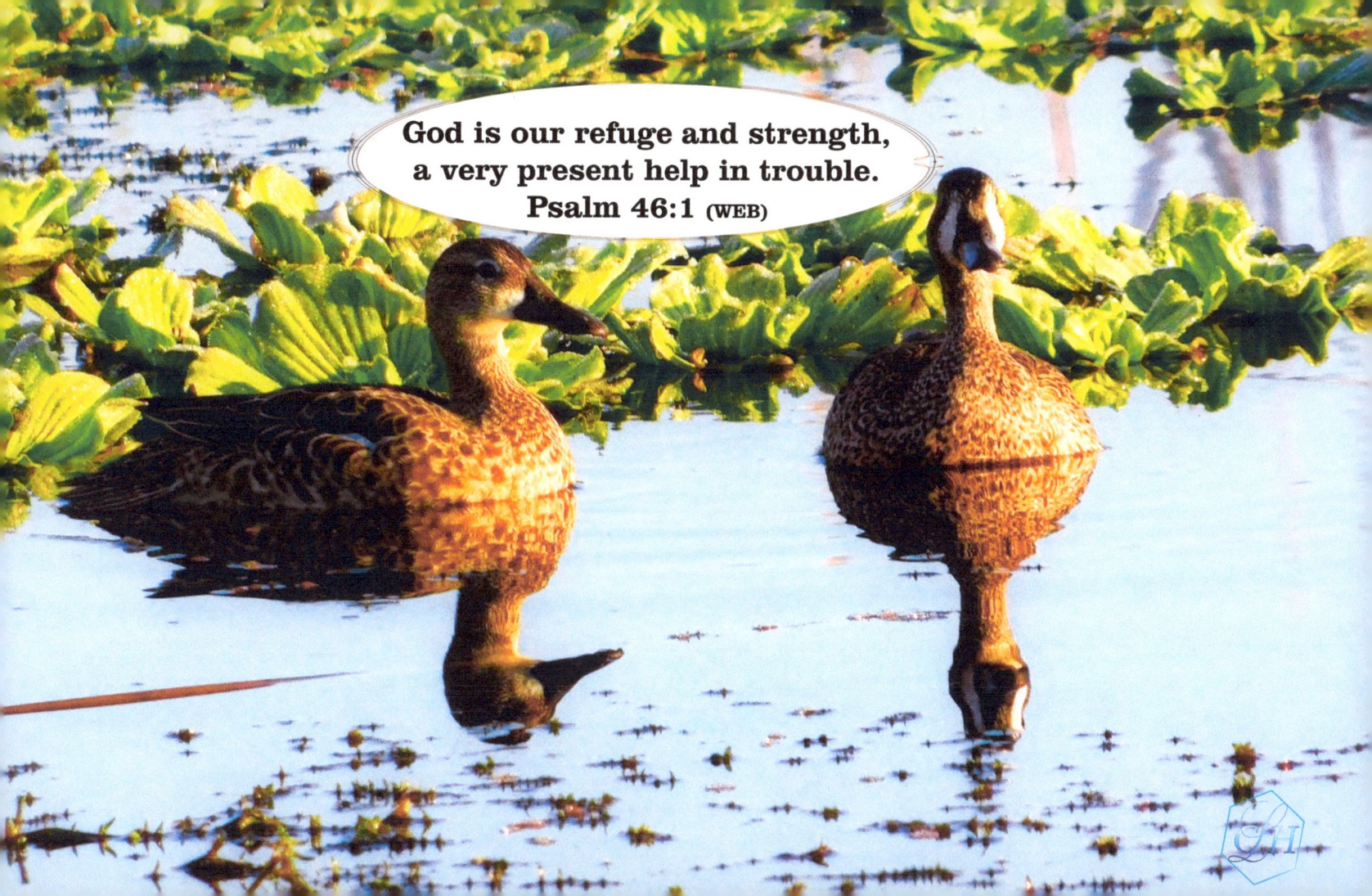

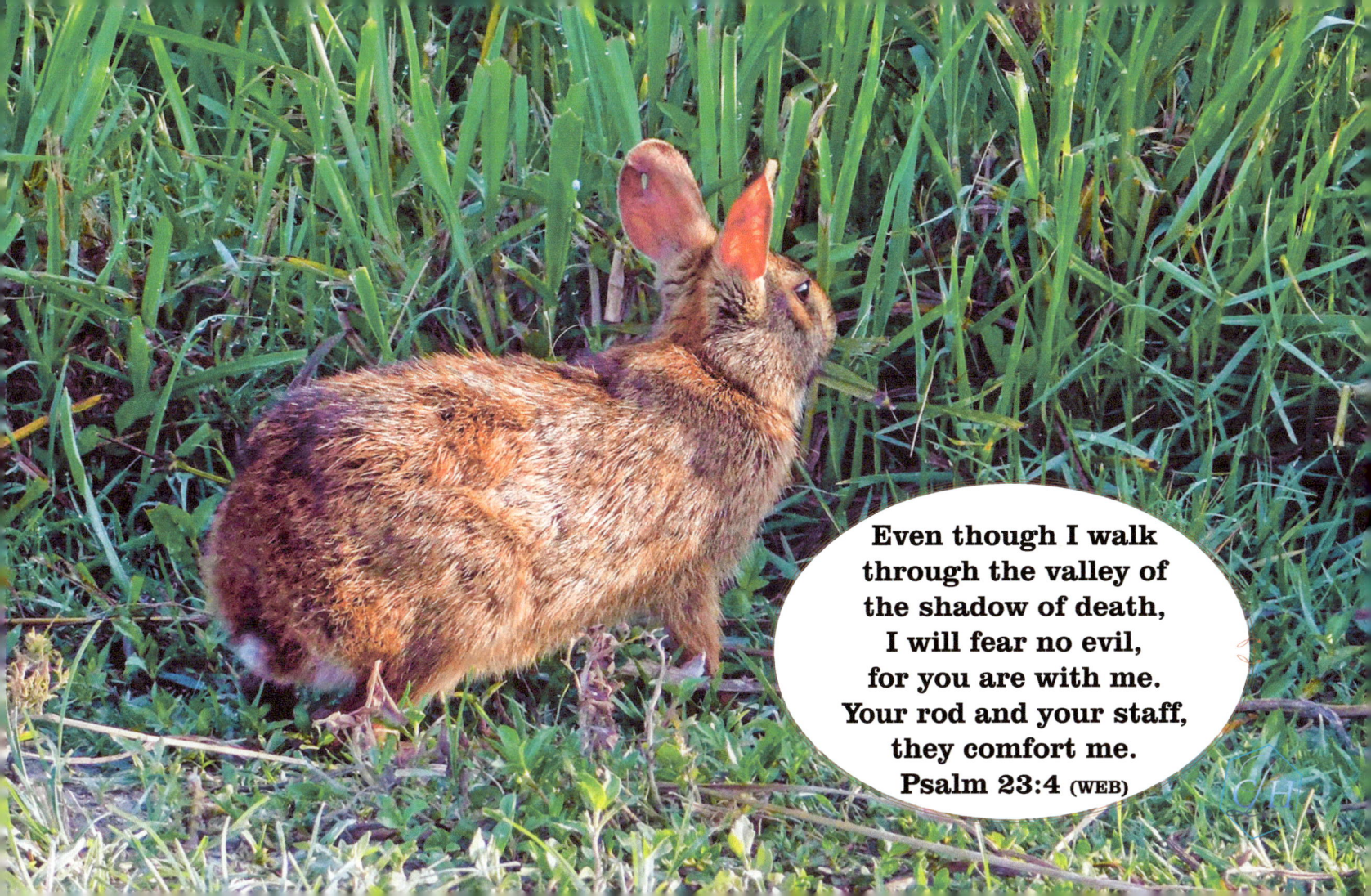

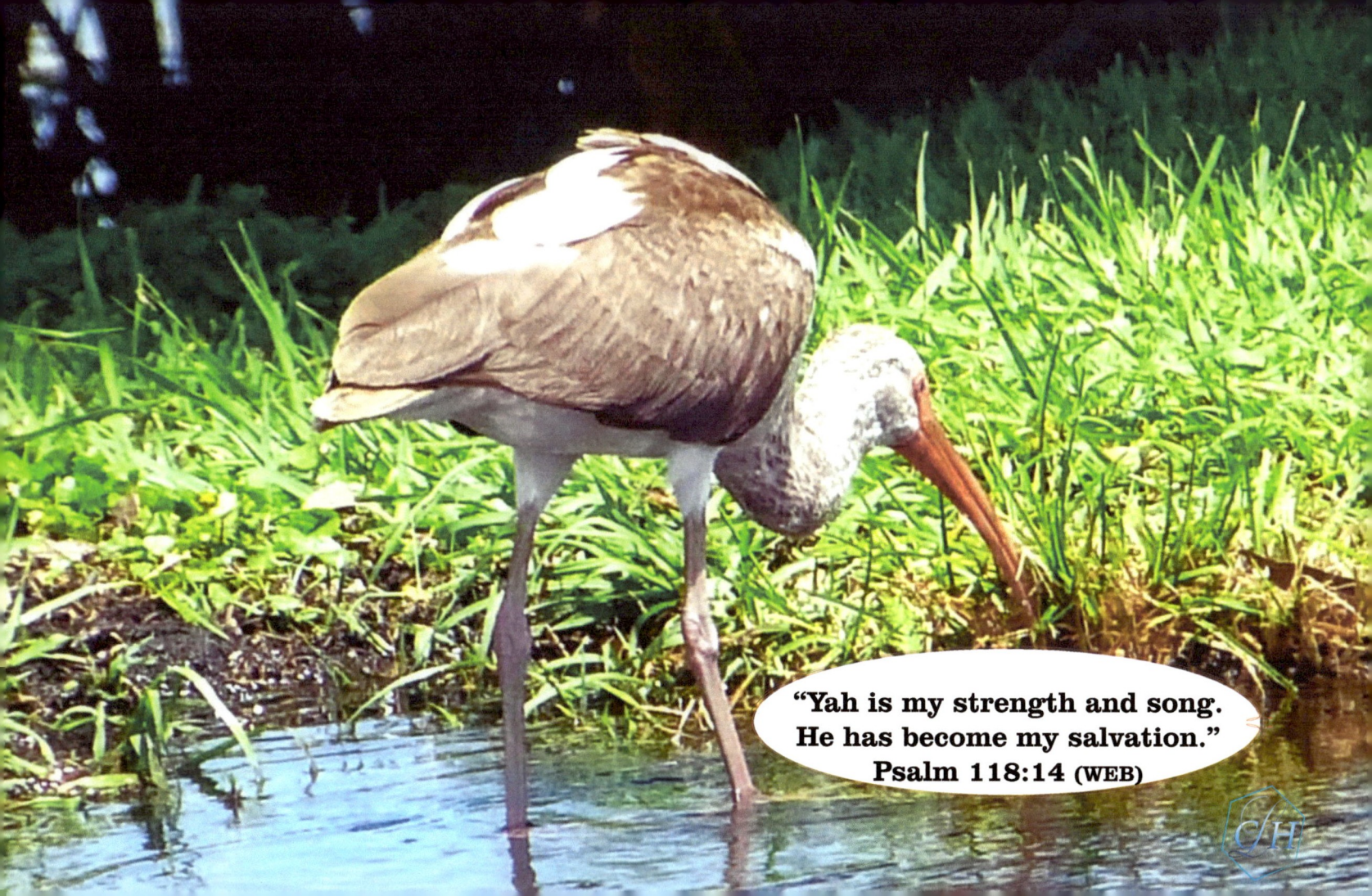

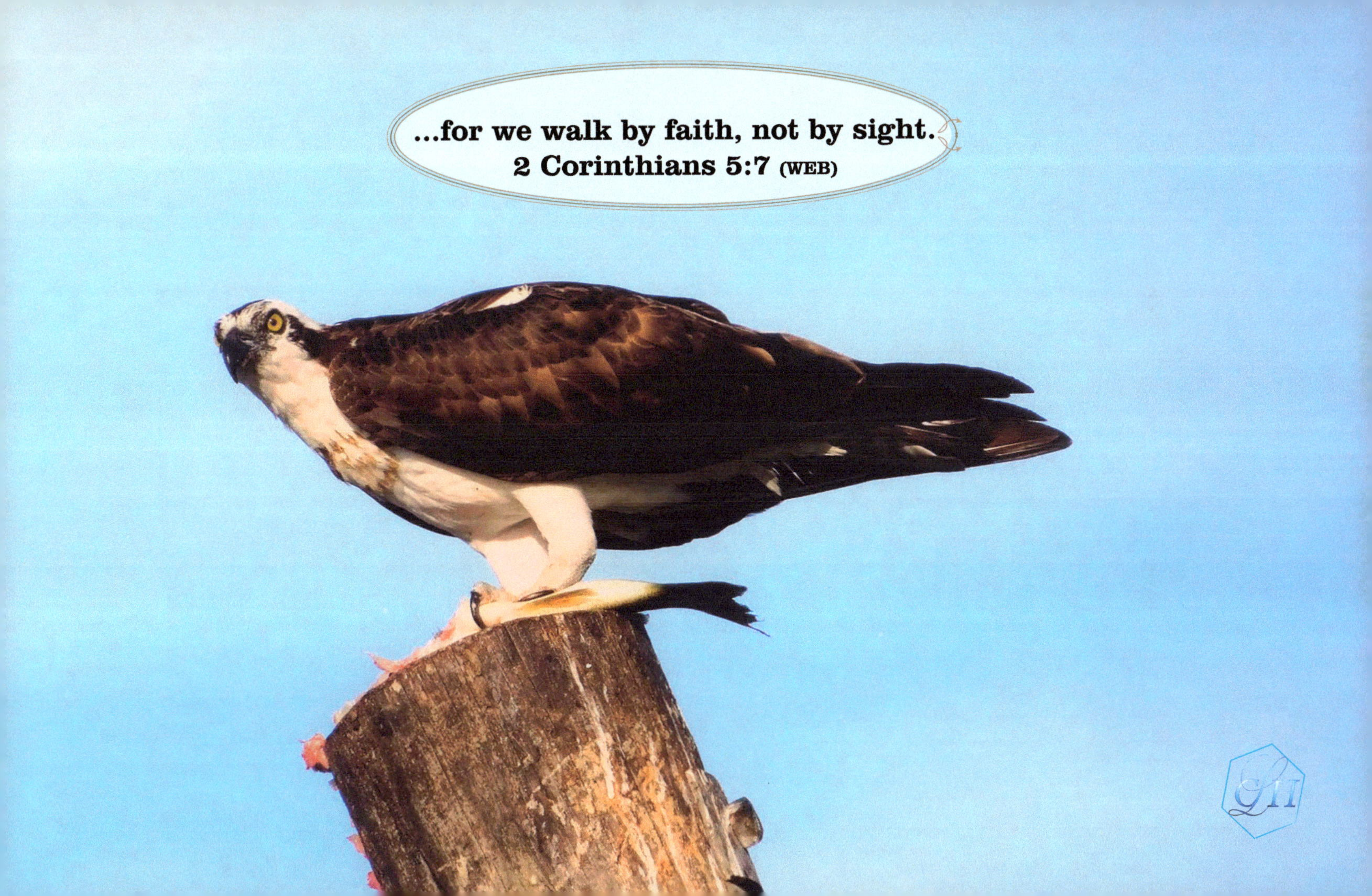

...for we walk by faith, not by sight.
2 Corinthians 5:7 (WEB)

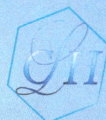

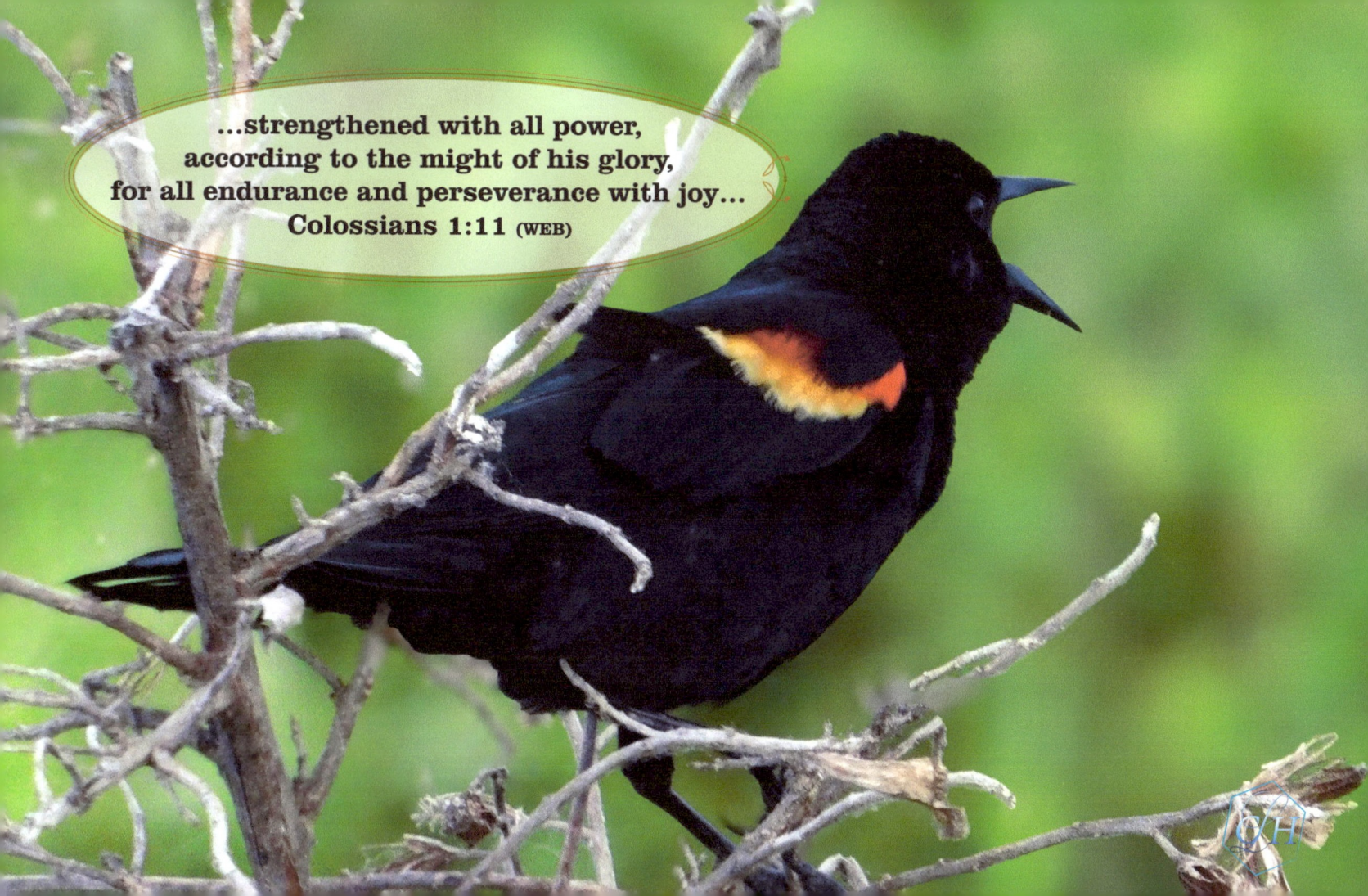

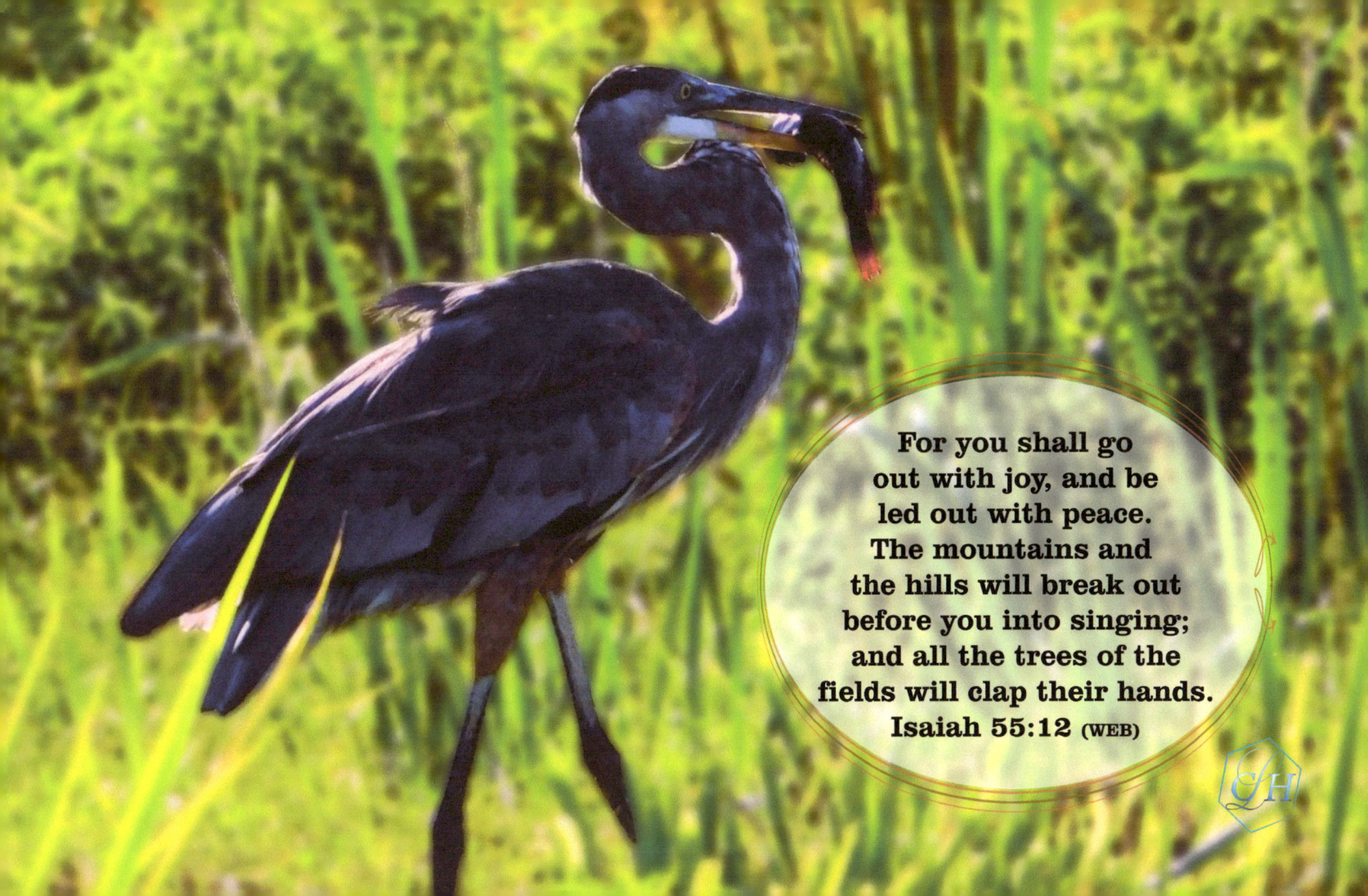

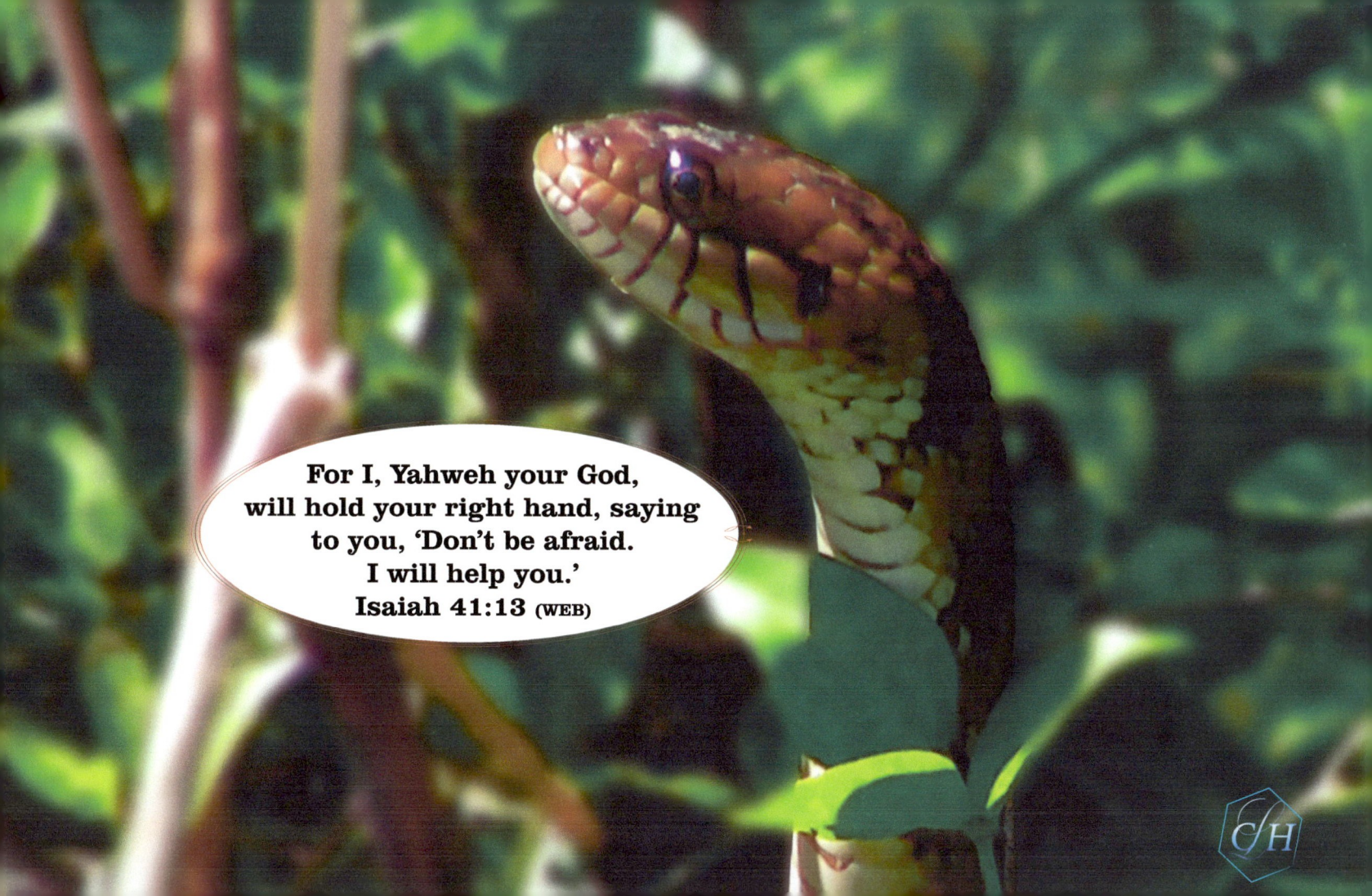

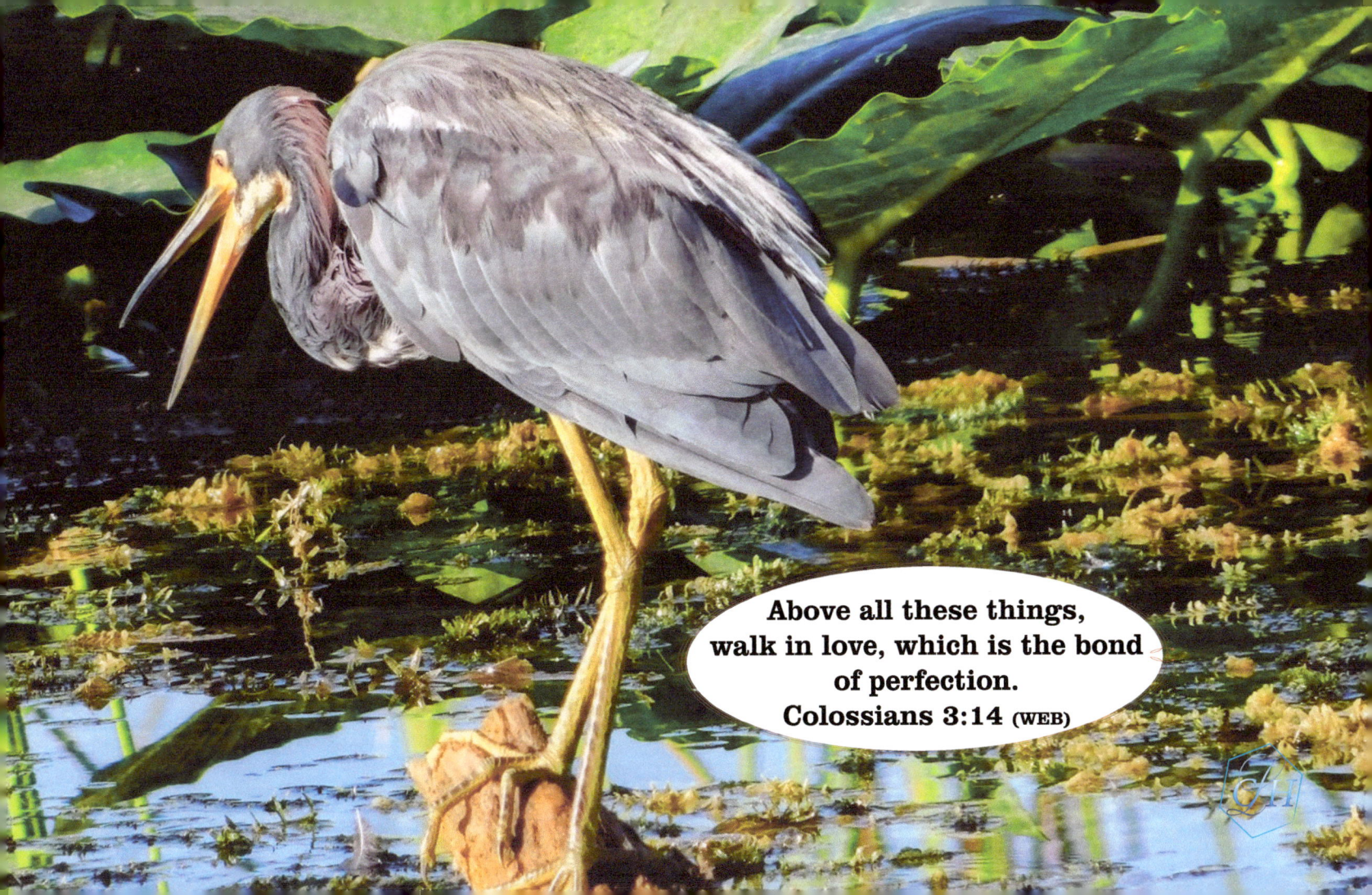

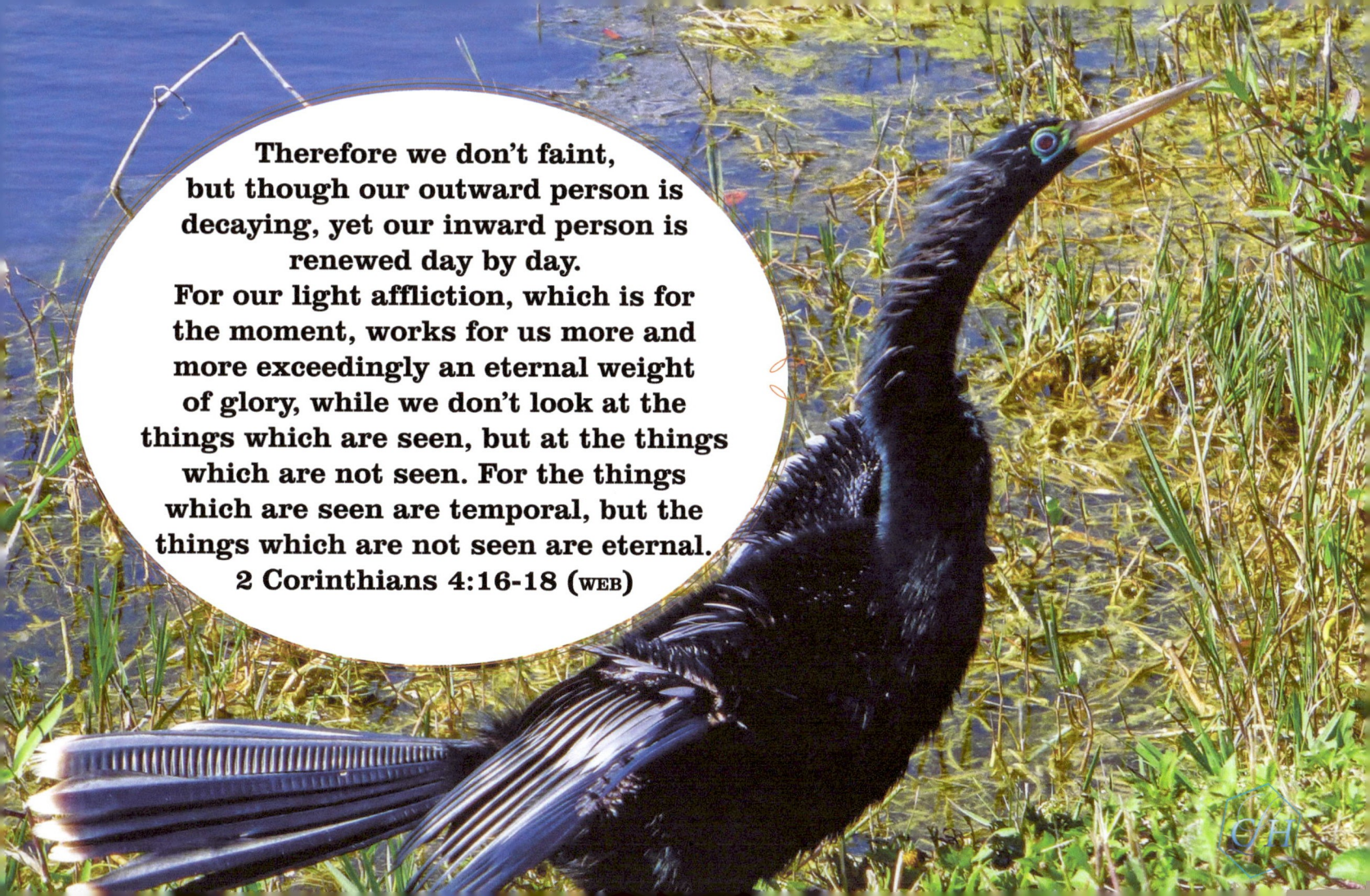

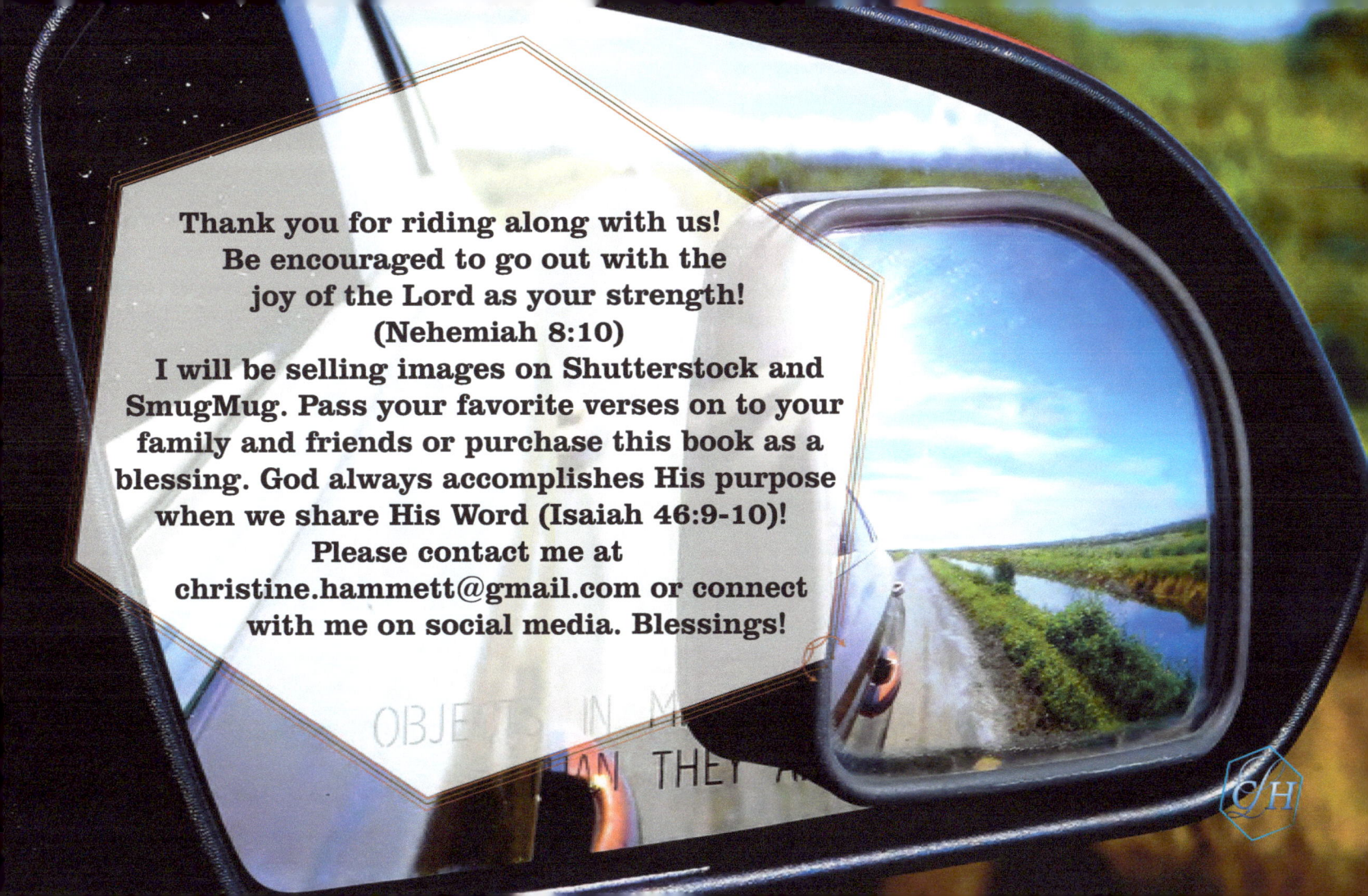

www.ingramcontent.com/pod-product-compliance
Lightning Source LLC
Chambersburg PA
CBHW040220220526
45473CB00001B/58

9 781934 194942